ANTHOLOGY
OF AN
EXILED AFRICAN DISSIDENT

*A Diaspora Movement That Toppled
a Government and Exiled a Dictator*

MATHEW K. JALLOW

ARCHWAY
PUBLISHING

Archway Publishing books may be ordered through booksellers or by contacting:

Archway Publishing
1663 Liberty Drive
Bloomington, IN 47403
www.archwaypublishing.com
1 (888) 242-5904

ISBN: 978-1-4808-8970-5 (sc)
ISBN: 978-1-4808-8969-9 (hc)
ISBN: 978-1-4808-8971-2 (e)

Library of Congress Control Number: 2020905394

Print information available on the last page.

Archway Publishing rev. date: 05/08/2020

CONTENTS

INTRODUCTION

The year 1994 was pivotal in African—and more particularly Gambian—politics. What happened that year, on July 22, was first welcomed by many Gambians, but that welcome soon soured. After thirty years in power, the president who led the Gambia into independence in 1965 was toppled by five renegade junior military officers. Before he was forced out of power, President Alhagie Sir Dawda Kairaba Jawara ushered in a period of stability, sustained by a democracy unrivalled on the African continent. President Sir Dawda stood out as a champion of democracy on the African continent, and even as many other African leaders turned to the harsh communist and socialist style economies, Sir Dawda Jawara never deviated from capitalism, realizing that only by providing opportunities and releasing the creative geniuses of his country's men and women could development be achieved. When, in 1992, Sir Dawda offered to resign, and his offer was soundly rejected, at the Mansakonko PPP party Congress, it created a backlash that left many Gambians dumbfounded. Despite enjoying a great degree of popularity, Sir Dawda had grown old and needed to retire from politics. That rest came two years later but not in a way Sir Dawda expected. The military coup, which occurred on July 22, 1994, unbeknown to Gambians, would turn out to be one of the biggest political tragedies on the African continent, for the next two decades. If a day deserved President Roosevelt's description of the

Japanese attack on Pearl Harbor, Hawaii, it was for Gambian, July 22, 1994. It was Gambia's day of infamy.

In November 1994, four months after the coup, the military regime, now headed by a recent high school graduate, Yahya Jammeh, a little-known colonel in the army, ordered the first executions of eight military officers, led by Lt. Basirou Barrow. This was soon followed by the execution of the beloved civilian finance minister, Ousman Koro Ceesay. Things began to look grim all across the country. But it wasn't until the massacre of demonstrating secondary students on April 10, 2000, that Gambians began to realize the destructive path of the military regime, headed by the coldhearted voodoo worshipper, Col. Yahya Jammeh, who was tightening his hold on power. Gambians needed to take drastic action against the new military regime, but as it would turn out, that would be easier said than done.

Two years after the 1994 coup, in 1996, I realized I had to move to a safer environment to continue my struggle against the regime. But before I finally flew to the US, I wrote two newspaper articles, for which I could have lost my life in another year when the national media became the target of the regime. In the first article, I reported the execution of the eight military officers on November 5, 1994. Later, I was alerted to the fact the Libyan mercenaries in Gambia were attempting to assassinate Lawyer Ousainou Darboe, the leader of a new political party, United Democratic Party. I could not get facts to ascertain this claim, and instead made the presence of Libyan mercenaries in the Gambia an issue of concern in an op-ed in Gambia's main newspaper, the *Daily Observer*.

Once in the US, I was introduced to Salieu Jallow, a Gambian in resident in Atlanta, Georgia, who started the first Gambian online newsletter. I continued the campaign against the Gambia's military regime and soon, there was a proliferation of online Gambians newspapers across the US and Europe. This was soon followed by the founding of the National Movement for the Restoration of Democracy in Gambia, (NRMDG, civil society organizations dedicated to the liberation of the Gambia from the tyranny of military rule). It was the first organization of its kind, but it wouldn't be for long. Across the US, Europe, and Africa, organizations dedicated to the restoration of democracy in the Gambia began to sprout wherever Gambians live in significant numbers. This book publication, the first of three volumes, captures the work, which inspired an international movement that won the struggle for democracy in the Gambia.

CHAPTER I

GOVERNANCE

JULY 22, 1994, MILITARY COUP THAT CHANGED EVERYTHING

The frail, dorky-looking man in military uniform who drove past me at the McCarthy Square turnaround in Banjul on a warm July afternoon in 1994 looked like an unlikely candidate for the president of anything, much less that of a country. But, since a sufficient number of Gambians were disillusioned with Sir Dawda Jawara's successive governments, citizens were willing to give the new military regime a chance. Not that anyone had the power to change the outcome of the coup itself, for no one did. In those days, and at that moment in history, Gambians were ready for something new and different—anything. Prior to the coup, more than one dozen government agencies worth billions of dalasi in assets had collapsed, one after another, and vanished with millions of dollars in assets. The unlikely collapse of the Gambia Commercial and Development Bank did not cause but seemed to have precipitated a domino effect that saw other government agencies crumble like sandcastles, and with them, a sizeable amount of Gambia's economic fortunes inexplicably disappeared in thin air. It was the classic case of state failure so common on the African continent.

On that hot July afternoon in 1994, as the military coup leader, Col.

Yahya Jammeh, escorted by an extravagant security detail, drove past me in a swanky SUV, his unimpressive, if not idiosyncratic personality left a bad taste in my mouth. For one thing, he did not look the part of a president of anything, but it was more than that. Though I was unable to figure out what it was about the awkward-looking military officer that spoke negatively to me, doubts of seismic proportion irritated my mind. Like most Gambians, my cerebral connection to Yahya Jammeh in the early days of the military coup was informed by my visual assessment of his demeanor and the persona he exuded, both in his speeches and demeanor. It soon became evident that his uncharismatic personality lacked refinement, exposing a typical African primitiveness that was a harbinger of things to come. A momentary glimpse and a few seconds of visual observation were all it took to form an opinion of the coup leader—an act of physiognomy that at the time did not do justice to his true character.

It did not dawn on me, at the time, that I was making a gratuitous and ad hominem intellectual critique, which could easily have been negated by further information, but frankly, I couldn't have cared less. It was not as if I could foresee what Yahya Jammeh was going to do in the future, but like many Gambians, the intellectual shallowness he exhibited bothered me, and challenged my biases and emotional objectivity. But I was by no means alone. Despite the fact that far too many questions, and even fewer answers, swirled around Gambians' troubled minds, there was still no need to panic—at least, not yet. The deluge of skepticism and uncertainty was not overtly disconcerting as yet, and Gambians by and large were also resigned to abstraction of the unfolding reality, as blind faith in a divine, celestial power took over. On the surface, it was working, as religious leaders soon began to embrace the military coup as an act of God. Behind the scenes and out of the public's unsuspecting imaginations, however, a brutal power struggle, which would change the course of Gambian history was brewing quietly among the small band of coup leaders.

The juxtaposition of egotism and ignorance, which was becoming more and more evident, exposed the gullibility, vulnerability, and intellectual immaturity of the five feuding coup leaders. The task that lay ahead was daunting. The Gambia needed a correction of course, both politically and economically. The totality of Gambians' collective disillusionment with the erstwhile Sir Dawda K Jawara's successive governments necessitated it. But for the ragtag high school graduates who knew as much about the complexity of the science of governance as they knew about neurosurgery, the challenges of governing that lay ahead was infinitely intimidating. This was the price they had to pay for taking on the gargantuan task of running a country, something that demanded tact and intellectual and emotional maturity, all of which the motley crew of five young military junta members copiously lacked. But as the sirens of the motor bicycle outriders escorting the new leader diminished into faint, mournful sounds and disappeared from view into the distant afternoon mist, a whimsical realization dawned on me that for a majority of Gambians, the military regime represented a promise that was out of their reach throughout the Sir Dawda Jawara presidency, hijacked by a mosaic of fractional, narrow-minded interest groups.

And soon enough, the internal power struggle among members of the ruling military junta would unexpectedly burst out into the open with the hasty arrest, trial, and incarceration of one of their strong men: second-in-command Sana B. Sabally. In the meantime, the US led Western governments' effort for a speedy return to civilian rule, and imposed strict economic sanctions on the new regime, further shaking the self-doubting, eclectic group of inexperienced coupists. These nerve-racking economic sanctions Gambia faced precipitated an ominous, if not intriguing, political sea change that Yahya Jammeh soon established. Members of the military junta began a series of overseas trips, deliberately targeting the world's pariah nations whose politics were on an orbit far removed from the civilized world: Cuba, Libya, Iran, Venezuela—regimes with impetuous leaders, incredible cruelty, reptilian savagery, and Cro-Magnon political worldviews. The groundwork for where the Gambia was heading was being laid down along the path that other ignominious African political characters of historical notoriety had dared to go.

The beginning of year 2000 was filled with trepidation as anxiety gripped the nation and froze the population into a heightened sense of vulnerability. The initial shock of the military coup had long ago waned, and the country's rhythm had returned to some semblance of normalcy. But politically, the embers were still burning furiously beneath the surface of tranquility. The finance minister, Ousman Koro Ceesay, had been murdered; in addition, a group of eight military officers were also executed on November 11, 1994, allegedly for attempted countercoup. Curiously, these cases failed to agitate Gambians into mounting any resistance to the increasingly maniacal regime. And soon, behind the scenes and out of the limelight, Gambians began to disappear in the dead of night, some never to be seen again. In the military, soldiers were increasingly singled out and blacklisted as potential threats to the military junta. Yahya Jammeh was growing increasingly comfortable in his dangerously reckless abuse of power. His mindless daring was exemplified by the broad-daylight, fatal shooting of Sergeant Dumbuya at the crowded Albert Market in the capital city of Banjul. Hundred eighteen miles south of the capital, Banjul, Kanilai village, the birthplace of Yahya Jammeh, was slowly transforming into the Gambia's de facto seat of government.

By the time the coup entered its first year; Yahya Jammeh had appropriated large swaths of Kanilai village farmland to himself, to build a seat of government, complete with a farm and a zoo and furnished with every modern amenity. His mad metamorphosis included an age-old African trick: retiring his military uniform in exchange for civilian robes. He soon styled himself after one of Africa's worst murderers—late president of Guinea-Conakry, Ahmed Sekou Toure. Luck was still on Yahya Jammeh's side, for he had managed to get away with the bloody murder of Gambians not once, not twice, but multiple times without suffering any adverse consequence for his actions. Gambians' collective failure to respond adequately to the threats Yahya Jammeh posed to the country was mind-numbing. It was such a crucial period, and the Gambian people failed the patriotic test as Yahya Jammeh and his regime tested the limits of the tolerance of the people. With the nation confronted with a stark and unbridled violation of human rights, our passiveness and political amnesia provided further impetus for Yahya Jammeh to usurp the authority of our system of government: the National Assembly, the Judiciary. And true to form, he was emboldened by a sense of invincibility brought on by the failure to put his power in check and his impetuousness under control.

The more power Yahya Jammeh acquired, the more he rubbed Gambians the wrong way. In conforming to the law of physics, "every action has a reaction," he began to manifest signs of paranoia, and his inclination toward sycophancy became disturbingly more pronounced. His evolution from a barely literate military recruit to a desensitized, tyrannical misanthropist was complete. Yahya Jammeh was the true embodiment of perversity, and his so-called revolution, the epitome of contradictions. He gradually transformed himself into a cruel demon, who, by dint of his Machiavellian predispositions, had long ago departed from the values of empathy and sympathy. And as his power grew and became more solidified, he no longer felt obligated by moral imperatives or simple human decency to honor his commitment to Gambians. For, having tasted the corrupting influence of absolute power, Yahya Jammeh embarked on a journey of emasculating and dehumanizing Gambians. Through his notorious manipulations and predilection to infidelity to the nation, he succeeded in reducing Gambians as victims of his idol worship and unbearable tribal bigotry. Yahya Jammeh's determination to subsume the larger national priority to his own selfish interest was manifesting itself in many ways. He took on the persona of a political pugilist who, in the process of remaking himself, plunged Gambia into the state of social, economic, and political quandary from which Gambians are still struggling to recover from.

As a paragon of moral insensitivity, Yahya Jammeh objectified an entire nation by subjecting Gambians to his whim and caprices, and turning the people into his minions and puppets. The insidiousness of his military regime came to a head on April 11, 2000, a day that will remain indelibly etched in Gambians' memories. The brutal massacre that hot summer morning of sixteen junior and high students became the national tragedy heard all around the world. The chilling story of that episode reads like the Gambia's answer to the Tiananmen Square massacre. The Yahya Jammeh revolution had come full circle. His rabid cruelty was unparalleled, and his bloodthirst in a country that only wanted to be left in peace was incomprehensible. Until then, nowhere on the African continent, had in recent memory, exercised such demonic cruelty and nauseating disregard for human life. Collective despair and helplessness were taking their toll on Gambians. Even by Africa's low standards of concern for upholding human rights, the depth and breadth of the cruel massacre of students provided a desperate and frightening look at the darkness developing in the Gambia. The irrational and fearful deference to Yahya Jammeh's maniacal propensity to extreme violence was gnawing at the very soul of the nation.

On that fateful day, April 11, 2000, Gambia lost more than just its precious young lives; Gambia lost what made it human and the values that distinguish the Gambians as one family. On that day, Gambians collectively personified the old adage "all that is necessary for the triumph of evil, is that good men do nothing." By condoning the April 11, 2000, savagery, Gambians exposed their serious moral deficit, having acquiesced to Yahya Jammeh's spite and depravity. The fate as a country was finally wrapped in the ebb and flow of Yahya Jammeh's moodiness and repulsive idol worship. April 11, 2000, metaphorically became the Gambia's longest day. It was one of those days in which the power of the moral belief system shifted unrecognizably to one of indifference and spinelessness, paralyzed by Yahya Jammeh's cruelty and greed, all in his pursuit of absolute power. It was a radical departure from the Gambia's customary civility. Perversion of the country's democratic system had taken center stage. It seemed everything about Gambia was a metaphor for disaster, an embodiment of the absurd. If Yahya Jammeh was fazed by the horrors unleashed by his reign, he did not show it. And any scintilla of hope of restoring sanity to Gambia's political system would remain a fantasy. Yahya Jammeh's distortion of the soul and character of the country was getting started. A new day had dawned on the Gambia.

By the time I snapped out of Yahya Jammeh's motorcade-induced daze, his convoy was long gone, and only the haunting, repetitive sound of sirens lingered on in my mind. And when I finally maneuvered the McCarthy Square turnaround and reached the *Point* newspaper, my friend Deyda Hydara was typing feverishly away on a laptop. He acknowledged my presence with a nod, and motioned for me to sit across the desk from him. He turned his attention to me as soon as he finished typing, and after placing the laptop at the base of his feet, under the desk. His face lit up with a half-smile, a smile restricted by the cigarette butt dangling from the right corner of his mouth. The cigarette was crowned with a half-inch-long ash that looked like it was about to peel off and crash on Deyda Hydara's crowded desk below. Mr. Deida Hydara, like everyone else, was caught between a rock and a hard place. In principle, he was unable to give his tacit and explicit approval to a military coup, but his position conflicted with his frustration with the plundering and pillaging under the Sir Dawda Jawara governments. The military coup in the Gambia had become as much emblematic of the tragedy of Africa as it was anathema to the democratic doctrine fronted by the Gambia's burgeoning media fraternity, headed by Deyda Hydara.

Ironically, for many Gambians, the coup was a cause for celebration of the demise of the thirty-year-old Sir Dawda Jawara reign. But as time went on, and the unlikely coup became a fait accompli, its novelty began to wear off, and with it, Gambians' wariness and apprehension toward the military coup slowly began to give way to acceptance. But the coupists, inebriated with newfound power, soon realized that governing was easier said than done. Months into the new regime, life was beginning to return to normal, but for a new regime vulnerable to the ebb and flow of international pressure, its actions highlighted a dissonance that subjected it to the discomfort of external political forces. Earlier, on the night of November 11, 1994, one of the most pivotal days of the early coup, bloodletting whose eerie story is yet to be told, further stained the image of the new junta and left Gambians dizzy with disbelief. According to the regime, a countercoup had been foiled, and a small band of soldiers, headed by Basirou Barrow, and including Dot Fall, Alpha Bah, and several others, were executed.

That incident, rather than purge the military of supposed rebellious elements, succeeded in heightening tensions among the coupists, the military, and the country at large. The glue that hitherto held the remaining coupists together was slowly disintegrating, and the camaraderie forged in political ignorance and cluelessness was crumbling, to the amusement of a watchful population. Of the original five members of the ruling junta, Sadibou Hydara and Sana B Sabally were arrested, tortured, and incarcerated in short order, following a brief trial in which both were found guilty of an unknown crime. A contentious power grab sealed Sana Sabally's fate and opened the way to the dangerous ambitions of the deadly Singateh brothers. A long, drawn-out struggle between Yahya Jammeh and a new nemesis, Edward Singateh, a Jerry Rawlings wannabe, was on. It was clear Yahya Jammeh had a profound distrust for Edward and his brother, Peter Singateh, and to protect his regime, he promoted his fellow Jola tribesmen to key positions in the military and the security forces. Yahya Jammeh also co-opted a fraction of the Casamance rebel movement into Gambia's security apparatus; and in so doing; he effectively neutralized the Singateh brothers' political ambitions.

The brutal execution on November 11, 1994, of so-called counter-coupists, in which both Edward Singateh and Sana Sabally are implicated, marked Gambia's baptism of fire, and its loss of innocence. It signaled a new era, alien in its brutality and disarming in its viciousness. (STOP)The uncharacteristic reservation Deyda Hydara injected in our discussions relative to the newly minted military junta was tragically Orwellian—a depiction of the cruel underbelly of the militarization of political life in Gambia. In the beginning, there was a paucity of information about Yahya Jammeh, but slowly and gradually, he came out of his shell: unsure, insecure, and scared. When Yahya Jammeh eventually began to come out, his visible nervousness betrayed his timidity. The expression of intellectual inadequacy written all over his scared face continued to haunt him. Everything the junta did earlier in the coup was unsettling and highly dramatic. Libyan agents sent by Muammar Gaddafi swarmed Banjul at the invitation of Yahya Jammeh. Unsavory characters from some of the world's worst nations came knocking. And at a time several when young military officers were executed in cold blood, the junta appeared to be falling into total disarray.

The first five months of 1995 began like the other months of the regime's previous year in power, but the night of June 13, 1995, went down as one of the darkest in the annals of Gambia's history. It was as if Gambians were living in the twilight zone and witnessing a horrifying experience that seemed impossible to capture in words. The scene of Ousman Koro Ceesay's assassination was a gruesome image that could only be captured vividly in dreams. It was another turning point in the junta's short history, but it had given Gambians a nasty preview of what was yet to come. Koro Ceesay's murder could only be depicted in narratives lifted right out of an Alfred Hitchcock horror movie, almost impossible to imagine in its sadistic cruelty. The proverbial train left the station on that day, and any opportunity for the regime to modify its irrational behavior was forever lost. Suddenly, Gambians were living a new dimension of reality that hitherto one only read about in other countries and dysfunctional societies far removed from Gambia's culture of caring and political cohesiveness. And as tragic as his death was, Koro Ceesay came to symbolize martyrdom, the iconoclastic central rallying cry of an anti-junta campaign whose efforts never took off the ground. Osman Koro Ceesay's murder triggered an angry battlecry for a war against military rule that would never to be fought.

If Ousman Koro Ceesay's assassination was meant to send a message to the Gambian people, it succeeded beyond the regime's wildest dreams. Threats and intimidation as a form of governance soon became the regime's de facto modus operandi. Murder, torture, and other forms of terror, as instruments of control and compliance, in a country once known as Africa's bastion of democracy, began to attract international attention. Fear as a political weapon took on the dimension of institutional policy, and tribal bigotry slowly began to take shape. In Gambia, death and disappearances became the natural progression to warrantless arrests, used as weapons to preempt effort to dislodge Yahya Jammeh from power. In order to bolster these efforts of power grab, Yahya Jammeh opened up new police stations and detention centers in remote places around the country, often in faraway places where the regime's atrocities would be out of the public glare. The regime that had come to rebuild a battered economy, as centerpiece of the rationale for the coup, was inexplicably turning into a liability. The Gambia was plunged in a political conundrum in which it remained hopelessly mired for the better part of two decades. The hopefulness Gambians experienced turned into a nightmare. But Yahya Jammeh had more surprises in his hat. The worst was yet to come.

THE GAMBIA DESCENDING INTO CHAOS

On a Monday morning in 2009, Gambians woke up to news of PDOIS's politician and leader of the now defunct National Alliance for Democracy and Development (NADD), Halifa Sallah's, arrest, but by the afternoon, more bad news were circulating around the world about the mass arrests and detention of innocent elderly civilians from the remote village of Sintet, in the Fonis. Similar recent and ongoing arrests in the towns and villages of Makumbaya, Barra-Niumi, Jambur, and Essau, left Gambians at home and abroad enthralled and incredulous, hoping it was all a dream. But however much Gambians wished this was only a bad dream; the reality was that Yahya Jammeh was once again demonstrating that he was unfazed and unrestrained by reasoned judgment. As Gambians began to come to terms with the apocalyptic nature of Yahya Jammeh's governing style, the country had reason to worry about what still lay ahead.

As the weeks and months progressed, it became apparent that the military's unfolding record was antithetical to our cultural values, and the only antidote to the APRC misery was disbanding the cabal headed by Yahya Jammeh, which is hell-bent on the destabilizing the country. The relentless effort to create permanent instability in the country fostered a climate that is conducive to the functioning of dictatorship, since it attenuates arguments for the maintenance of civil order. Yahya Jammeh has so far survived and thrived in a state of social and political anarchy, but in the end, it is the people with nothing to lose, and everything to gain, who will prevail over the regime's tedious exercise of absolute power. The prolongation of Yahya Jammeh's hold on power will depend very much on how Gambians' respond to the provocations of his insanity, but judging from the venality of his Machiavellian outlook on politics, it is hard not to believe that the end is drawing near for the military regime.

If we have learned anything from the events of the past several weeks, it is that as a country, we must jettison our fears in order to confront Yahya Jammeh and put an end to his senseless barbarism. At this juncture, the most effective way to address Yahya Jammeh's proclivity to violence and the abuse of human and civil rights is to reciprocate with a ferociousness designed to stop his madness. Yahya Jammeh's rapacious behavior has taxed the limits of Gambians endurance and impoverished our country for so long that, given the social and economic paralysis Gambia is in, our country can only gain from the demise of his regime. Today, apart from a few ignorant dawdlers, we have arrived at a general consensus that Yahya Jammeh's anachronistic regime has overstayed its welcome, and it is time to reclaim our country from the despair and chicanery of his perfidious regime. Any effort to dislodge Yahya Jammeh from power will not come easy, as the natural law of self-preservation dictates that he will use a cornucopia of lethal weapons that he has amassed to suppress our people.

This notwithstanding, no overthrow of a dictatorship has been a cakewalk, but we must mobilize the Gambian people in the effort, because in the final analysis, it is to them that we must bequeath a far better and hopeful world. The sum total of the events that began a decade and a half ago, culminating in the arrest of thousands of innocent, older citizens in a witch-hunting exercise, serve to drive our seemingly docile military and security forces into the corner of patriotic Gambians, motivated by a sense of duty and moral obligation to fellow citizens. No one can pretend to understand Yahya Jammeh's illogical thought processes, but what we do know is that his actions have depleted any hope of successfully expurgating his character of the demons that have destroyed his humanity. After fifteen years of unrelenting abuse, the forbearance of our people is being tested once again, but we have nothing more to give, for we have cringed and cried, fretted and prayed, spilled blood and seen our neighbor's blood spilled. We have been shamed and seen our pride and dignity denigrated, but still Yahya Jammeh's hubristic tendencies will not give us our peace.

The Gambia, once a political paradise, is today descending into a state of anarchy; defaced by cruelty, its innocence has been lost to actions that are inimical to the nature and character of civilized society. Yet, in spite all this, Gambians are not helpless and still refuse to give up. More importantly, each time Yahya Jammeh conjures up penurious ways to disturb the tranquility in Gambia with the stresses of his unbearable tyranny, we as a people must forge a cohesive and determined unitary body of defiance against his regime. So far, the paucity of courage of the military and security forces is very deafening, but knowing how such dictatorships function as factories of fear, this opinion of the military should not be construed as passing judgment; rather, the purpose is to encourage the fearlessness in order to harden their resolve in the effort to remove Yahya Jammeh. At this juncture, without pretending to speak for Gambians, it is reasonable to assume that our citizens are willing to extend immunity to the military for minor infractions and grant immunity from prosecution to those members of the military in exchange for the removal of Yahya Jammeh.

It is a trade-off that Gambians both at home and abroad feel comfortable with and can hopefully accommodate. At this time, no one will deny the level and gravity of the situation our country is faced with. Gambians call on the men and women in uniform to work with civil society in order to deliver our country from the senseless killings of innocent citizens. As a country, Gambians are comforted in the knowledge that Yahya Jammeh is his own worst enemy, and his eminent downfall is the creation of his own genius. For no matter what happens, in the end, the Gambia will survive these dark days of our painful history when Yahya Jammeh is finally driven from power under the weight of his madness.

GAMBIA IS BLEEDING: YAHYA JAMMEH MUST GO

In 1994, when five young military officers took over the reins of power, there was widespread jubilation by a disillusioned Gambia public. I had previously witnessed riots in Brikama town over water and electricity shortages under deposed President Sir Dawda Jawara. I survived a lynch mob who thought that I belonged to the enemy—the government, that is. I was just a reporter trying to get the story of the people to the *Daily Observer*, the newspaper where I worked. Those were trying times; I remember the rolling blackouts and darkness that blanketed entire towns, the endless water shortages, and the ugly street fights at public water standpipes all across villages Kombos, from Brikama to Bakau. Not long after the riots in Brikama, the military took power and promised change. The promise of a better future filled the air, and the dreams of a new tomorrow permeated the air. Hope was reborn. We clung to it. More than ten years later, it was déjà vu all over again. Little had changed. The blackouts and water shortages were back. The people are as frustrated as they had been before, perhaps even more so. Yet Brikama, the revolutionary trendsetter, under the previous government, is sitting tight-lipped, this time. What changed is that the constitutional freedoms Brikama youth exercised in turning out into the streets in large numbers to vent their anger and frustration against the former government has been taken away.

The new military gang in power in Banjul had an exaggerated sense of their power. It didn't take long before citizens began to forfeit liberties that rightfully belonged to them, as enshrined in the constitution. Then came April 10, 2000, when young schoolchildren were massacred by Gambian security forces. It was a turning point in the country's history, a low point, gruesome and barbaric, which will forever haunt Gambians for decades to come. The day was a harbinger of the Machiavellian style of government that the military regime would later apply to maintain its tenuous hold on power. Before he was forced out of office, Sir Dawda was, in the end, out of touch, either through indifference or senility, or both, and so he allowed the country slip into the hands of bitter and competing hodgepodge of tribal interest groups. There was jockeying for power and the wealth that went with it. In the process, several state agencies were looted and bankrupted: The Gambia Commercial and Development Bank (GCBD), National Trading Corporation (NTC), Gambia Produce Marketing Board (GPMB), Public Works Department (PWD), and Gambia Fish Marketing Board (GFMB).

As a result of bankrupting these institutions, which had performed much-needed services to the nation, many former officials under Sir Dawda were brought before a commission of inquiry, and their properties confiscated by the new regime. One difference between the military regime and the ousted government of Sir Dawda, was Yahya Jammeh's level of corruption. Whenever he travels to his home village, Kanilai, the entire government follows him there. And nowadays, Kanilai village is also the Gambia's party town; it's Las Vegas. While the level of corruption in Gambia increased exponentially, there was a new dimension in the way the military regime operated. Yahya Jammeh who turned civilian and was elected in 2006, was morphing into a despot. He was acquiring limitless power, and there was no boundary to the things he could or couldn't do. His cruelty had no parallel. Given the nature of Gambia's cultures and what death means in society, the regime had turned what was rarity into a norm. Killings, maiming, and torture had become commonplace in the Gambia. To make matters worse, Yahya Jammeh was answerable to no one, not even the judiciary, but more; the military exists exclusively to protect and perpetuate his bloody thirsty leadership. Under the regime, human life no longer mattered, and everyone danced to Yahya Jammeh's tune. Hardly a week went by without someone, somewhere, being arrested, killed, or fired from their prized government job, under false pretenses.

Today, if there are no qualified Gambian citizens left to run the country, it is because Yahya Jammeh has no clue what the Gambia needs in terms of skill sets in order to move the country towards economic development.

Yahya Jammeh's ignorance, paranoia, and shaky emotional state, combine to make him susceptible to making onerous public policy decisions. This lethal combination often manifests itself, because each time Yahya Jammeh speaks, he doesn't seem to make sense. In his book, *Africa in Chaos*, Professor Ayittey laments that African leaders are so engrossed in the business of fighting their perceived political enemies that they have time for little else. Yahya Jammeh is locked in an unending battle with so-called enemies, and more than a decade on, it is the battle that preoccupies if every waking moment. He has made many enemies. In his book *Things Fall Apart*, Chinua Achebe quotes Irish poet W.B. Yeats's "The Second Coming"" "turning and turning in the widening gyre, the falcon cannot hear the falconer, things fall apart; the center cannot hold, mere anarchy is loosened upon this world."

The previous ten years were a nightmare, and Yahya Jammeh lost his way in trying to navigate the complicated labyrinth of governing, which he knows nothing about. Running a country through the barrel of a gun has no place in modern society, and there is always a tragic end to his style of governing. Dictators around the world who to perpetuate their hold on power, eventually always fail. It is an error in judgment to think that a people can be kept in subordination in perpetuity. I believe Gambians have reached the limits of their tolerance, when they hate their government more than they fear the guns of the military. The lessons of history have taught Gambians that when angry people stand up to tyrannical governments, because they have nothing to lose, mighty armies retreat and fall. The Gambian military regime is only as strong as the people allow. As the population becomes more pregnant with angry and disillusionment, a groundswell of anti-dictatorship protests have bugan to manifest at home and around the world. It has become inevitable for Yahya Jammeh to begin preoccupying himself with the thought of how he could fall victim to an angry nations. Yahya Jammeh must realize that each of the people he killed, beginning with eight military officers in 1994, and former finance minister, Koro Ceesay, in 1995, to Solo Sandeng, in 2016, will be avenged. President Eisenhower once said, "The buck stops here." The ultimate responsibility for every crime of murder and violence that occurred in Gambia rests squarely on Yahya Jammeh's shoulders.

THE DANGEROUS INTERSECTION OF POLITICAL PROPAGANDA AND IGNORANCE

Political propaganda has a capacity to elicit reactions that almost defy reason. As a tool of mental and intellectual suppression, the primary objective of propaganda is to deny citizens their rights to independent thinking, for safer and easier subjective reasoning. A scrutiny of African politics does uncover an uncanny similarity between the autocracies that dominated East Europe in the 1980s and existing African monocracies that inhibit independent thinking and economic progress. This paucity of intellectual freedom, the thread that weaves through a complicated social and political fabric, relegates African governance to demonic irreverence, and kept its politics on the apocalyptic margins, for decades. The divine reverence, in which African political leaders are viewed by their populations, is axiomatic of a culture that encourages the emergence of cult personalities of clueless political leaders. As a microcosm of African politics, a case study of the Gambian politics showcases violence to the intellect that is both enduring and often less obvious, even in its pervasiveness. The deep psychological impacts of the consequences of dictatorship, in Gambian, have not been studied in any detail, but its unflattering dimensions include the mental conditioning that desensitizes citizens and numbs them to the catastrophe of the existing political tyranny. At another perceptible level, the prevalence of the denial of reality, across tribe, geography, and social and economic status, compels the obvious search for an answer to the baffling question of how a segment of the Gambia's population can reconcile between what exists in reality, and what exists in their minds.

Not far from the surface truth is the ability and willingness of Gambians to deny acknowledging the chaos in the country's body politics. Material rewards, used to incentivize officials to look the other way, is intended to sap their moral dignities and places them on the wrong side of history. This has degenerated into a polarizing and unhealthy adversarial relation between citizens, which cannot be easily swept aside by the mere force of will. Pivotal in the Gambians ideological straightjacketing is the forced grounding to an irrational single-mindedness that more attuned to the pathology of selfishness than the human morals inherent in the Gambia's religious and cultural beliefs. And ironically, the divergence in political opinions, often inimical to the national interest, has created irreconcilable barriers to citizens' consensus by hemorrhaging the crucial trust and goodwill necessary in homogenizing Gambian society. In-depth understanding of the ramifications of tyranny in the Gambia cannot preclude the natural tendency of significant number of Gambians for the sanguinary, not because of succumbing to outside forces, but because of the independent capacity for evil. Complicity in the evil often expressed in dramatic extrajudicial force, a hallmark of Gambia's contemporary politics, is underpinned by the existential threat that the state poses. The challenge to push back on the toxicity and bitterness in the Gambia's politics cannot be informed by tepidity and fear, but by galvanizing the national conscience against the crippling social, political, and economic degeneration of the past two decades. The banality of the brutal and often deadly show of force, designed to instill fear and terrorize citizens, and thus preempt insurrection against state tyranny, has created a radical, even revolutionary strain of nationalistic patriotism that is deadly in its manifest rage.

If Burkina Faso reminds the Gambians of anything, it is to recommit to the groundswell that seeks to reanimate the sanctity of our humanity, after decades of brutal, relentless dehumanization. The arch of history plays to the advantage of a national resistance designed to change Gambia's pitiful political circumstances by leveraging the power of the greatest force of all—the people. The demonstrations, radio shows, newspaper articles, and photo opportunities, have powerful benefits in the struggle for political change, but the culmination of our combined effectiveness must be to create a popular resistance movement to change a regime that elections have consistently failed to remove from power. The Gambia's slow drift towards political anarchy can be averted by a resolution that measures up to the challenges forced on us as a nation. A political culture that is devoid of morality and fueled by pure greed, rather than being a challenge, actually presents an opportunity to reject the degenerate tyranny that has trapped the Gambia in a state of moral decadence, for the better part of two decades. The Gambian people, suffering under the weight of political tyranny, and locked in a perpetual struggle for change, see the path to freedom blocked by greed, and fueled by the intersection of ignorance and political propaganda. The rich tapestry of Gambia's homogenized cultures, the lynchpin of intertribal harmony, must be fully revived to break down the barriers to peaceful coexistence erected by the military regime. The divisiveness of the military regime will remain seared in Gambia's consciousness for a very long time, but not even the regime's provincial mind-set and ideological rigidity can deter Gambia's return to its proud democratic tradition. As a beacon of hope to our fellow countrymen and women yearning to be free, the moral sanctimony among a significant number of Gambians remains incorruptible. This serves as a kryptonite to Gambians who, by dint of greed, willfully fall victim to the dangerous abyss of propaganda and ignorance.

SUBVERTING THE CONSTITUTION AND PUTTING A PRICE ON DEMOCRACY

On the surface, the presidential elections fee hike, and its affordability, may seem like only a benign financial matter, but it is far more complicated than its surface appearance. It is, first and foremost, a withering indictment of the regime's mind-set, and citizens' complicity by indifference, which has enabled Yahya Jammeh, time and again, to undermine the capacity of the Gambian Constitution to regulate the political atmosphere and ensure civility in the political discourse. It challenges Yahya Jammeh's disregard for the Constitution as a living document replete with unwritten laws, which assign social and political behaviors in the bargain for the fairness of the electoral system. But, far worse than the fact that Yahya Jammeh's arrogance is grounded in an ostentatious show of power, his habitual flaunting of Gambia's laws and Constitution, with reckless abandon, is unprecedented, both in its scope and frequency. Yahya Jammeh's bizarre clown shows, which strike most Gambians as needless buffoonery, are, above all, extremely damaging to Gambia's image in the international community. The many dumb ideas conceived by Yahya Jammeh's rash decision-making, now include the arbitrary increase of the fees for potential presidential candidates. There is pervasive hostility among Gambians to a gutless idea that departs from custom by needlessly making political engagement and the electoral process onerous. The sweeping impeachment of the fee hike for aspirants to the presidency has generated unanimous international condemnation and spun a serious conversation around the legality of the fees, seen by many as a form of taxation. The fact that this terrible idea grew out of someone's dim brain is, by itself, incredibly troubling, and above all, it demonstrates a painful lack of fairness in the political system. In Senegal, where citizens understand their roles at the apex of the political food chain, unjustifiable trampling on the rights of citizens often sparks public objection and widespread unrest, as a way to reassert the supremacy of people's collective voice. The fee increase idea, intended as punitive measure, for diaspora contribution to opposition political parties, puts a price on democracy, apart from posing an existential threat to people's rights to choose their leaders, unencumbered by the imposition of malicious financial barriers. Yahya Jammeh's intent to scrape funds out of his primary opponents in the diaspora is a classless act of political thuggery. The financial burden that the fee increases will put on opposition political parties, apart from being totally unfair, is completely at odds with the democratic processes and, therefore, has no place in the Gambia's political system. The Gambia's slide into a one-man rule, and Yahya Jammeh's transformation, characteristic of Africa's tyrannical regimes, first started with the assassination of former finance minister, Ousman Koro Ceesay, and continued with the April 2000 student massacre, the execution of nine Mile 2 Prison inmates, the kidnapping and disappearance of Gambian citizens, and hundreds of similar human rights violation cases. Clearly, Gambia's descent into a state of chaos defies the law of physics, which dictates that for every action, there is a reaction. Like many other nations that have historically suffered the burdens of political tyranny, Gambians have fallen short of their patriotic obligation to remove Yahya Jammeh, and have only themselves to blame for it.

After each heinous crime Yahya Jammeh ordered, his actions are met with total and complete silence, and morbid fear, rather than the wrath of citizens. The threats of violence that still loom large over Gambian's of consciences, have forced citizens into fear-induced self-censorship, the denials of reality, complacency, and radio silence— acts of moral cowardice that have buried Gambians in shame. The nexus between complacency and Yahya Jammeh's predilection to buy silence and indifference form the basis of his shiftiness and disastrous, unilateralism. In 1661, King Louis XIV of France declared, "L'État, c'est moi" ("I am the state"), and three hundred fifty years later, Yahya Jammeh can declare that he too is the state, and he will be absolutely right. The power Yahya Jammeh wields is unparalleled in Africa, South of the Sahara, and the fact that Gambians still cower in fear of one man who, in reality, is fearful of them, represents a profound logical absurdity. For enraged Gambians to rise up against a political tyrant who will not stop murdering, disappearing, and incarcerating them, should be a no-brainer. It is not. And that is the sad part. But it is never too late to stand up to a vicious regime that has little regard for human life. Understanding the price he has to pay for the carnage in the Gambia, Yahya Jammeh is literally fighting to stay in power in order to save his life. But the day of reckoning cannot be delayed forever, and the writing is on the wall for all to see.

CHAPTER 2

TRIBALISM

YAHYA JAMMEH'S OBJECTIFICATION OF GAMBIANS

It was a time of great upheaval, an era fraught with danger, but also of promise. Even more important, it was a world deeply divided by political chicanery, and desperate ambitions, and Africa, not surprisingly, was home for some of the worst excesses of political imperiousness. In Oslo, groups of Asians of Indian origin descended on the city late one summer night, courting unsolicited attention and leery looks, even as their uneasy smiles provoked sympathy of a discombobulated public. But that is not the story. Their expulsion from Uganda by Dictator Idi Amin Dada is the story that made the international news headlines around the globe, and this morning, the experience of being an acquaintance to one of those Indians brought back the haunting memories of a long ago era. As I watch a YouTube clip someone posted on one of their timelines, I was mesmerized by how eerily similar in behavior Yahya Jammeh is to General Idi Amin Dada, Africa's inarguably most savage dictator. Their similarities are not mere coincidences. It is evident from the anecdotal evidence that Yahya Jammeh consciously modeled himself after Dictator Idi Amin Dada's rude eccentricity and nauseating misogyny. Yahya Jammeh's total indifference and objectification of the Gambian people, mimics the actions of a character of notoriety who once ruled Uganda with abominable fanfare—Idi Amin Dada. Like Idi Amin Dada, Yahya Jammeh decided to transform his birth village, Kanilai, into the de facto seat of government from where he will compel the entire civil service and a cross section of the nation's population to join what has developed into an extravagant tradition of self-celebration, typical of African dictators. Yahya Jammeh's narcissistic impulses and predatory instincts are the character of a person determined to dishonor his covenant with the Gambians people. This week, the Gambian public sector was grounded to a halt, because Yahya Jammeh's indifference to reason and malicious disregard for the public has hampered his ability to empathize with the broader interest of the country. Instead, slowly but decidedly, he continues to methodically cultivate a cult like personality in the Gambia, as an instrument of repression and domination. His political calculations mirror the modus operandi of totalitarian dictatorships around Africa. Equally important, Yahya Jammeh's claim supernatural powers, in a country where superstitions and the ancient voodoo practices still remain stronger belief systems than Christianity and Islam. In Gambian culture where supernatural power is equated with deities, Yahya Jammeh in effect seeks to be worshipped, not unlike the dictators in North Korea, where the rulers are worshipped as deities. Nothing represents the outwardly manifestation of contempt that Yahya Jammeh holds toward Gambians than his abominable practice of throwing biscuits at people lining the streets, in fear, as his motorcades drive past, often at a high rate of speed. As Yahya Jammeh sits on the celestial pedestal that he has created in his mind, he is comforted by a sense of invincibility. In actuality, he knows he is merely putting up a front to mask his fear of the Gambian people. The next two weeks Yahya Jammeh will spend in his hometown, Kanilai village, are designed merely to give him a platform to test the depth and breadth of his hold on power, overwhelm and diminish the pride of the Gambian people, and expose their weaknesses for the purpose of reducing them to the service of his singular interest. Make no mistake about it; Yahya Jammeh will leave office either Uganda's Idi Amin way, or the Bissau's Nino Vierra way. The choice is his.

But even as Yahya Jammeh's quackery and megalomania smudges the image of our country and turns the Gambia into another failed African state, Chongan's book, *The Price of Duty*, has opened up a new front of attention. It is evident that dealing with Yahya Jammeh's erratic behavior is of overriding interest to our country. Reactions emanating from the pungent divide between supporters of the regime and the Gambian dissident movement have generated attention at a time when Gambians should be preoccupied with the challenge of overthrowing Yahya Jammeh's regime. Is it the right time to revisit our recent past by drawing our precious attention away from Yahya Jammeh's deadly rule? I think not. This week saw the relaunch of another new website in the regime's effort to control the political narrative. The efforts at whitewashing the actions of the regime with this new website will likely fail too. If it could succeed, we would have seen it happen from the efforts of the regime's mouthpiece, the *Daily Observer* newspaper. The military regime is inclined to believe they can hoodwink the Gambian people with the pro-regime propaganda splashed on a shiny new website created purposely to misrepresent the facts and distort the truth. Only Gambians who lack objective judgment will take the regime's propaganda with any seriousness. The regime's effort to conceal its crimes; its narcotic trafficking, and the insufferable corruption, which have become an integral part of the totalitarian regime, will likely fail. With the Gambia turned into a drug cartel, using the port of Banjul as a transshipment of cocaine for notorious South America cartels, and with a significant number of state employees working with drug barons in this lucrative transatlantic drug trade, no amount of websites can help the regime hide the character stain Gambia represents in the sub-region. Gambians are fed up with Yahya Jammeh's criminality, and are bound by patriotism to want to report the regime's transgressions on the online papers operating in the diaspora. The regime's first website failed to promote the good image of this nihilistic regime; it is foolhardy to think designing another new website will be any different. This website represents government's waste of time and scarce resources. Yahya Jammeh exhibits paranoia, even as his deranged supporters abroad are engaged in futile efforts to insulate their leader from his corruption crimes and from his history of criminal abuse power.

YAHYA JAMMEH'S DIVISIVE TRIBAL BIGOTRY AND THE NEED FOR POLITICAL CHANGE

It is a word pregnant with historical innuendos and carries a stigma that correlates with bitterness and suffering. The devastation it has caused in Africa is horrendous. In many ways, it is perhaps the dirtiest word in Africa's sociological lexicon, still used by political demagogues to resurrect ancient tribal feuds and foment tribal discord, but don't tell that to the Gambia's disreputable mafia capo, military leader, Yahya Jammeh. In his twenty-one years of torture, killings, and economic pillage, he has persistently used tribalism to create potent, but invisible divisions along tribe, with reckless abandon. Yahya Jammeh's tribalism is less than subtle; in fact, it is indiscreet, duplicitous, cruel and downright repugnant and counterproductive. Last week, when Yahya Jammeh's tribal bigotry burst out in familiar dramatics and antagonistic polemics, he betrayed more than just his loathe for Mandinkas; he exposed his spinelessness and not so veiled attempts to pit Mandinkas against Gambia's other tribes. Inflaming tribal bigotry is dangerous and cowardly, but most Gambians have by now overcome that pathetic chapter of history defined by tribal wars and forced subjugation into slavery. On a campaign tour back in 2011, Yahya Jammeh first made his strongest, unprovoked tribe-motivated attacks on the UDP party leader, Ousainou Darboe. On that occasion, like all the other times he displayed profound fear of the Mandinkas, he again threatened to kill, in his effort to induce fear, stave off political dissent, and remain in power in perpetuity. Yahya Jammeh exemplifies an unhealthy obsession with Mandinkas, and his frequent anti-Mandinka outbursts are not unlike his unprovoked attacks on the West—in particular, the Gambia's historic partners and benefactors, the USA, UK, and the EU. The residue of inter-tribal quibbles that remains in Gambian society does so within the parameters of the law, and has never escalated into violence, since the advent of colonialism centuries ago. But it seems Yahya Jammeh is seeking to reverse that peaceful history by foisting acrimony and tensions among Gambia's various tribes. Yahya Jammeh's ignorance is truly emblematic of tyrants whose failures intersect with their insatiable lust for political power, which compels them to reach back into history and revive an old African orthodoxy based on intertribal conflicts, war, and enslavement. Disgraceful tribal politics is being practiced in the Gambia as the bedrock of Yahya Jammeh's dangerous, and unforgiving political ideology.

Yahya Jammeh's stroking inter-tribal rifts in Gambia, and his determination to stay in power, is not new. The purpose of the regime is premised on exercising the worst form of tribalism known to Africa, guaranteeing favorite to the Jola tribe, who consists of 7 percent of the total population, key positions in government and more than 75 percent of the senior positions in the civil service and other ancillary agencies. The Gambia long ago unwittingly became West Africa's face of political embarrassment, but it wasn't always like this. Two decades ago, only Senegal rivalled Gambia as an oasis of democracy and the rule of law, on a continent first mired in endless tribal strives, and later subjected to harsh military dictatorships. Gambia is a shell of its former self—an unfolding dystopia still writing its own story, and more history still waiting to be written. The days of tribal homogeneity may soon be over, and the peace and tranquility that gave rise to Gambia's name of endearment may soon lose its magic. The Smiling coast of Africa, a name created for tourism marketing, reflects the friendly nature of the people attracts hopeless romantics, sandy beach lovers, and adventure seeking tourists, has now become an absurd characterization of the Gambia. In the short space of two decades, Gambia has achieved notoriety as the last remaining hellhole in a sub-region still crawling out of the trenches of civil strife. In a sub-region once coursed by the prevalence of devastating political turmoil, tribal wars and military dictatorships, West Africa is gradually transforming itself into Africa's epicenter of democracy and the rule of law, reluctantly adapting to the politics of the time. But, fear-induced political ambivalence still predominates in pockets of Africa, and no country exemplifies this quandary than Gambia. Yahya Jammeh's resistance to the emerging political paradigm sweeping across Africa has left the Gambian military regime extremely petrified, and ECOWAS saddled with crippling moral dilemma. As Yahya Jammeh guiltlessly attempts to resurrect the Gambia's ancient tribal animosities, ECOWAS remains stuck between a rock and a hard place—very reluctant to confront Yahya Jammeh and help force political change, on the one hand, and passively watching the Gambia unravel and descend into political anarchy. The ECOWAS leaders' awareness of Gambia's political crisis and their disinclination to engage Yahya Jammeh is perplexing in its total lack of objective reasoning.

The deafening silence of ECOWAS and the AU does not portend well for Gambians, ECOWAS and the AU. While the group of ECOWAS leaders was meeting in Dakar, Senegal, last week, for the forty-ninth Extraordinary Summit of the Economic Community of West African States (ECOWAS), across the border in Gambia, Yahya Jammeh was again threatening the Mandinkas, and instigating the deafening uproar of Gambians all across the globe. And, as ECOWAS and the international community remain focused on the fantasy of peaceful, free, and fair elections, their ignorance of the oppressive nature politics in Gambia was on full display. Election rigging and denial of access to free and fair electoral process was entrenched in a recently promulgated law. But, the divisive tribal bigotry Yahya Jammeh is propagating is further cementing the will of the Gambian people to deny him another term of mayhem and catastrophe—killings, disappearances, mass incarcerations, mass exodus, corruption and cannibalization of the Gambian economy. Recently, Yahya Jammeh unilaterally raised the fees for presidential candidates by 10,000 percent, from \$250 in 2011 to \$25,000, effectively pricing the opposition out of the democratic process. Anecdotal evidence suggests that elections 2011 will be unacceptable, considering the rigged electoral system and the demands for Yahya Jammeh to step down. Most recently, apart from vowing to kill members of the majority Mandinka tribe, Yahya Jammeh also threatened to ban public protests, which are constitutionally guaranteed. Yahya Jammeh's threats of violence against Mandinkas were, in past instances, shrouded in ambiguity, but his threats last week was different, explicit and reaffirm his imperviousness to reason. It is not possible to overstate Yahya Jammeh's ruination of the Gambia's body politics, and after so many years in power, his insensitivity to the suffering of Gambians is frighteningly familiar. With his recent assault on the Mandinkas, most Gambians have reached the breaking point in their tolerance of his regime. It has to be said that beneath the superficial tranquility across the country, the underbelly of Gambian society is an earthquake of rage and bitterness. The fact still remains that the Gambia is a place where dabbling in politics is a dangerous enterprise, and even political neutrality is similar to walking on eggshells, guaranteeing no insulation from state sanctioned physical harm. In the binary choice between living free, and under a tyranny, Gambians will always choose freedom. The monotonous chorus demanding 'no to the sham elections' grows louder and bolder every day, and the familiar refrain, "Yahya Jammeh Must Go," is pervasive and ubiquitous in Gambian online for, and among the population. From the serene shore of Kartong, to the hills of Sare Gainako village and beyond, the yearning for a Gambia free from the permanent nightmare of political tyranny and divisive politics.

YAHYA JAMMEH'S TRIBALISM AND THE TYRANNY OF THE JOLA MINORITY

As this year's meet-the-voters tour comes to an end where it began, one of Yahya Jammeh's messages around the country has become not only a strikingly familiar refrain but the chorus of a sickening melodrama of his own making. For many years, Yahya Jammeh's signature political posture has centered on the evils of tribalism, a hot-button issue, which, by all accounts, is both a social and cultural anathema. Much to the amusement and consternation of Gambians who watch the Gambia's slide into a Jola hegemony, Yahya Jammeh's anti-tribalism sermons portray a quintessential African political animal, characterized by denial of reality that borders on delusional. Yahya Jammeh's ubiquitous tribal messages bear no resemblance, whatsoever; to the reality he created, epitomizing instead, relentless propaganda that has already been debunked by anecdotal evidence. As much as the politics of tribe in Gambia is a sensitive issue, it's the undeniable hallmark of the Yahya Jammeh regime—a divisiveness unrestrained by ethical impartiality. Yahya Jammeh's obsessive fidelity to his Jola tribesmen and rants about the vices of tribal bigotry are a lesson in contradiction. The insidiousness of Yahya Jammeh's tribal politics is memorialized in Gambia's body politics and is designed exclusively to place social and economic barriers on Gambia's majority tribes, in order to render unfair advantage to the minority Jolas. After many years, Yahya Jammeh has not departed from his messianic vision to economically elevate his fellow Jola tribe to a power status that excludes Gambia's majority tribes. Today, Gambia's majority tribes are marginalized to a devastating degree of neglect and in so doing; Yahya Jammeh has effectively decided the fate of a post–Jammeh politics in Gambia for decades to come.

Yet, despite the fact that Yahya Jammeh's Jola tribesmen consist of the majority of murdered, disappeared, and incarcerated Gambians, their support for him has helped create the phenomenon of the "tyranny of the minority." Yahya Jammeh has courted the eerie of the disadvantaged majority victimized population. And nowhere is the Yahya Jammeh's tribal hypocrisy more reflected than in the military and security services, where for more than a decade, it remained a national policy to elevate Jolas to the highest echelon of military power, at the expense of far more qualified non-Jola citizens. And to buttress his Jola tribesmen's military resumes, Yahya Jammeh disproportionately assigns them to overseas peacekeeping missions, most notably in Liberia and Sudan, where they benefit not only from lucrative United Nations pay and bonuses, but also acquire warfare experience in order to support Yahya Jammeh's grand ambition of entrenching his apocalyptic regime under Jola domination for decades to come. It would be easy to sneer at accusation of Yahya Jammeh's tribalism if it were not such a socially, politically and economically debilitating factor of Gambian life. The damage is already done, and Yahya Jammeh's unapologetic veering into the political wilderness is destined to cost Gambia more than just unfair economic deprivation of non-Jola Gambians, but propagate a hostile mind-set among other tribes, which threatens to destabilize post–Yahya Jammeh Gambia. By institutionalizing tribalism, Yahya Jammeh has probably created the marginalization of the Jola tribe from the broader Gambian family, even if only a minority of them have benefitted from his largesse, in hiring and promotions, in the civil service. Yahya Jammeh's tribal preference includes education where the regime's investment in free education for girls worth billion dalasi, provided by the Taiwanese government, is extended primarily to Foni area school girls, where the Jolas are geographically concentrated. In the civil service, Yahya Jammeh's tribal philosophy underpins his every action, and informs his political worldviews.

Yahya Jammeh has pursued a self-serving and egotistical agenda, which has less to do with tribal pride, and more to do with his determination to exploit the Jolas in order to help keep him in power. His distrust of many other Gambians due to their unwillingness to acquiesce to his nefarious political agenda is evident. Only two years ago, the sickening confessions of a young Manjago man, who, in a stunning admission, narrated how Yahya Jammeh recruited Jolas and Manjagos to harass and falsely accuse Fulas, Mandinkas, and Wollofs in the civil service of crimes they did not commit. The purpose, according to him, was to get them fired, dragged through the Gambia's kangaroo courts, and eventually replaced by Jolas. This behavior has defined Yahya Jammeh's regime, and put absolute power in the hands of the minority

Jola. Today, Jolas dominate in the leadership positions in every sector of the Gambian bureaucracy; from the military and security services and the civil service. Yahya Jammeh's self-serving pontification against the evils of tribalism, therefore, ring hallow, are disingenuous and rigged with hypocritical inconsistencies. It is preposterous for Yahya Jammeh to think he can pull the wool over the faces of Gambians. He may play dumb, but the injustice he has inserted in Gambian politics is far too serious. As Gambians watch his every move, they are reminded of an age old adage, "every action has a reaction." That applies to Yahya Jammeh's blatantly discriminatory tribal bigotry. One thing is certain; post Yahya Jammeh, the Gambia will have a lot of fence-mending to do, for if there is one thing in which there is universal agreement, it is that Yahya Jammeh has managed to sow seeds of discord among Gambians, in doing so destabilized the multi-tribal diversity and cohesiveness that existed in Gambia for centuries. In today's Gambia, Yahya Jammeh is the wrong messenger for a cause that is so fundamental to the Gambia's peace and stability, now and in the future. Until then, the Gambia is trapped under the tyranny of the Jola minority, and the one person who more than anyone else shoulders the blame for this unsustainable social phenomenon, is none other than Yahya Jammeh himself.

TRIBALISM: BLAME YAHYA JAMMEH

The ascendancy to power of Yahya Jammeh's Armed Forces Provisional Ruling Council (AFPRC) ushered in Gambia an era of unprecedented tribal bigotry and political paternalism. Regrettably, this regime-sanctioned tribal preference has never been discussed in any detail in the past, but that all seems to be changing now. The past couple of weeks have seen *Gambia Echo* newspaper and *Freedom* newspaper cast the spotlight on the vexing problems of Yahya Jammeh's tribal bigotry. The indifference to Yahya Jammeh's tribalism by most Gambians is the product of Islamic beliefs, which teach subservience and submission to political leaders as Allah's choices. The majority Islamic country indoctrinates believers that every word or action emanating from political authority must be regarded as gospel truth, and obeyed without question, irrespective of the pain and suffering inflicted on society. Since 1994, tribalism in the Gambia has not been an abstract concept; rather, it's a humiliating and dehumanizing practice that exposes the ugly underbelly of bigotry. Yahya Jammeh's regime has over the past years perfected tribalism in Gambia and used it as a means to ensure that his regime continues to survive.

The past thirteen years of the regimes rule has witnessed the domination, in all aspects of Gambia life, by Yahya Jammeh's preferred tribe, the Jolas. The Jolas constitute a minority of the Gambian population, but their total control of life and politics is possible in spite of the Gambia's remaining majority tribes. It is also true that without the collaboration of self-serving elements of the Gambia's remaining tribes, the Jolas could not sustain the oppression of the other tribes for so long. The real irony is that by collaborating and protecting Yahya Jammeh, Gambia's other tribes inadvertently support the murders, tortures and forced disappearances of their fellow tribesmen. Most Gambians admit that not all Jolas are in cohort with Yahya Jammeh, but those who are—and are flaunting their power and wealth—need reminding about a simple life lesson, "what goes around comes around." Sooner rather than later, Yahya Jammeh's inevitable demise will come, and when it comes, Yahya Jammeh's collaborators will be the objects of public scorn.

After the coup and Yahya Jammeh's ascension to power, Gambia's Asset Management and Recovery Commission (AMRC) laid claims to properties that originally belonged to public officials under Sir Dawda Jawara government. That bitter experience should serve as a reminder to those who are unfairly benefitting from the corruption of Yahya Jammeh's ruling military regime. The properties of corrupt officials of the ruling AFPRC military party, and all the wealth they have accumulated, belong to Gambians and should, after Yahya Jammeh's downfall, be seized and returned to the people. Clearly, not all Jolas are being blamed for Yahya Jammeh's tribal bigotry, but to the extent that they enabled his bigotry to continue, bear culpability for what happens and cannot be ignored. The years of military rule have encouraged the rise of corruption to incredible levels no one thought possible. One of the indicators of the regime's corruption is the way in which civil servants and public officials are appointed and promoted. Yahya Jammeh's insecurity, paranoia, and distrust of Gambia's other tribes is evident in the way he surrounds himself with Jolas, who he appoints to positions of significant authority where they wield unprecedented power. The long list of Jolas appointed to prominent positions in the regime, in comparison to other majority tribes, speaks to the hatred Yahya Jammeh has for Gambia's majority tribes. For now, until this regime changes, the vast majority of Fulas, Mandinkas, Wollofs, Sereres, Akus, and Serahules are mostly excluded from sharing in the Gambia's limitless opportunities.

YAHYA JAMMEH'S MILITARIZING THE JOLAS OR JOLANIZING THE MILITARY

It is a common strategy African dictators have so often used to prolong their stay in power. But it is divisive. It has a corrosive effect on the fabric of any society where it is practiced. Sectarian politics, which in the Gambia is exemplified by the tribal preference Yahya Jammeh has introduced, is not based on simple differences in political beliefs, but on the exploitation of the worst human instincts. Liberia's Samuel Doe practiced tribalism for years before his gruesome slaughter. Iraq's Saddam Hussein used tribalism to bring about the gory bloodbaths of innocent Kurds and the Shi'a Muslim populations, before his public execution. Libya's leader Muammar Gaddafi swore by it and used it effectively to suppress dissent, only later to be dragged out of a rat-infested sewerage hole and shot in the head. Adolf Hitler and Idi Amin Dada practiced it with senseless brutality to devastating effect. Artificial divisions based on religion, tribe, race, and other bigoted social differentiations, apart from eventually resulting in power struggles, tend to always mature into conflicts, which bring out the reptilian nature of the human character.

It is with considerable alarm that we witness how Gambia is spiraling out of control into shocking tribal bigotry. Tribal preference is now entrenched in the Gambia's body politics as an overarching policy objective of the Yahya Jammeh military regime. As sensitive and exceedingly difficult it is to talk about tribalism, and even harder yet to accept tribal bigotry, Yahya Jammeh has elevated tribal preference to a whole new level. Granted that most Gambians choose to ignore its existence, precisely because it deals with human emotions that have the potential of flaring up into conflicts, it is nonetheless alive in the Gambia, slowly tearing apart the social cohesiveness across tribes in the most insidious way. The difficulty of discussing tribal politics in the Gambia is predicated on the assumption that it could instigate tribal discord in the country. This is possible, but highly unlikely; moreover, it is not borne out by historical evidences. On the contrary, to discuss tribal bigotry before it escalates into tragedy has been proven an effective antidote to the possibility of conflicts and civil strife. Instead, pretending that tribalism does not exist in Gambia poses greater existential threat to the Gambia's future political stability.

Clearly, Yahya Jammeh has over the past decade deployed an unseemly policy objective that has seen the systemic purging and abdication of non-Jola Gambians from most senior position within civil service, replacing them in short order with Jolas who possess neither the education nor the capacity to man those positions. And if this does not constitute criminally corrupt practices, then nothing else does. Moreover, in our lifetimes, we have witnessed many human tragedies—including Syria, Libya, Democratic Republic of Congo, Rwanda, and Iraq, to name just a few—all of which arose from the kinds of disaffections Yahya Jammeh is, by sheer negligence, causing in our until recently peaceful country. The bigotry he introduced in the Gambia is truly alarming both in its divisiveness and moral bankruptcy, with the potential for unintended consequences. This is disastrous to a country that has historically prided itself in its tribal cohesiveness. There are plenty of life lessons to learn from so that history's darkest hours are not repeated in our country, but Yahya Jammeh's intoxication with power, his pursuit of momentary gratification, and his intellectual myopia have blinded him to the consequences of his unprecedented tribal bigotry and precludes any reasonable chance of reversing the decade-long tribal purge and victimization that is causes the deprivation and psychological traumas among Gambia's other tribes.

Yahya Jammeh, having tasted power, has no design to relinquish it, and coming from a minority tribe lacking the numerical advantage to keep him in power, he devised many brutal and corrupt ways to perpetuate his rule. This is the origin of his distrust of non-Jola Gambians, a fact that has conclusively been established. The driving force of Yahya Jammeh's tribal politics and examples of his irrefutable Jola bias are evident everywhere one looks—in the civil service, parastatals, foreign missions, and government projects, among others. In a country with several tribal groups, the probability that the heads of Intelligence, police, and the military will belong to the same tribe, which incidentally comprises a minority of the total population, is zero. This degree of probability becomes impossible to fathom, considering also that nearly all the heads of government institutions and parastatals are Jolas. This kind of chance does not happen in nature. Consequently, the overwhelming occupancy of senior government positions by Jolas is a social construct by a person sworn to marginalize Gambia's other tribes to exclusively benefit his fellow Jolas tribesmen.

The argument that we ought not to talk about Jolas' biases is ridiculous. But Yahya Jammeh has also killed and incarcerated more Jolas, and most of the twenty forced disappearances since in 2005 are Jolas from the Fonis. Yahya Jammeh's destabilizing biases; promotions of Jolas' interests and his brutalization of fellow Jolas who do not subscribe to his tribal inclinations are not mutually exclusive. In other words, because Yahya Jammeh promotes Jolas' biases does not mean he will not also murder Jolas. The two often happen simultaneously, and if the atrocities committed against the Jolas can be discussed, it stands to reason that there is an obligation to highlight his tribal bias, as well as his exclusive promotion of Jola interests. Yahya Jammeh has created the tyranny of the Jola minority, something the Gambia has grappled with for the last two decades. But the idea that Yahya Jammeh is doing this to avenge the way Jolas were treated in Gambia under the previous government is, on its face, downright ridiculous. The Jolas who worked as maids and house servants in Gambia were from Senegal, Casamance, and the government owed them no legal responsibility as it does to Gambian Jolas. The Gambian Jolas did not become maids or servants in Gambian households; instead, they got educated and enjoyed the same privileges and opportunities as the rest of Gambians. Even Yahya Jammeh, as a Casamance born, grew up to enjoy the same privileges as the rest. The idea that the Jolas were victimized under Sir Dawda Jawara is ridiculous.

Finally, by his policies and bigotry, Yahya Jammeh has engineered a new culture of militarizing Jolas on both sides of the border, effectively purging the security forces and military of non-Jolas and replacing them with Jolas. And even with being a minority, Jolas hold all the senior military and security positions. The policies the military regime introduced are stunting the intellectual and economic development of Jola youth by steering them toward military and other security services, rather than promoting their development in other areas of endeavor. While many Jolas are disproportionately benefiting from overseas education; their limited population means they can never overwhelm the numerical advantage of other tribes. Yahya Jammeh has, however, created a new mind-set in which Jolas' role is now as Yahya Jammeh protectors. This brainwashing is not limited to Jolas in the military and security services alone, but affects the way many Jolas perceive themselves in Gambian society. This was recently exemplified by a blanket ban of opposition party campaigns throughout the Fonis. This manifestation of Jola militancy is dangerous to the future stability of the nation. This tribal opportunity imbalance in our country must be echoed so as to empower all Gambians to resist falling into Yahya Jammeh's divisive tribalism. For not only is Yahya Jammeh Jolanizing the military, he is also militarizing the Jolas.

KANILAI: CAPITAL FOR EXECUTIONS, IMMORALITY, AND GUT-WRENCHING DEBAUCHERY

A Freedom Radio interview of a young Gambian female tells about her experience in Kanilai village. For in Kanilai, the times they are a changing. In fact, in Kanilai, they began to change more than a decade and a half ago. Situated in the southern forest region of the Gambia, the changes in Kanilai are not of the good type. This unlikely southern Gambia village, where collapsed straw fences and mangled mud walls once complemented windowless mud huts and grass houses, blusters with the endless celebration of life, but it's also a place of nightmare that plays out much like a horror-filled dream.

Among the treetops in and outside of Kanilai village, parades of colorful birds, in fewer numbers, continue to chirp as purposefully as the classical concert music of yesteryear. Around the village, the ever-diminishing forest cover, which served as a buffer zone between Kanilai and its neighborhood villages, the once untouched virgin land now represents the tragedy of the disappearing flora and fauna in the Fonis. At a different time and under different circumstance, Kanilai village could have indulged in joyous celebration of a different kind, promoting Gambian culture and other national interests; instead, debauchery, immorality, and secret executions have turned a once unassuming rural village into an intemperate place of crime and fornication.

And now, like Bonto village, in the Kombos, made infamous by the touch of South American drug cartels, Kanilai village has been branded an unholy place where marriages are wrecked, relationships broken, women gang-raped, school-age girls impregnated, and babies born to fathers that they may never know. The transformation of Kanilai village from innocence to a place of abomination did not take much effort.

Yet today, the village qualifies as the Las Vegas of West Africa, and the Gambia's Sodom and Gomorrah of Old Testament notoriety. But, unlike Kanilai, Las Vegas offers opportunities to the millions of dream chasers who swell its crowded streets to patronize the cozy, glitzy nightlife that encapsulates the vibes of Nevada. The untold and still unreported murders and executions that have taken place in Kanilai have easily qualified the village as the Gambia's village of death. And from historical perspective, Kanilai village only recently turned dirty, because its native son, Yahya Jammeh, notoriously drunken with power and ignorance, and consciously decided to transform his hometown into an open brothel in the service of the pleasures of those who come there to worship at the altar built to his own honor. But Yahya Jammeh's motivations in turning Kanilai village into a den of prostitution are purely political.

In his role as Kanilai's benefactor, Yahya Jammeh plays pimp to hundreds of females who go there to answer to his coercive invitations. By providing for his bloated military, security officers, civilian officials, and ordinary Gambians an avenue for free exercise of carnal pleasure at the expense of our sisters, daughters, mothers, neighbors, aunts, and other females, Yahya Jammeh seeks to cultivate loyalty and support from beneficiaries of his immoral largesse. To perpetuate its notoriety as a brothel, Yahya Jammeh organizes long sojourns to the village where the senior civil service and tens of thousands of people migrate to. In addition, his entire civil service follows him to Kanilai under the guise of government retreats, which is a misnomer characterization considering what really goes on there. The public infatuation with Kanilai is not without ulterior motives, and for a place where the skeletons of countless Gambian victims lie buried in unmarked graves, Kanilai ought to be the one place where only sadomasochists would want to go. Beyond that, Yahya Jammeh is increasingly feeling insecure being in Banjul, where escape from an eventual overthrow is far less likely than in Kanilai. To the many upright and decent natives of Kanilai village, Yahya Jammeh is a bad dream they wake up to each morning, a kind of native son they would rather not have.

There is no denying the fact that Yahya Jammeh has turned into the curse of the Fonis and Kanilai, and the reality of Kanilai's debauchery and immorality will remain to malign the character of the village for generations to come. In time, more salacious and damning revelations about the debauchery, murders, tortures, and fornication that occur there will come to light. In the meantime, the midnight tortures continue, the unmarked graves remain untouched and hidden from public view, fatherless babies continue to be made, gullible wives are coerced into joining Yahya Jammeh's party train, spouses abandon their husbands for a little pleasure, once secure marriages fail, relationships collapse under the weight of the scandals of unfaithfulness, and the tormented Kanilai villagers shudder in pain and disgust for their once quiet community. It is apparent that Kanilai village has turned into a place of abomination, where fornication, debauchery, and immorality have become the only way of life. Yahya Jammeh the idol-worshipper decided long ago to turn his place of birth into an open brothel where Gambians go for carnal pleasure, and for the citizens of Fonis, Kanilai, the village also represents a place where relatives and family members still go to die.

THE POWER, THE WEALTH, AND THE EXCESSES OF YAHYA JAMMEH

The adjective *absolute* does not even begin to qualify the depth and breadth of power wielded by Gambia's Yahya Jammeh. Yahya Jammeh's power is enough to make the powerful Medici family of medieval Italy, to whom Niccolò Machiavelli dedicated his controversial political thesis, *The Prince*, green with envy. The ideas and theories behind Machiavelli's *Prince* have over the past five centuries been studied, dissected, and applied in their literally context by tyrants and dictators alike, but the supremacy of brutal power advocated in *The Prince* has, in most parts of the world, been rejected by political doctrines attuned to a more enlightened world. In the intervening years since Machiavelli published his exceedingly self-serving work in 1572, the Gambia has experienced the destructive forces of tribal wars and the devastation of slavery, but even those chapters of our history have not taught Yahya Jammeh's regime the lessons of civilized human behavior. Instead, Gambia remains one of the few countries in Africa still burdened with the crushing weight of political tyranny, and the erstwhile Niccolò Machiavelli must be smiling in his cold grave.

But, while Yahya Jammeh probably never heard of Niccolò Machiavelli or his infamous hardline advocacy of brutal force in *The Prince*, he has, nonetheless, inadvertently become one of Africa's last remaining disciples of Machiavelli's Orwellian dystopia. The Gambia under Yahya Jammeh truly exemplifies the old adage that "power corrupts, and absolute power corrupts absolutely," a truism Gambians know all too well. Yahya Jammeh's exercise of the excesses of power, designed primarily to entrench his reign of terror and amass wealth for himself, has succeeded only because of his unchallenged flaunting of the laws and Constitution of the Gambia. More particularly, Yahya Jammeh's brutal exercise of power, an aberration in the new and emerging Africa, has made the world community take notice of Gambia's slow drift into political anarchy and administrative chaos. The self-serving motivations that define Yahya Jammeh and his anachronistic regime are saddled by the painful interface between greed and stubborn lust for power, exacerbated by the divisiveness of the tribal bigotry that has turned Gambians' frustration into an intense desire for radical change, by any means necessary.

Today, more than a decade and a half into Yahya Jammeh's reign of terror, his futile fantasy of Jola hegemony in our sub-region may have died long before it even began, but his ruination of Gambian society continues unabated. Gambia's story under Yahya Jammeh's rule is like a storybook prefaced by an impossible reality that can only be imagined and illustrated with a phantasmagoria derived from Yahya Jammeh's narcissistic delusions of grandeur. To understand how Gambians surrendered their freedoms to the perverse Yahya Jammeh regime, one has, among other things; reflect on the gruesome assassination of

Gambia's late civilian finance minister, Koro Ceesay, in the early days of the coup in 1995, which was followed by the senseless massacre of sixteen high school students. The fear and terror these two senseless episodes generated in the hearts of Gambians provides the backdrop to the capitulation from which Gambians are still trying to recover from. It is against this background that Gambians continue to battle the demons of Yahya Jammeh and his cabal of mean-spirited lackeys and political prostitutes.

The failure to muster enough courage to end the political nightmare in Gambia is exacerbated by the deafening silence of ECOWAS and the African Union. Additionally, the indifference of Senegal, Gambia's neighboring sister country, with which Gambia shares cultural values, tribal lineage, and geography, has hitherto been deafeningly loud in its unforgiving silence. Seventeen long years after political power was handed to Yahya Jammeh by a feckless group of young, predacious soldiers, Gambia's unlikely story is so incredibly unbelievable that it looks like something out of a Leo Tolstoy novel; something that can only be created by the fertile imagination of a sadistic mind. But, Gambia's story, with all its cruel manifestations of absolute disregard for human life, is real and marked by the disintegration of social cohesiveness and the dysfunction of the mechanisms of governance. It is the enduring legacy of a regime handicapped by catastrophic exposure to mortifying ignorance and provincial demeanor of the eclectic group of apprehensive military coupists. But the disquieting gullibility and puerile reticence exhibited by the military coupists was short-lived, as Yahya Jammeh gradually solidified power through a process of elimination that continues to devastate the Gambian family.

Yahya Jammeh's accumulation and consolidation of power represents the most wretched chapter in Gambia's history. Gambia represents the most fitting case study in misanthropy; for our country has become a glaring manifestation of the desensitization embodied in Yahya Jammeh's reptilian exercise of brute power. The last decade and a half of our history have accentuated Yahya Jammeh's criminal mind and illustrated his capacity for graphic display of demonic cruelty. But while the summary executions, murders, maiming, tortures, incarceration, and intimidations of perceived political enemies and innocent citizens alike embody the worst of Yahya Jammeh's instincts, his excesses reach far beyond the frivolous effort to entrench his reign of terror. To understand the depth and breadth of Yahya Jammeh's power, it is necessary to examine the totality of his activities both inside and outside the realm of governance. A representative sampling of his conspicuous abuse of power below does not even begin to tell the full story of the abuse under Yahya Jammeh. Below is a list of what we now know, a list that is exhaustive, but far from complete.

1. Yahya Jammeh is the wealthiest man in the Gambia and its biggest land and property owner. Yahya Jammeh owns more than a hundred farmlands dotted around the country, in addition to close to one hundred developed properties around the Greater Banjul Area and other parts of the eastern end of the country.

2. Every vehicle and equipment for use in public service in departments and agency of government, including uniforms and vehicles supplied to the military and security services, is represented before national television cameras as a gift from Yahya Jammeh.

3. Yahya Jammeh is the only authority who can hire and fire public servants, and fires and hires from the same qualified and unqualified group of people with frequency that bothers the imagination. Since 1994, nearly eighty cabinet ministers have been hired and fired, some multiple times, and others were fired even before they ever set foot in their new jobs. As for other areas in the civil service, including the diplomatic Corps, the hiring and firings are in the hundreds.

4. To date, dozens of poems, songs, and community projects have been dedicated to Yahya Jammeh by a fearful public as a way to secure financial assistance and other favors.

5. Around the country, scores of newborn babies and edifices such as hospitals, health centers, and police stations, to name just a few, have been named after Yahya Jammeh or his family members.

6. Yahya Jammeh frequently gives out hundreds of thousands of dollars to praise singers and select groups of Gambians whom he perceives as useful to his aspirations of entrenching himself in power.

7. In every past election cycle, Yahya Jammeh has fired his party's National Assembly representatives, and replaced them with even more subservient candidates.

8. Yahya Jammeh controls the Gambia's Central Bank, its staff, and the money saved in it, and uses its funds as a piggy bank to bribe foreign dignitaries with supervisory authority over Gambia.

9. The entertainment parties Yahya Jammeh holds at his adopted village are funded by the government's income-generating public agencies, which include Gambia's Ports Authority, the Gamtel, the National Telecommunications agency, and the Customs and Excise Department, to name just a few.

10. Yahya Jammeh's incorporated company, Kanilai International, was until recently an importer and re-exporter of military weapons and a partner of the notorious Russian arms dealer Victor Bout. The consignment of arms apprehended in Lagos, Nigeria, in 2010 represents only a fraction of the weaponry imported and re-exported in the name of Kanilai International.

11. Gambia's main newspaper and Radio and Television Services (GRTS) have become around-the-clock propaganda instruments for Yahya Jammeh and his military regime.

12. Yahya Jammeh's minority Jola tribesmen hold nearly 70 percent of the senior civil service jobs at the expense of the other major tribes in the country.

13. Yahya Jammeh is said to own an eight-story hotel tower in Guinea-Conakry, where his wife's family comes from, a mansion in one of the affluent parts of Washington, DC, and a supermarket and other properties in Morocco, where his wife's family lives.

14. Yahya Jammeh dictates what the Justice Department and the Gambian judiciary does, and only last week, the so-called chief justice of the Gambia shamefully described Yahya Jammeh as "my boss" in an answer to a journalist.

15. Posters of Yahya Jammeh hang all around the country, but mention of his name in public that is not flattery may result in arrest, detention, probably torture and incarceration, and perhaps even death.

16. Gambia's main Islamic body, the Supreme Islamic Council, Students' Union, the trade unions, nongovernmental organizations, the National Women's Council, and other civil society organizations are all controlled by Yahya Jammeh.

17. Yahya Jammeh is known to oversee between two and four ministerial portfolios for which he was financially compensated.

18. As we speak, nearly twelve senior civil servants, half of them holding doctoral degrees, are being tried on trumped-up charges of corruption and replaced in their positions with what can only be described as Jola analphabets.

19. Until President Macky Sall was elected, Yahya Jammeh destabilized the southern region of Senegal, supplying the arms to the rebels, providing them training, and offering them a base in Gambia, from which to launch attacks into Senegalese territory.

20. Yahya Jammeh suddenly saw religion and became peacemaker in a region in Senegal he spent more than a decade destabilizing,

even masterminding the assassinations of the late president Nino Vierra and Guinea-Bissau's Gambian-born Guinea Bissau military leader, Ansumana Manneh, but now with ECOWAS and Senegal watching, he has no choice but to desist from such activities.

21. To date, the number of Gambians who were murdered, on orders of Yahya Jammeh, is in the hundreds, with nearly twenty forced disappearances, not to mention the massacre of sixteen high school students, yet none of these deaths have been investigated, no family has been compensated, and no one has been held accountable for any of these murders and disappearances.

22. As we speak, more than two dozen students and their teachers have been arrested for staging a peaceful demonstration against a corrupt administrator recently appointed to head their establishment.

23. The Gambia's main prisons, full to capacity, have become death traps where innocent political prisoners languish, emaciated and helpless, yet one dares protest this abuse of power.

24. The massacre of forty-four Ghanaian immigrants on Gambian soil remains uninvestigated and unresolved, and both Presidents John Atta Mills and his predecessor, John Kafour, have done a lousy jobs demanding answers from Yahya Jammeh, despite the fact there are living witnesses ready to testify against the Gambian regime.

Clearly, Yahya Jammeh's holds immense power, with absolute authority and any challenge that authority can result in arrest, detention, and incarceration, or worse— death at the hands of the notorious National Security Agency. But since the election of President Macky Sall as Senegal's new president, Yahya Jammeh's power has been slipping, and it is only a matter of time before Gambia explodes into civil disobedience. With no friends in sight, perhaps soon Yahya Jammeh's grip on power, like other dictators who came before him, will come to an end. And when it does, his fate will be in the hands of the Gambian people, a people on whom he has visited untold misery and suffering. For every long night has a day.

AN OVERVIEW OF YAHYA JAMMEH'S MILITARY REGIME'S HORRIBLE LEGACY

The story I wanted to write this week was going to be extremely flattering yet not superfluous. It was going to be a glowing tribute to a great president, without being a canting exposé of his still-untold story. It was to be about Sir Dawda K Jawara's extraordinary legacy and the myth and excruciatingly painful mendacity of Yahya Jammeh's so-called regime's achievements. It was to be a story that showcases the infinite admiration and adulation of the three decades that made Gambia, like its sister neighbor, Senegal, stand out as a rare bastion of democracy and the rule of law in an Africa wrecked by greed, corruption, and citizen murders. For Gambia was a country where refugees from conflict zones and political exiles from across the continent found sanctuary away from the bloody wars of imperialism and African neocolonialism. And it was going to be a bombastic eulogy to the brilliant foresight of the man who understood the existential threat dictatorship and political tyranny posed to the stability of the state and cultural homogeneity of Gambian society.

Unlike most African countries, Gambia was a country that provided safety and security to those touched by the cruel hands of political tyranny and injustice: Liberia's preeminent journalist Kenneth Y Best; South Africa's distinguished development expert Mosebyane Malatsi; Guinea-Bissau's anticolonial Amilcar Cabral's PIAGC fighters, among many others. It was a country where Liberia's future president, Ellen Johnson Sirleaf, alienated from her chaotic homeland, also often visited her countryman Kenneth Y Best. Up until the outrageous dismantling of the legitimate Gambia government, by the military, Gambia was one of perhaps five countries on the African continent that remained untouched by the intolerable ignorance of military rule and reptilian brutality of intellectually stunted dictators who ruled Africa's political landscape. But all that changed when the group of unformed and barely literate high school graduates decided they wanted to run a country even before they learned how to run their own unaccomplished lives.

In the seventeen years since Sir Dawda K Jawara was removed from power, the Gambia has gone through grueling social, cultural, political, and economic transformation, a baptism of fire that questions the sanity of Yahya Jammeh and casts the Gambia as a pariah nation under the painfully agonizing stranglehold of an exceedingly vexing, egomaniacal military ruler. The fallout from seventeen years of political repression, wanton corruption and mindless looting of a nation has easily fostered a climate of a post–Yahya Jammeh disintegration of Gambia's social fabric as disgruntled citizens seek to settle scores in an effort to once again find their rightful places in Gambian society. The cohesiveness and cultural homogeneity that until recently distinguished Gambia from the sanguinary nature of African politics may be dealt a devastating blow as Gambians seek to sort out Yahya Jammeh's mess in an effort to bring the country back from the abyss of ruin and disintegration.

This story about the morally bankrupt buffoon, who, undeservedly and by a stroke of bad luck, ascended to the pinnacle of power in our country, is also about the completely transform Gambia into a society forever changed by the high level of collective moral deficit—a place where human conscience and the moralizing power of religion have become valueless. In new Gambia, under the dehumanizing power of fear, self-preservation has become a valuable currency, even as others are crushed by the vile, nauseating power of tyranny. To understand what Gambia has become, one is compelled to revisit a past that made Yahya Jammeh his own worst enemy. And now, even if he wanted to, Yahya Jammeh cannot walk back the utter psychological devastation he brought upon the collective mind of the Gambian people. Everything Yahya Jammeh did has done is geared towards enhancing his standing both in terms of raw power and material wealth, and national issues take a back seat to his greed and insatiable lust for power.

Today, the Gambian civil service has become exceedingly bloated and the wealth of the nation rests in the hands of one person. Yahya Jammeh is the only voice in the country that counts, and beneath the surface, and under Gambia's veil of secrecy, social decadence has set in as the morally and socially destructive vices of prostitution, the scourge of drugs, and criminality have brought devastation to a whole new generation of Gambians who have never experienced the infinitely empowering joys of living in a free society. The legendary rants and raves that have made Yahya Jammeh look like a clown come from a heart of darkness that typifies the perniciousness of a Frankenstein monster. Last year, Yahya Jammeh tried to entice diaspora Gambians into investing at home, even as he and his wife squirrelled out billions of the nation's wealth into foreign bank accounts.

Recently, Yahya Jammeh established what is universally regarded as witch-hunting Tax Commission, yet his vast business empire—in particular, his import and empire enterprise—is exempt from taxes and other liabilities. Additionally, his Land Commission, another witch-hunting exercise, made exceptions for his vast property and land holdings, much of it stolen from Gambians, in particular, those who fell on hard times. Currently, Gambia is changed by the influx of foreigners who can afford to buy up lands to replace Gambians fleeing to the safety of foreign lands. This is unsustainable and is a likely tipping point that will bring the post–Yahya Jammeh era to a head as another land reclamation commission is set up to oust foreigners and return lands to their rightful owners. The heart of the problem now is how Gambians will oust Yahya Jammeh by any means necessary, because to do that, we are put in a position where we will be on a confrontation course with the military itself.

It is a paradox, albeit not an unfamiliar one, that our military, the single most embattled government agency is also Yahya Jammeh's main protector. But how much longer will those serving in the military continue to be murdered and fired from their positions without fighting back is the question on everyone's mind. The fact that Yahya Jammeh has turned the military—our sons and daughters, brothers, sisters, aunts and uncles, nieces and nephew, neighbors and class mates—against citizens is itself frightening, to say the least. But one thing is certain; no condition is permanent, every dictatorship has an end time, and Yahya Jammeh's end days are closing in on him. Like every dictator and murderer before him, he too will face the day when the ground under him will give way to the violent retribution of the nation he has reduced to fear, terror, and complacency. As it stands, no prayer, no *jalang* sacrifices, or devil worship can change the course of this eventuality.

YAHYA JAMMEH TO EU: GO TO HELL; MILE 2 EXECUTIONS BLOWN OUT OF PROPORTION

Yahya Jammeh's shocking statements last week that the execution of innocent Mile 2 Prison inmates 'was blown out of proportions,' and telling the European Union "to go to hell," veered towards insensitivity, and close to insanity. The twisted mind-set that compelled Yahya Jammeh to even enunciate such sanguinary comment is more than callous; it's demented. Like everything else, Yahya Jammeh is merely putting on a brave face to projects calm comfort to give the impression that he can stand up to the powerful European Union, but deep in his guts, he is a nervous wreck, in despair due to the intense political pressure being brought to bear to expose the ruthless underhandedness with which he exercises political power. Nowadays, Yahya Jammeh is a man consumed by severe internal turmoil and on the verge of buckling under the weight of an unforgiving external pressure. For a universally hated person as Yahya Jammeh, with everything to lose, the veneer of numbness and detachment from the Gambia's state-sanctioned murders, forced disappearances, and the constant arrest and detentions of the innocent, which have profoundly tortured the Gambian psyche, illustrates the depth of Yahya Jammeh's apprehension about his regime's future survival prospects. For years, the overarching concern for Yahya Jammeh has not been the business of governing; instead, he is consumed by political tyranny and economic exploitation of the state. Today, a year after the national elections, not one cabinet portfolio has survived one month without the notorious reshuffling exercise that has bedeviled this listless regime. Not unlike everything else he is doing, the frequent cabinet changes are far from being just tangentially related to the perennial chaos and crisis pervading every aspect of life in our country. The familiar, and crippling ministerial musical chairs, like a country under martial law, is a disastrous conundrum emblematic of the dysfunction of the regime.

Last week, an internet video of Yahya Jammeh, fecklessly ranting against the European Union, surfaced to the complete and utter dismay and disgust of most Gambians. The video exposed his discomfort, and the visible disconnectedness of the eclectic group of miserable cabinet ministers hunched, humped, and crouched in total filial silence. In his monotonous hour-long soliloquy, Yahya Jammeh's stunning lack of any sense of reality was an eerie reminder of Idi Amin Dada's infamous ministerial meetings that so often ended in the deaths of some of his cabinet ministers. But Yahya Jammeh's defiance of the EU is a losing proposition, yet a déjà vu likely to condemn Gambia to the specter of economic sanctions not unlike those that collapsed the Iraqi and Iranian economies. The prospect of Yahya Jammeh condemning the Gambia to punishing economic sanctions must be a wake-up call to all Gambians, but it is common knowledge that he is totally impervious to reason, besides lacking the intellectual fortitude to make sound judgments. The EU's capacity to wreck economic havoc and totally incapacitate Yahya Jammeh's regime is not in dispute, and his defiance and downright disrespectful posturing will not make sanctions less likely. The European Union's recent groundbreaking commitment to the Gambia's interest is underpinned by a commitment to the rule of law. As determined and as focused as the EU is, Yahya Jammeh's posturing will likely push Gambia toward the brink of economic catastrophe in the event he does not relent in the ongoing dispute with the EU over human rights. EU bureaucrats cannot be bribed, as Yahya Jammeh does with breathtaking frequency to selfish IMF and World Bank officials from corrupt third world countries. The EU will never capitulate to Yahya Jammeh's madness, narcissism and charm offensive. Moreover, Dr. Momodou Sedat Jobe, Gambia's internationally renowned political and diplomatic luminary, will not make it easy for Yahya Jammeh as he travels around Europe to encourage its leaders to address Gambia's bloody, long, drawn-out struggle against political tyranny. In addition to Dr. Jobe's ongoing tour, Dr. Amadou S Janneh, Civil Society Associations-Gambia's (CSAG) newly elected strategist, and Mr. Banka Manneh, CSAG's chairman, have planned travels this summer to meet with European and US officials and Gambian communities aimed at uniting Gambians in the struggle against Yahya Jammeh's dictatorship.

Yahya Jammeh's declaration that the universally condemned executions of innocent Mile 2 Prison inmates on August 23, 2012, 'is blown out of proportions' is disgusting abstraction of reality. If anything, it demonstrates a stolid mind-set, and questions his intellectual fitness to serve as president. Tabara Samba's brutal gang rape before her executions, the execution of a mentally ill inmate, and the execution of Momodou Darboe, whose death sentence was commuted to life more than twenty years earlier, are all snapshots of the sheer lawlessness and screaming madness that surround their executions. The legal remedies the law allowed were ostentatiously abrogated with mindless impunity. Needless to say; the executions were a tragic national aberration of monumental proportion, besides being a glaring exhibition of an unmitigated disregard of the Constitution and the laws of the land. Even today, nearly six months later, the Mile 2 Prison executions still defy imagination. The European Union's recent demand for the disclosure of the burial grounds of all the executed, comes in the wake of the incessant demands by Gambians for the retrieval of the corpses of the dead in order to grant them decent religious burials. It is understandable that European Union may be skeptical about Yahya Jammeh's human sacrifice practices, primarily because, it sounds too farfetched. Nearly twenty children have so far been sacrificed in staged motorcade accidents in which they are lured into locations they were vulnerable, leading to their merciless deaths. Rush for the biscuits Yahya Jammeh that throws out from heavily armoured speeding motorcades have so far claimed the lives of more than a dozen children, and the primitive tribal practice of child sacrifice ended only after the media realized that these accidents were human sacrifices, not accidental deaths. But these are uncommonly difficult days for Yahya Jammeh, and with internal and external pressure mounting, he is likely to execute more Gambians again to ward off 'evil spirits' and 'save' his regime from collapse. Gambians must, therefore, be vigilant, but above all, mindful of Yahya Jammeh's effortless capacity to kill more. We are in the nexus between EU's determination and Yahya Jammeh's familiar stubbornness, and the Coalition for Change Gambia and Civil Society Associations-Gambia urge the European Union to never succumb to Yahya Jammeh's puerile rants and banal threats. EU's position must be the unequivocal support of the Gambian people in this time of desperate need for political change. And for the Gambian people, going forward, fear is no longer an option.

CHAPTER 3

NEIGHBORING SENEGAL

MESSAGE OF SOLIDARITY TO SENEGAL FROM ACROSS THE BORDER

This year, after more than fifty years of relative political stability, Senegal is in the spotlight for all the wrong reasons. With barely two weeks to the divisive elections of March 18, the whole world is holding its collective breath, waiting, watching, anxious, and hopeful—hopeful that five decades of exemplary political leadership will not descend into chaos or mire Senegal in a state of political quandary.

Africa's premier democracy is facing the greatest challenge of our lifetime, a baptism of fire that will test the limits of Senegal's endurance. Little wonder then that the eyes of the world are focused on Senegal, Africa's last bastion of democracy, a country that boasts Africa's most robust and open political system, a true democracy untouched by the vicissitudes of tyranny and untainted by the loathsomeness of political dictatorship.

Fifty years of unprecedented political stability is at stake, and Senegal's calm demeanor and moderating influence on the tripartite Senegal, Guinea-Bissau, and Gambia tripartite could be at risk of degenerating into a political morass characterized by civil unrest and political strife. And with Yahya Jammeh arming, training, and supporting an insignificant group of Casamance separatists on the southern border with the Gambia, one more hotspot in the Senegambia/Guinea-Bissau region is a thing Africa does not need.

In this brave new era of transformative global politics, the people of Senegal are not standing alone. But amid all the international attention, one country, the Gambia, more than any other, has more to lose from Senegal's most violent political season in recent memory. And unlike the rest of the free world, Gambians, lacking a legitimate government to speak on their behalf, have taken the liberty to extend our unwavering support to the Senegalese people in their unrelenting desire to keep their traditional democratic values alive.

Senegal represents a determination to maintain the sanctity of the democratic system supported by the free world and envied by the rest of Africa. It is a struggle of the emerging new Africa devoid of the old mindset where lifetime leadership and endemic corruption serve the few at the expense of the majority. And as the international community mobilizes to give moral support to Senegal's opposition forces, Gambians join the chorus of voices to express sympathy for the lives lost.

The bloodletting brought on by the incredible intransigence of the senile eighty-five-year-old Abdoulaye Wada did not have to happen. Any rule without the consent of the governed is doomed to fail, and in the struggle between the forces of tyranny and government by the people, Gambians are unequivocal their support of the collective opposition's effort to deter hereditary political leadership in Senegal.

Today, a new paradigm shift in consciousness is gaining momentum across Africa, and Mali, Guinea-Conakry, Ivory Coast, and now Senegal are leading the charge against the entrenchment of political leaderships that have turned Africa's republican constitutions into de facto monarchies. But more than that, President Abdoulaye Wada's cunning attempt to position his son, Karim Wada, to succeed him, is doomed to fail, because the Senegalese will not tolerate the repeat of

Faure Gnassingbe or Joseph Kabila in our midst. In the challenge to keep the integrity of their democratic heritage, when the dust settles, Senegal will come out injured, but not substantially harmed by the cruel intransigence of outgoing President Wada.

This optimism was recently bolstered as the opposition coalesced around Macky Sall's candidature in the second round of elections. Moustapha Niasse, Ousmane Tanor Dieng, Idrissa Seck, and Chiekh Tidiane Gadio, and the rest of the opposition, not only made the world proud, but ensured the failure of President Wada's aspirations to be succeeded by Karim Wada. The Senegalese opposition has exercised political maturity and selflessness in their collective representation of Senegal's opposition forces. And who can forget the steadfastness with which Singer Youssou Noure and Alieu Tine inspired sacrifice and played a pivotal role in rallying the Senegalese people around the battle cry for political justice.

Today, with the blood of innocent Senegalese spilled over President Wada's attempt to entrench his rule, he has lost an opportunity to emulate Senegal's former iconic leaders—the nobility of late Leopold Sedar Senghore, the quite charm of Abdou Diouf, and the alluring enigma of Mamadou Dia. What Abdoulaye Wada did to Senegal over the past weeks was typical Machiavellian heavy-handedness. But then the pervasion of Senegal's democratic process has not gone unchallenged, and the consequences of President Wada's actions may come back to haunt him. Senegal was pushed to the brink, until a coalition of opposition forces brought the country back from the proverbial cliff edge, and delivered the country a prideful moment in political transition. In Senegal, a new generation of democratic leaders is ascending to power, and political change is coming to Africa, one country at a time.

WELCOME, PRESIDENT MACKY SALL: NOW
THE BITTER TRUTH ABOUT GAMBIA

The Republic of Senegal and Gambia—two countries, one nation, and this is not political pandering. It is a fact grounded in our shared heritage—language, culture, geography, and history. It is the social fabric bequeathed by our ancestors and seared in the traditions inherited from our past. The shallow view of the Senegal and Gambia dichotomous identities that today define the two nations as separate entities is forced colonial legacy and ridiculous invention of long-ago geopolitical interests, which nonetheless have miserably to blur the reality of our common identity. More than ever before, the convergence of shared interests encapsulate more than just the primordial instincts we share as one people, but also the political objectives assigned by the manifestly compelling social and economic interests that are now at the core of our different political and governance systems. For even as two countries, the two countries are forever condemned to live as one nation and no amount of personal interest and political machinations can change that.

Yet, in spite of all that joins us as one people, the political world that defines our common interests has created gaping dissimilarities in the quality of life of our two people. In Senegal, the elections have just ended, and the political struggle that led to the opposition's landmark victory is yet to be inventoried into a history written in the blood of those who sacrificed their lives so Senegal will remain free. But even as the memories of Senegal's dead are yet to be eulogized, the legacy of the elections has put Senegal on a pedestal all its own: unique and different from any other African country. Senegal has once again proven what we in the Gambia knew all along; that it is a rare gem in expanding the democratic tradition, a beacon of hope for the survival of a democratic space which every country envies, and every government should be aspire to emulate. On President Macky Sall's historic visit to the Gambia, he can soak up the superfluous pump and pageantry that will greet him, but he should also be mindful that beneath the superficiality of it all is a country locked in an eternal struggle to be free from the banalities of military rule.

Ours is a history haunted by the painful memories of years of political criminality under the menacing shadow of brutal military regime, a regime so corrupt and clueless that it makes the barbarian regime of Idi Amin look like the true emblem of Jeffersonian democracy. The last decade and a half has left Gambia demoralized by a sanguinary past, and the military regime loathed for the shameful notoriety of its recent history. For far too long, the murders, forced disappearances, executions, arrests, intimidations, detentions, and incarceration of innocent citizens and noncitizens alike have remained Yahya Jammeh's claim to fame. And even then, in their small way, Gambians continue their defiance in the face of the naked mismatch between the cabal of armed thugs who have turned the country into a haven for the transshipment of South American drugs, and military weapons bound for other failed regimes like Guinea-Bissau. Coincidentally, the week of President Macky Sall's visit to Gambia also marks the twelfth anniversary of the massacre of sixteen schoolchildren, mowed down by the military regime on the orders of Yahya Jammeh and VP Isatou Njie-Saidy, children killed for merely protesting the death of a fellow student at the hands of the Gambia's "Gestapo" police force. This week, Gambians everywhere remember them and honor their memories.

Even as we remember that fateful day, April 10, 2000, so long ago, we will focus attention on the atrocities of a misanthropic regime whose unforgivable cruel ignorance has undeservedly turned a once admired country into one of Africa's last remaining pariah nations. For seventeen long years, Yahya Jammeh led a gutless regime whose claim to fame is a shameful history of brutality, mendacity, deceit, and today, the Gambia remains haunted by the tragedy of the student massacre, a day that will long be remembered as a watershed event in the Gambia's tortured history under Yahya Jammeh's unbearable military regime. On his memorable visit to Gambia, President Macky Sall should be reminded that Yahya Jammeh's words are worthless and that he is extremely deceitful—in fact, so deceitful that he makes Judas Iscariot of Bible notoriety look like a saint. In the coming weeks and months, Yahya Jammeh will manifest what we in Gambia know him all too well for, the use of financial and material bribery to buy loyalty, influence, and indifference from Senegalese officals. This is a forewarning to President Sall and his emissaries who will have the misfortune and the curse of interacting with Yahya Jammeh in different bilateral interest situations.

Beyond that, Yahya Jammeh will whisper into President Sall's ears what he thinks he wants to hear, but it would all be habitual lies that will have no bearing on reality, tales that are politically expedient to utter as a way to blind President Sall to the reality of Yahya Jammeh's nefarious intents, given his unapologetic sponsorship and perpetuation of the conflict in southern Senegal. If President Sall wants to understand who the real Yahya Jammeh is, all he needs is look no further than the crowded streets of Dakar; for somewhere among the mass of humanity in downtown Dakar are hundreds if not thousands of Gambian refugees who fled their country, not to mention the exodus to Europe and America of the country's best and brightest. But as Yahya Jammeh's notorious military regime continues its mindless victimization of innocent citizens, Gambians will continue to resist the train wreck that is Yahya Jammeh. For now, suffice it to remind President Sall that even in the face of his blatant support of the rebels in southern Senegal, Yahya Jammeh managed to disarm former president Abdoulaye Wada with lies and empty rhetoric. Our hope for Gambia is that President Sall will become Yahya Jammeh's kryptonite, the power that will compel him to change his ways or else.

MACKY SALL'S BLUNDER AND SENEGAL'S DESCENT INTO FAMILIAR POLITICAL APATHY

Will he or will he not? The intensity of the speculations and counter speculations were not unlike a moviegoer's burning desire to unlock the mystery of who shot J.R, in the movie *Dallas*. In the end, it did not take long before this nagging question was answered. And to say the answer was distressing to Gambians would be the understatement of the decade. It was like seeing the Gambia's next twenty years of history flash right before our eyes: more murders, more executions, more disappearances, more forced exiles, more wealth accumulation, and the cruel perpetuation of the tyranny of a family dynasty. The man who, less than a year ago, was widely cast as the embodiment of Jeffersonian democracy in Africa, and a possible catalyst in the Gambia's liberation from political tyranny, suddenly turned into the naive antihero. The rage over Senegalese President Sall's attendance of the Gambia's forty-eight-year independence anniversary exploded into accusations of receiving funding from Yahya Jammeh in Senegal's last presidential elections. But a former Gambian foreign minister and diplomat, based in Dakar, Dr. Momodou Lamin Sedat Jobe spurned such recriminations as baseless innuendos, preposterous at best and downright fictional, at worst. Notwithstanding, President Macky Sall is yet to prove that he is imperviousness to the influence of money, and Gambians who are all too familiar with Yahya Jammeh's predilection to buy loyalty, apathy, and indifference, are wary that President Sall could succumb to Yahya Jammeh's charm offensive and the habit of bribing those who, on moral grounds, reject his tyrannical regime.

The once cultural and diplomatic intimacy between the Gambia and Senegal has, since Yahya Jammeh came to power, descended to the dark depths of political cataclysm, making relations between the sister countries prone to the devastating military conflicts. A case in point: the perennial MFDC rebellion in South Senegal has intensified in recent years with the acquisition of modern Iranian weaponry, which has shifted the conflict from sporadic to an unprecedented level of carnage and bloodletting. The historical ties that glued Gambia and Senegal together have devolved into chaos as Yahya Jammeh's heavy-handedness and interference in aggravating the Southern Senegal conflict intensifies. For years, Yahya Jammeh unbendingly pursued provocation and coercion as diplomatic cudgel over Senegal, but Senegal and Bissau have been cynically deferential to Yahya Jammeh's duplicitous Casamance policy. And sensing Abdoulaye Wada's senile old age and susceptibility to Yahya Jammeh's fairytales, coupled with the near collapse of civil order in neighboring Guinea-Bissau, Yahya Jammeh found a niche that will enable expanding his sphere of influence in the region; from Gambia to Guinea-Bissau. The case of the MFDC in Casamance and the seizure of arms in Nigeria, bound for the Gambia, further complicate the relations between Senegal and Gambia. These and the recent execution of two Senegalese nationals and the murder last week of Amadou Bah, another Senegalese citizen, combined to cloud President Macky Sall's Gambia visit in controversy—perhaps deservedly. Criticism of President Sall is, to many Gambians, characterized as harsh and unforgiving, in some quarters, but others view President Sall's cavorting with Yahya Jammeh insensitive to Gambians and beneath the dignity of the Senegalese president.

President Macky Sall's Gambia visit strikes Gambians as an alarming and a calculated disregard of the Gambia's political nightmare; the festering horror of Yahya Jammeh savagery and withering contempt for human life. Use of Gambian territory as epicenter of the protracted, but devastating Casamance rebel activity, and Senegal's failure to contain Yahya Jammeh's willful and dangerous adventure into political anarchy, call into question Senegal's diplomatic approach to Yahya Jammeh's perpetuation of the unending Casamance conflict. Moreover, the use of Gambian territory as an MFDC rebel base is a flagrant violation of Gambian law and the sovereignty of the Gambian state, apart from illustrating the powerlessness of Gambia's lawmaking body. Containing the alarming excesses of the Yahya Jammeh military regime must be a goal for President Macky Sall. In any way one looks at it, the Gambia is now engaged in acts of war against Senegal by providing sanctuary, weapons, and recuperative facilities to injured MFDC rebel fighters, but Senegal has yet to reciprocate in equal measure to this jaw-dropping menace emanating from Gambia. Additionally, juxtaposing the Casamance discord and the casualness with which several Senegalese were executed in the Gambia provides overwhelming evidence for Yahya Jammeh's disdain for President Sall and the Senegalese government. Yahya Jammeh's social and political bend is informed by his divisive nationalist ideology, and his deranged tribalism has percolated into the consciousness of Gambians, to arouse deep sense of alarm in a country long united by a common national identity.

Yahya Jammeh's pedestrian worldview and his knee-jerk, sorcery-driven decision-making process have reduced Gambia to a regional pariah administered by dark forces and the magical powers of witchcraft. For a person so incredibly steeped in primitive idol worship, the banality of Yahya Jammeh's provincial mind-set is reinforced by an astonishing indulgence in cannibalism and human sacrifice. True, given the circumstances, carrying weight for Gambians is worthy of President Sall's consideration mainly, because family ties across the border bear testimony to the mutual affinity Gambians and Senegalese share. The gravity of the human rights abuse in Gambia needs no embellishment to put in proper context, because Yahya Jammeh's story is written in the blood of citizens and noncitizens alike. Already, Gambians traumatized by years of ruthlessness read too much into President Sall's every action, characterizing Senegal as a country in denial of the political scourge in the Gambia, yet former Gambian diplomat and foreign minister Sidi Moro Sanneh forcefully rejects unsubstantiated charges against President Sall, citing his entourage to the Gambia as indicative of his displeasure with Yahya Jammeh's regime. President Sall's relations with Yahya Jammeh or lack thereof, is scrutinized with revolutionary vigor by many Gambians who see Senegal as the key to resolving the Gambian tyranny and humanitarian crisis. Gambians' strident opposition to the Gambian regime is driven by the reptilian brutality with which Yahya Jammeh exercises authority. Partnering with neighboring Senegal to restore sanity and the rule of law in Gambia is desirable, if not inevitable. For now though, the ball is in President Macky Sall's court. At the very minimum, President Sall should relax on his opposition to Gambians' use of Senegalese territory to liberate their country. If anything, Gambian territory is being used by Yahya Jammeh to destabilize South Senegal. For now, whether Senegalese President Macky Sall has also blundered into Senegal's familiar political apathy, only time will tell.

GAMBIA'S STATE CRISIS AND SENEGAL'S IMPOSSIBLE SECURITY

"I tremble for my country when I reflect that God is just; that his justice cannot sleep forever." If Thomas Jefferson's premonition more than three centuries ago seemed sagacious and even prophetic, it was because he understood the enduring power of freedom. Even after the elapse of so much time, Thomas Jefferson's ominous maxim puts in proper perspective the inevitable demise of the Gambia's pungent military regime. But Thomas Jefferson's divination only reinforces the human desire for liberty, away from the strains and stresses of political abuse that continue to consume the Gambia. And as Gambia sinks even deeper into political and economic paralysis and political insanity echoes ever louder, the nobility of being free people will continue to challenge the pervasive cannibalization of Gambia's political and economic life. This week, as Senegal's new Prime Minister, Aminata Touré, visits Gambia to partake in the questionable celebration of twenty years of disastrous and divisive tribal politics, the uneven Senegal and Gambian relations will once again surface to the forefront of the political conversation. The failure of Senegal to articulate clear public policy toward Gambia where military dictatorship flaunts unsettling reptilian brutality presents serious challenges which interrogate Senegal's dispassionate response to the Gambia's toxic military regime. Senegal's commitment to social order and political sanity in the Gambia will have profound implications for Senegal, where the decades old low-intensity civil strife in Casamance, masterminded by Yahya Jammeh, contravenes the sovereignty of Senegal boundaries and sub-regional stability. Colonial interests created shocking limitations to Senegal and Gambia's political intercourse; nonetheless, Senegambia is not a mere slogan that will wither with time. It is a living reality of the cultural bonds that predate the shared Senegambia colonial experience.

But to bring historical perspective to the nagging Senegambia relationship, one has to harken back to the 1970s when Gambian students foist a massive riot to retaliate in the murders of Dakar University students, which cut short President Senghor's three-day state visit to the Gambia. It was Gambians' way of honoring the dead and the living at Dakar University and to the entire people of Senegal. For when justice demanded it, young Gambians stood up to state overreach in Senegal and inflicted massive damage to state property in Gambia. In this period when Machiavellian politics in Gambia are underpinned by the regime's existential fear of the demonstrably dehumanized Gambian people, Senegal's unresponsiveness to Gambia's political challenges is borderline reckless, and demonstrates a diplomatic bungling that is both negligent and downright incompetent. Senegal's inability to conceptualize a future beyond its false sense of security, in pursuing shortsighted political expedience, tests the mental dexterity of its leaders' abilities to rationalize Gambia's existential problems within the context of Senegal's own political and economic security. And if there is one constant not subject to manipulation and diplomatic nuances, it is the unique Senegambia bloodlines and spatial twinning, powerful forces that combine to resist efforts to create the superficial decoupling that continues to corrupt the neighborliness between the two sister nations. At a time Senegal and Gambia bogged down by divisive, politically motivated, cross-border transport ruckus, it seems preposterous for a Senegalese leader to grace the Gambia's wasteful independence celebration, when thousands of Gambians have fled the country for the safe haven of near and distant lands. Today, the arrogance and arbitrariness with which the Gambia is governed by the military regime has mobilized citizen resistance of the dangerous pitfalls of autocracy and degrading subordination to Gambia's social divisions and economic plunder.

Based on anecdotal evidence, the history of Gambia's lethal regime has yet to be persuasively seared into the political consciousness of the broader segment of the Senegalese and their government. At this juncture of diplomatic relations between the two sister countries, Senegal may use the reverse rationale of non-interference due to bloodlines and spatial geography, to justify indifference to the Gambia's political crisis. Yet, to date, the havoc wreaked by the Gambian military regime is compounded by an absolute disregard for the sensibilities of Gambians, and with prisons overflowing with innocent victims; the key question is whether Senegal has the moral capacity to reverse its frame of mind on the Gambia's destructive politics and catastrophic tribal divisions. Gambia's blundering military rule and Yahya Jammeh's relentless ad hominem attacks on innocent Gambians notwithstanding, radical change of attitude is manifesting, as more Gambians are being persuaded to testify to the regime's sickening politically motivated atrocities.

These shifting loyalties in Gambia portend the most basic measure of the inevitable demise of the military regime, a paradigm shift unheard of just three short years ago. But until real and substantive change comes to the Gambia, the population will still latch onto hope, even as the country continues mourning the staggering loss of life under the tyrannical military regime. After nearly two decades, the Gambia's shaky diplomatic ties with Senegal, motivated by Yahya Jammeh's illusions of grandeur, have not taken into consideration the passions of the history, geography, and culture of the sister nations. In a commentary last year, the Senegalese government was challenged to reconsider the political morass in Gambia and its effects on to the prolonged civil strife in Casamance, With Gambia in the grip of a madman, peace in southern Senegal will continue to remain a pipe dream. As Gambia deteriorating into a permanent state of crisis, peace in Senegal will factually be impossible to achieve.

YAHYA JAMMEH IS DESTABILIZING
SENEGAMBIA/BISSAU TRISTATE REGION

A recent *Daily Observer* newspaper editorial, captioned "Senegal continues to destabilize Gambia," was rather baffling. Evidently, the *Daily Observer* newspaper is suffering from political myopia. There is one person destabilizing the Senegal, Bissau, and Gambia tristate region, and it's not Senegal or President Macky Sall. No one in the international community takes Yahya Jammeh's whining seriously since his regime has lost credibility at home and around the world. The Gambia's accusations that the Senegalese Jakai rebels helped Col. Ndure Cham escape, do not shock anyone; on the contrary, if it's true, then Gambians thank the rebels for that act of kindness. Gambians hail Jakai rebels as partners in the struggle against Yahya Jammeh's dictatorship. Gambians are thankful that Col. Ndure Cham escaped with his life; otherwise he would be one of the regime's statistics. Gambians express gratitude to the rebels for extending a helping hand to Col. Ndure Cham, but the rebel's job is not quite done yet, because more of our citizens may flee into Casamance to escape Yahya Jammeh's murderers: the NIA, Jugglers, and the Green Boys.

It is dumbfounding that the *Daily Observer* has sympathy for the innocent civilians and villagers caught in the crossfire between warring Casamance rebel factions. This humane side of the *Daily Observer* has not been evident in recent memory as the carnage continues in Gambia, but the fact that the paper now speaks out on behalf of Casamance citizens, who may collateral damage in this fractional strife in Casamance, is laudable. For Gambians, these misplaced sympathies beg the questions: Where was the *Daily Observer* when all the politically sanctioned murders, attempted murders, and tortures were being carried out by Yahya Jammeh's NIA, Jugglers, and his Green Boys? Where was the *Daily Observer* when Daba Marenah and five other young Gambians were murdered without the benefit of a judicial process? Where is the *Daily Observer* when so many of our fellow citizens are still disappearing from the face of the earth? Where was the *Daily Observer* when Yahya Jammeh's henchmen executed Private Camara and military service men and women?

But even more than that, where is the *Daily Observer* when scores of Gambians are being arrested and detained for no legal reason, and without due process? Where is the *Daily Observer* when Gambia's educated citizens languish in our prisons or fleeing the violence in Gambia for the safer havens of Senegal, Europe, and the US? Where was the *Daily Observer* when Yahya Jammeh's regime murdered nearly four dozen innocent Ghanaians and dumped their bodies in a well in Casamance? Yahya Jammeh and his regime and the *Daily Observer* complain and whine about the sad predicament facing Casamance villagers, but where is their compassion for Gambian families whose, sons and daughters, fathers, mothers, uncles, and friends are being murdered or thrown in jail on Yahya Jammeh's orders? No one knows how many Gambians are packed in the nation's dirty, stinking, mosquito- and rat-infested prisons system. It is clear, however, that over the past years, nearly a hundred inmates have been known to die of hunger and diseases there. Besides, many more have been tortured, and some are destined to carry the trauma and scars of tyranny for the rest of their lives. These atrocities happen as a matter of routine, right under the nose of the *Daily Observer*, but the paper ignores it to instead sympathize with villagers in Casamance. The *Observer* ignores far worst atrocities within the Gambian borders. It is hypocrisy when the *Daily Observer* chooses to ignore the murders, tortures, and disappearances in Gambia. If the *Daily Observer* hopes to arouse the sympathies of the international community as a mouthpiece of the Gambian regime, that's unlikely ever to happen. In light of this, it is my opinion that its way overdue for Gambian dissidents to meet and discuss the future of our country and the transition to a multiparty democracy. Because Yahya Jammeh has the national elections locked in his favor, the Gambian people must figure out how to remove him from power by any means necessary. For, every day Gambian people do not act, is a day wasted and another Gambian murdered by the military regime.

SENEGAL'S CONTINUITY OF INDIFFERENCE
OR ARTICULATION OF NEW POLICY

To many political observers in Gambia, the sudden changes in Senegal's cabinet have once again stirred the dominant viewpoints emblematic of Gambians' recent attitude toward neighboring Senegal. The diverse Gambian viewpoints, informed by Senegal's Gambia policy, or lack thereof, in the recent past, suggests either a radical change likely to define Senegal's new policy toward the Gambia or inadvertently bolster a regime that long ago lost its moral grounding. The absurdity of Senegal's failure to clearly articulate a Gambia policy, since the military coup in 1994, spawned speculations about Senegal's political detachment, punctuated by sporadic optimism about the likelihood that Senegal may succumb to the agony of the Gambian people. By virtue of geography, every minuscule change in Senegal's cabinet profile provides opportunity to articulate a Gambia policy that defines the future of Senegambia relations. President Macky Sall's appointment of a renowned human rights activist, anticorruption campaigner, and former justice minister, Ms. Aminata Toure, as head of government, could color the future of relations between Gambia and Senegal and usher in a new paradigm likely to alter the strained relations between the sister nations. The new prime minister of Senegal boasts a resume that more broadly speaks to the needs of ordinary Senegalese, and is more likely to focus more attention on its Gambia neighbor. Moreover, the significance of Prime Minister Toure's appointments of the International Federation of Human Rights former boss, Sidiki Kaba, as justice minister, Augustine Tine, armed forces chief, and Abdoulaye Daouda Diallo as interior minister, is not lost on Gambians. If anything, this has heightened Gambians interest in Senegal's new cabinet and, above all, deepened the curiosity about a new Senegal policy on Gambia. And as long as the political situation continues to worsen in Gambia, Ms. Aminata Toure's new cabinet will be the subject of relentless speculations and mindless conjectures if Senegal continues to ignore the embattled Gambian population. Over the past decade and a half, Senegal and Gambia barely coexisted under a cloud of suspicion over the Gambia's unapologetic support of the decades old low intensity rebel insurrection. But the Gambia's support of the Casamance MFDC rebels is not supported by the Gambian people, recognizing that supply of weapons, offer of training bases, and medical facilities on Gambia territory violates the Gambia's sovereignty. The downward spiral in Senegal and Gambia relations, since 1994, was recently propelled into a crisis situation with the unchallenged execution of Senegalese nationals by a regime that puts no value on human life. Recently, three Gambian dissidents, Ndure Cham, Saul Ndow, and Mahawa Cham, were abducted in Dakar and returned to face torture and certain death in Gambia, yet not even this international scandal of about Gambia breaching Senegalese sovereignty seemed to matter or arouse President Macky Sall's fury.

Clearly, President Sall appears totally indifferent to the lives of Gambian dissidents under Senegal's protection. And that said; Gambia's belligerence toward Senegal culminated in the supply of sophisticated military weapons to Casamance rebels, some of which were apprehended in Nigeria, three years ago. In total, Senegal inaction in the Gambian regime's destabilization of the Casamance region ignores Senegal's ability to influence the Gambia's politics. Due to its geography, economic, and demographic superiority, Senegal's indecisiveness on Gambia is driven by the failure to invest in Gambia's long-term democratic agenda, focusing, instead on accommodating the tyrant in Gambian. But Senegal's celebrated linkage to Gambia, rooted in the shared cultural heritage, does not seem to persuasively permeate into the minds of Senegal's decision makers. Consequently, to President Macky Sall and his predecessor, Abdoulaye Wada, the military regime in Gambia may appear benign, but to Gambians, the scars of tyranny are profound, and the trauma of emasculating a nation runs deep. Perhaps, President Macky Sall's policy on Gambia is underpinned by his fear of initiating a broad Senegambia conflict. The realization that Gambians don't have the support of Senegal in their ongoing political crisis further spurns hatred of the military regime. Now whether the new government of Prime Minister Aminata Toure will bring attention to the Gambia's crisis remains to be seen. One thing is self-evident: there can never be peace in the Casamance region as long as there is political turmoil in Gambia is not resolved. The two, political stability in Gambia and peace in Casamance, are inextricably linked, but whether President Sall sees the situation the same way as the Gambian people, is another matter.

TERROR IN DAKAR AS GAMBIAN REFUGEES REASSESS MACKY SALL'S REGIME

The night sky was ablaze with radiant fireworks, but the ephemeral pump and pageantry only masked the drudgery of life on the mean streets of Serekunda. Just two miles east of the center of the Gambia's largest metropolis, Kairaba Avenue teemed with charming Gambian girls whose angelic innocence encapsulates their preordained drift toward the social and economic periphery of Gambian society. But the lavish birthday bash, which military ruler Yahya Jammeh threw for himself at the Coco Beach Hotel to solemnize his egoism and commemorate Gambian life in slow drift toward the edge of political insanity, heightened the excoriation of the military regime. Yahya Jammeh's lavish birthday bash showcased his irrational detachment from the grind of daily life in Gambia. But, in the midst of so much mindless celebration of Yahya Jammeh's life and bursts of the colorful fireworks, an incredible story was unfolding 165 miles north of Banjul. It was characterized as blatant disregard for Senegal's sovereignty, an act of criminality so daring; it had a chilling effect on Gambia's dissident community throughout Senegal. It was a daring episode that shifted the Gambia's deadly political center from the narrow, blood-drenched alleyways of Kanilai village, to the bustling streets of Dakar, Senegal, and in so doing, tested President Macky Sall and the Senegalese resolve to engage the regime of Yahya Jammeh. The kaleidoscopic city of Dakar was, as always, iridescent with vibrant fireworks of its own, not in wasteful celebrations and merrymaking, but in displaying Senegal's proud cultural heritage. Only a little over a year ago, the Gambia was shrouded in boundless optimism, and giddy with the hope for a future painted in the vivid imagery represented in murals festooned on the walls of the Gambian imagination.

And that was only the beginning. Around the world, Gambians lavishly eulogized newly elected President Macky Sall in essays and on the radio airwaves, celebrating Senegal and Gambia's common identity, and cultural homogeneity. Even the invisible forces of nostalgia for bygone Senegambia, and the compelling desire for political change in Gambia did much to cast Senegal's President Macky Sall as a paragon of political virtue. Gambians were on desperate search for a hero to rescue Gambia from the clutches of a tyrant and Senegal's new President Sall seemed like the man to do it. But it did not end there. Without ambiguity, many Gambians elevated President Macky Sall to a messianic pedestal reserved for the exclusive few political illuminati. Not all Gambians were generous with flattery without the advantage of knowing Macky Sall. The reticence of the vocal few has been consistently borne out by the evidence, which created revulsion for President Sall's shocking indifference to Gambian tyranny. Specifically, President Macky Sall's decision to seek Yahya Jammeh intervention to resolve the Casamance crisis was a crushing blow to Gambians who expected Senegal's retribution against the Gambia for arming the Casamance rebels and their use of Gambian territory as a military base. Gambians' disfavor of the nauseating relations between Macky Sall and Yahya Jammeh is aggravated by Senegal's trivialization of Gambia's political quagmire. Not since Senegal's student protests were met with police violence and destruction of public property in Banjul had such antipathy toward Senegalese's leaders been so intense among Gambians. And not unlike the 1970s bloody Banjul riots in support of Dakar University students, Gambians again question Senegal's disregard for the safety and security of Gambian refugees in Senegal.

Last week, the kidnapping and disappearance of Mahawa Cham and Saul Ndow, Gambian refugees, and the muteness of Senegal over this extremely serious international crisis, caused alarm and violates the 1951 United Nations Convention for the protection of refugees. Since the abduction of the two dissidents in Dakar, Senegal, the uncharacteristic nervousness of Gambian refugees in Senegal speaks to Macky Sall's dismissiveness of Yahya Jammeh's misanthropic regime and Senegal's unwillingness to protect Gambian refugees from harm. The vulnerability of the Gambian refugee community in Dakar in the face of the insecurity, threatens to unravel the common identity and cultural cohesiveness that outlived generations of Gambians and Senegalese. The reckless kidnapping and forced disappearances of Mahawa Cham and Saul Ndow has the handiwork of Yahya Jammeh vengeance, and it also challenges not only Senegal's sovereignty, but Senegal's obligation to protect Gambian refugees as enshrined in the 1951 UN Convention. The audacity with which Yahya Jammeh's undercover agents snatched Gambian refugees from the streets of Dakar is a callous move designed to instill fear among the Gambian refugee community in Senegal. The common identity Gambia and Senegal share cannot be underestimated, but the lingering effect of President Sall's disregard for Yahya Jammeh's vexing abduction of Gambian refugees from the streets of Dakar, is an abdication of Senegal's responsibility. The blistering criticism of Macky Sall on the blogosphere is not mere bluster, and his failure to support the return of the rule of law in the Gambia may cause his forfeiture of the right to the presidency. Until then, President Macky Sall must seek the safe return from the Gambia and Yahya Jammeh's custody of Mahawa Cham and Saul Ndow. Gambians expect nothing less from the President of Senegal.

CHAPTER 4

ECOWAS, AU, AND INTERNATIONAL COMMUNITY

OPEN LETTER TO MS. REINE ALAPINI GANSOU, CHAIRPERSON OF THE AFRICAN COMMISSION

Ms. Reine Alapini Gansou,
Chairperson of the African Commission
C/o Kairaba Beach Hotel
April 26, 2011

Dear Ms. Gansou,

This no-confidence protest letter is addressed to your honor in your capacity as chairperson of the African Commission. The aim is bring the spotlight on the African Centre for Democracy and Human Rights Studies (ACDHRS), which is located in Banjul. And the intent is for you bring the concerns of the citizens of the host country for the Forty-Ninth Ordinary Session Gambia, to the African Union body in order to educate policy makers about what sham the ACDHRS has become. First, allow me to diverge into another important area of concern to Africans all across the continent. As observers of the shenanigans that dominate the operations of the African Union and its predecessor, Organization of African Union (OAU), Africans have become frustrated with the redundancy, wastefulness, and utter uselessness of the continental body and regional institutions such as the Economic Community of West African States (ECOWAS). The picture that has emerged is that the African Union and its predecessor, the OAU, have existed solely to serve the interests of the leaders of its member states. To that effect, these institutions have become white elephants where millions of dollars are wasted each year for the purpose of preserving the selfish interests of corrupt leaders and brutal regimes. The past five decades have seen African leaders and their corrupt regimes squander the goodwill and economic fortunes of African countries and reduce their people to devastating poverty far worse than the one left behind by our colonial experience.

It is an absolutely disgraceful paradox that the continent with the largest share of the world's natural resources also shamefully boasts its poorest people. After fifty years of political independence, this lunacy and the political conundrum our continent is plunged into by the cruel machinations of greedy and self-centered despots and wayward bureaucracies defies imagination. This selfishness and greed, which cuts across Africa's failed regimes, is inexplicable in any rational way. Each year, for the past fifty years, the United States and European powers transferred billions of dollars to regimes all across the continent, yet we have seen nothing to show for it. Instead, Africa's worsening poverty, which has generated civil wars and created civil strife in countries across the continent, will continue to fester and claim the lives of more Africans. And this is just the beginning. In the 1960s and 1970s, Africa was economically far better off than the vast majority of Asian and Latin American countries, such as China, India, Vietnam, and South Korea, but today, African leaders visit these countries with their hands tucked between their legs, shamefully begging for charity aid. Almost every country in sub-Sahara Africa is dependent on foreign aid to survive, and some, like the Gambia, depend on foreign aid from the United States and Europe for up to 80 percent of annual national budgets. Institutions like the AU and ECOWAS are still funded directly by benevolent Western governments and the United Nations. Despite this transfer of wealth to the poor African countries, a World Bank study found that in 2005 alone, African politicians and bureaucrats looted $148 billion from their countries and stashed these funds in foreign bank accounts. This amount was more than the total foreign aid transfer to African countries for that year. This staggering amount is absolutely mind-boggling; yet it's true.

It is in this regard that the African Centre for Democracy and Human Rights Studies (ACDHRS), an organization that has been in existence for nearly a quarter century, but which has done nothing to challenge the human rights violations of one of Africa's last despots, in particular, the idiot in Gambia—Yahya Jammeh. The ACDHRS has never issued a press release to condemn any of the murders and executions of Gambians, Senegalese, Nigerians, and Ghanaians. In particular, the Ghanaians, headed to the Canary Islands, met their fate at the hands of Yahya Jammeh's agents of death; the Gambian military and the jugglers. Never once did the ACDHRS publicly condemn or produced documents that challenges Yahya Jammeh's criminal regime for its gross human rights violations. Meanwhile, the murders, executions, tortures, arbitrary arrests, detentions, and other violations perpetrated by Yahya Jammeh, continue unabated. The ACDHRS has turned into a white elephant despite the forums and seminars the agency frequently organizes, such as the Forty-Ninth Ordinary Session taking place in Banjul. Each year, millions of dollars are wasted in meaningless meetings and seminars that produce no worthwhile result, as far as African are concerned. It appears like people who attend these useless meetings do so for the per-diem money and other the perks they receive. Given the history of the ACDHRS's uselessness in the face of the ongoing human rights violations, which include extrajudicial executions, forced disappearances, tortures, and incarcerations in Africa's worst prison, Mile 2 Prison, Gambia no longer deserves the privilege to host the African Centre for Democracy and Human Rights Studies (ACDHRS). Consequently, Gambians demand that the ACDHRS be moved to another country that deserves the unique honor of hosting the center. As it is, the African Centre for Democracy and Human Rights Studies (ACDHRS) exists to throw away millions of dollars down a bottomless pit. The money wasted to pay unearned salaries and other perks could be better utilized to serve other useful projects. Since Yahya Jammeh uses the ACDHRS to project an image of the Gambia as meeting international human rights standards, Gambians demand that the ACDHRS be defunded and relocated to a more deserving country.

Sincerely yours,
Executive Secretary
Gambia Consultative Council (GCC)

GOOD MORNING, JONATHAN GOODLUCK: SEVERED HEAD OR CUT-OFF BREAST FOR LUNCH

I have to say, I kind of liked you the first time I heard about you. From afar, you embodied both the bleak present and promising future of black Africa, and it has nothing, whatsoever, to do with Nigeria being Africa's biggest economy. I will explain. But first, allow me, on behalf of Gambians across the world, to welcome you to this long-ago, lost oasis of peace and tranquility, this place, this land where democracy and the rule of law burgeoned, and a people thrived to display the limitless joys of liberty and freedom. Allow me to take you back through the sweep of history to a land that proudly became the sanctuary of victims of South Africa's bloody apartheid war, a Gambia transformed by necessity into the safe haven for Guinea-Bissau's anti-colonial PIAGC freedom fighters and a Gambia once dubbed "the smiling coast of West Africa," by tourists who flooded its pristine coastline and giddily scavenged the treasures in open village markets, where they smell the odor of bad breaths and the nauseating stench of rotten fish, which innocently permeated the humid air in an ephemeral mixture of rebellion and revulsion. Come with me on a journey to a forgotten past where the proverbial desert flower sprouted and flourished out of the nothingness of the sheer will and vision of a people once so prideful of this land they call home. And walk with me into the blank stares of a people whose death and dying has reduced a once proud people into worthless objects, marked for a life on the borderline of social and economic disintegration. Today, only the nostalgia for the distant past, with its boundless opportunities and infinite spread of freedom and liberty, remains—reminders of the calm beauty of the interminable freedom, that once was.

Mr. Goodluck, the title of this article is tinged with wittiness, deliberately designed to offend the mind and sensitize the soul. And it is offensive for a reason, to guarantee that the underlying catastrophe that prevails in Gambian society is not parodied into oblivion by the bombastic manipulations of the regime's mendacious insensitivity. Gambians, by dint of their collective efforts to restore the rule of law and the democratic experiment, are engaged in a perennial struggle to irritate the consciences of those gifted with the treasure of human souls. The footnotes of history are replete with efforts of both the willing and the reluctant who seek to justify the carnages of the evil and soulless, in ways that defy comprehension. The insensitivity to the plight of the defeated and demoralized has often manifested intermittently around the world, to create the ugly stains in the meandering story of the sad of the human past. But, coming back to the issue, Nigeria and Gambia share historical bonds that showcase the bloodcurdling savagery of those who seek to impose their will on an unwilling people. The Nigeria and Gambia story, a history once built on the solid foundation of shared values and common colonial identity, is slowly rotting due largely to the universal hatred of Nigerian judges who Yahya Jammeh uses as instruments of terror and repression in a country that deserves neither

Yahya Jammeh nor judges who enable the violent inclinations of a drug dealing regime of murderers, and rapists—a regime whose dependence on primitive African human sacrifice has seen Gambian soil drenched in the blood of children and adults alike, and witnessed the unostentatious rivers of blood of transients that no one knows, and who will not arouse suspicion, because they have no Gambian family.

President Goodluck, after all the preceding postulation, it boils down to one simple thing: what will West Africa do to ameliorate the plight of a people locked in an impossible struggle for political liberty from a repressive regime that foments ugly tribal bigotry and inadvertently promotes the disintegration of social order? Will ECOWAS break through the sanctimonious diplomatic lingo to see the reality of the ugliness to which Gambia is held captive by the threats of a war machine the regime built? Today, Gambians are not unmotivated by fear of Yahya Jammeh, but are rather taken aback by sights and sounds of West Africa leaders gracing Yahya Jammeh's regime with visits and in doing so, give fortuitous diplomatic cover to the rapes, murders, economic plunder of Gambia's meager resources. Similarly, Yahya Jammeh's fearsome attachment to absolute and unfettered power precludes holding free and fair elections, which prompted His Excellency Hon. James Victor Gbeho, former ECOWAS Commission president, to boycott Gambia's elections in 2011. The situation that gave rise to that ECOWAS decision in 2011 elections has not changed; in fact, Yahya Jammeh still seeks to further entrench a government system that surrenders all state power to him to decide who lives and dies. It is a bit of an irony that while Great Britain, United States, EU, and human rights and democratic institutions around the world forcefully support Gambians in the effort to restore democracy and rule of law, African countries exhibit sickening lack of interest in the Gambia's ongoing maladministration. President Jonathan Goodluck, as you visit the Gambia to savor the beauty and splendor of the land, take time to listen to the fearful silence of a people to hear the haunting laments that loudly cry out: no more severed human heads and cut-off female breasts for the primitive monster of Kanilai. No more.

PRESIDENT JOHN MAHAMA AND GAMBIA'S TYRANNY AND STATE-SANCTIONED TERROR

In the aftermath of the effort to restore democracy and rule of law in Gambia, the regional body charged with ensuring regional political stability and economic integration did something rather dramatic, and an antithesis to the objectives of the organization. The recent visit to Gambia by ECOWAS chairman, President John Dramani Mahama, to solidify diplomatic relations with the Gambia's murderous regime, highlights the pervasive pathology of indifference among the cabal of African leaders. Ghana's President, John Mahama, buried his head in sand to be so clueless about the gristly crimes sanctioned by the Gambia's military regime, or perhaps, he represents a case of lethargy to the Gambia's ongoing mass murders. In either case, President Mahama's unflattering solidarity visit to the Gambia's Yahya Jammeh must be seen against the backdrop of the slaughter of forty-four Ghanaian immigrants bound for Spain in 2005. The carnage on that day has never been fully investigated to anyone's satisfaction, and as the third president since that senseless slaughter, President Mahama's visit resurrects old questions around that episode. Gambians are aware that Yahya Jammeh is inclined to bribe as an instrument of securing influence and detachment from Gambia's state-sanctioned murders and mayhem. President Mahama's sickening appeasement of murderer Yahya Jammeh, undermines the credibility of ECOWAS as an empowering its vast impoverished citizens. For far too long, ECOWAS and AU have served the interests of African leaders, rather than its citizens. This is self-serving abuse of office, and needs to end. Africans, and in this case Gambians, deserve more.

The gallant effort to return democracy and rule of law to Gambia suffered a devastating blow, but this dark hour in the Gambia's history has, more than ever, brought citizens across the globe together around the common cause of regime change. The international coalescing of different voices truly reflects the suffering of the Gambian people and their burning desire for political change. Gambian security forces, in denial of the brutality and dysfunction of the military regime, are forced to swearing allegiance to the source of Gambia's misery; Yahya Jammeh. This unbecoming behavior of Gambia's military and security forces is, of course, the manifestation of their collective low self-esteem, due largely to the lack of education and political awareness. This is, because Yahya Jammeh has, for many years, systematically whittled down the Gambia's military and security forces of its best and brightest, leaving behind mostly his fellow Jola tribesmen and women, who support his grip on imperial power. Notwithstanding Ghana's President John Dramani Mahama's manifestation of intellectual myopia, cowardice, and complete indifference to Yahya Jammeh's brutality, Gambians at home and across the world will not relent in the commitment to save Gambian lives by removing the country's sadistic military ruler by whatever means necessary, regardless of what ECOWAS and the AU do. The indifference to Gambia's continuing carnage, and the efforts of the AU and ECOWAS to deter the Gambian people from liberating their country of the scourges of state-sanctioned brutality, will bring to a head, their relations with Gambia in the future. The strategy of non-violence advocated by these two bodies is unlikely to have an effect on the broader Gambian perspective of regime change.

The Gambian carnage offers repudiation to President Mahama's gratuitous effort to straitjacket the Gambian people into submission to state brutality. The attitudes of the AU and ECOWAS represent the sickening abstraction of the Gambian reality that is still prevalent among the international community. Most Gambians view President Mahama as just another spectacle of African ineptitude and incompetence, and Ghana, the flagship of a country drowning in corruption. The bottom line is this: if ECOWAS lacks empathy for what Gambia is enduring under the military dictatorship, Gambians will have no compulsion in rejecting the regional body's ground rules as unreasonable in their brazen disregard for the existential threat that the ruthless regime poses to the integrity of the Gambia. The emerging political paradigm compels organizations like the AU and ECOWAS to encourage political change that supports citizens' economic development, and if that fails, to force it. And after twenty years and hundreds of Gambians and non-Gambians dead, thousands incarcerated and thousands more fled, Gambians see no redeeming grace in the military regime and are unforgiving in the deaths and destruction to Africa's formerly most peaceful nation. But, having failed to restore the rule of law, more than once, Gambians have more arrows in their quiver. If the powerful Gambian dissident movement has its way, Yahya Jammeh will be barred from contesting the 2016, under the pain of Burkina Faso–type popular rebellion. Hopefully, the political parties at home recognize the futility in contesting in the rigged 2016 elections. Political consensus between political parties at home and the diaspora dissident movement is necessary to bring this into fruition the idea of a broad liberation movement.

AN ECOWAS AND AU DISASTER, IGNORED FOR FAR TOO LONG

Last week, two different reports focused on separate aspects of Gambia's political quandary, yet the reports are similar in a major way. Human Rights Watch's blistering criticism of Gambia's decades of political tyranny and administrative malpractice, and the *Standard* newspaper's shocking revelations of the mind-boggling state of mental health in Gambia, encapsulate tragic human devastation in a country that still continues to veer dangerously towards self-destruction. The Gambian denial of brutal human rights abuses, repeated with amazing frequency by Yahya Jammeh's lapdogs, has not hindered international efforts to delving deeper into the rule of terror that continues to scream for regional and international attention. In addition, the *Standard* newspaper's report on a critical health issue that has evaded media and public scrutiny adds a significant new dimension to the core issues confronting Gambia. The public executions, killings, tortures, forced disappearances, mass incarcerations, and arbitrary arrests and detention, which haunt a traumatized population, combine to make Gambia a living hell; a place where citizens, vulnerable to political stress, physical harm and psychological violence, have become easy victims to the ravages of mental illness. The *Standard* report of 91,000 mentally ill citizens roaming the streets and alleyways of Greater Banjul, apart from being alarmingly high, exposes the agonizing human tragedy and monumental dehumanization of citizens by a regime steeped in Machiavellian ruthlessness. All put together, Human Rights Watch and the *Standard* newspaper reports confirm the online media characterization of Gambia as a massive gulag prison camp, not unlike North Korea, but the reports also provide a palpable sense of how two decades of political repression underlie the severe mental health crisis in Gambia. This loss of human capital is a withering indictment of the regime that is numb to tragedy and hopelessness that emanates from its policies. Besides, providing adequate mental health services to such a large population of mentally ill, in a country with acute lack of mental health resources is exceedingly difficult, if not downright impossible.

In its damning country report, *Human Rights Watch* may not have made any new revelations that have not already been known by Gambia's online dissident media and other human rights institutions sympathetic to the Gambia's political debacle. But by adding voice to Gambia's political disaster, Human Rights Watch will help raise the profile of the Gambia as a new bastion of riveting human rights abuses. If ECOWAS and the African Union had done half as much as Amnesty International, Human Rights Watch, Committee to Protect Journalists, and Media Foundation for West Africa, to address Gambia's festering human tragedy, it could have made a tremendous difference in restoring power to a traumatized citizenry. The Human Rights Watch report was the rave of the week, yet Gambians are also mindful of the arduous diplomatic offensive launched to misinform the public and sway the public opinion from an unbending position on Gambia's human rights catastrophe. In a recent case that is as baffling as it is incomprehensible, an email addressed to the Gambia's DC Ambassador, Omar Faye sought clarification on the issue of withholding funds from the Gambian regime. Clearly, withholding funding and the imposition of a travel ban on Yahya Jammeh and his cabal of hoodlums is an objective of the Gambia's dissident movement, supported by many rights organizations. Consequently, Corinne Dufka, HRW associate director for West Africa's email to Amb. Omar Faye is unprecedented in the sense that it tries to explain and placate the fears of officials of the regime complicit in commission crimes against Gambian citizens. Human Rights Watch must not be seen as playing footsie with such a national tragedy, and the Gambian dissident movement and many rights organizations unequivocally support the demands to withhold Western funding to Gambia's murderous regime, in addition to imposing a travel bans on Gambian officials. This is necessary and imperative punitive measure against a regime that continues to defy the international community. Notably, a cabal of turncoats, whose judgment is clouded by corrupt self-interest and propensity to deny reality, recently, launched a sustained Soviet-style misinformation campaign, funded by the Gambian to counteract the diaspora dissident voices.

The futile attempts to conceal the atrocities in the Gambia include bribery to buy silence and indifference of diaspora opponents of the regime who refuse to look the other way in the Gambia's political tragedy. The Human Rights Watch eighty-one-page, jaw-dropping report, catalogs, in detail, the extent of human rights violations in Gambia, but as comprehensive as the report is, the specifics of the gruesome and deadly rights abuses across the country largely remain swathed in secrecy. A universally fact about the horrifying rights abuses in Gambia, however, is that the known tortures, forced disappearances, executions, killings, terror, and mass incarceration, pale in comparison to what is still unknown to Gambians and the international community—particularly, the human and child sacrifices, female body mutilation, and feeding human corpses to Yahya Jammeh's crocodiles. As incredible as it might seem, these acts of criminality are part of an elaborate human sacrifice ritual said to have the powers to prolong Yahya Jammeh's hold on power, despite the pervasive public clamor for regime change. Human sacrifice rituals are part of Africa's primitive shamanism belief system, which the Gambia's online dissident media is still reticent to cover for fear of looking ridiculous to a skeptical international community. The human sacrifice rituals conducted by Yahya Jammeh are real and supporters of the Gambia's return to civilian rule should believe in the veracity of the human sacrifice stories. Gambian defectors who participated in the horrendous violence against citizens can attest to the veracity of Yahya Jammeh's human sacrifice practices as motivator in the state-sanctioned killings of innocent citizens. And apart from that, the *Standard* newspaper report shows how two decades of systemic oppression in the Gambia have been saddled with enormous mental health crisis. Negligence of the human rights crisis in the Gambia borders on detachment from reality and now that Human Rights Watch has added voice to the Gambia's imperious military misrule, hopefully ECOWAS and the AU too will begin to pressure Gambia to allow transition to civilian rule as the only guarantee to peace in the Gambia. For one person to remain in power for twenty-one years is ridiculous, and to ignore the executions, murders, forced disappearances, and mass incarceration of innocent Gambian citizens is absolutely insane. In light of the fact that peaceful political change is impossible under current circumstances, both ECOWAS and the AU have an obligation to intercede and demand change on behalf of the Gambian people. The Gambia is not a monarchy. It is a republican constitution, which requires regular political change. After twenty-one years of one man's rule, it's time for Yahya Jammeh to go—now.

THE AFRICAN UNION AND THE TRIUMPH OF EVIL IN GAMBIA

After more than twenty years of tyranny, the single most consequential blowback on the Gambia's murderous regime, under Yahya Jammeh, was the regional body, ECOWAS, rejection of observer status to Gambia's predetermined presidential elections.

That was back in 2011. The Honorable James Victor Gbeho, then president of ECOWAS, personified the kind of moral rectitude desperately lacking among Africa's institution leaders. In that instance, Mr. Gbeho became the instant hero in Gambian's relentless search for political liberty. For a people sold to the idea of an African Union wedded to the irrational impulses of indifference and moral myopia, Mr. Gbeho embodied sagacity and fortitude and, in the process, conferred on the Gambian people a break from the pathology of despair and helplessness.

As the African Commission on Human and Peoples' Rights again convenes another meeting in the Gambia, the human rights body's insensitivity to Gambia's relentless search for freedom is pretty much established. If Gambians are baffled by the ACHP sponsored international congregations in the Gambia, it is because the organization's paradoxical relationship with Gambia's military regime borders on the absurd.

The blight of moral courage the ACHPR has exhibited since Gambia strayed into dark depths of military rule has direct correlation to Yahya Jammeh's ability to bolster the crippling image of his undeniable internecine regime.

The rationale and justification for the ACHPR's continued presence in the Gambia, as Africa's premiere human rights body, contradicts the spirit of the AU Human Rights Charter, but equally importantly, it manifests the recklessness of the ACHPR's cover for a regime that has willfully perverted the ECOWAS, AU, and UN missions, to which Gambia is a signatory. As AU's human rights defender across the continent, the reason for the ACHPR's domicile in Gambia is overtaken by adverse political circumstances and turned into a spectacle that demonstrates a moral aberration unworthy of an organization with such laudatory objectives.

If the AU and ACHPR leaders seem disposed to hero worshipping Africa's political leaders, the grounds for establishing the ACHPR as custodian of human rights in Africa will be called into question. The silent majority, the bedrock of African society, from the blue Atlantic, to the tsunami-prone Indian Ocean, have, for decades, lamented the cluelessness of their political leaders.

In the Gambia, the adversarial nature of the relations between the governed and governing showcases a deep divide that has generated a dangerous political climate marked by Yahya Jammeh's appropriation of total power, and assumption of imperial authority, in total disregard for the Gambia's republican constitution. Over the past two decades, the ACHPR's lack of empathy has rubbed Gambians the wrong way and caused disinterest in the organization's irreverent activities, despite its headquarters being in Banjul.

The failure of the AU to enforce human rights for political dissidents and desperate poor, reinforces a perception of the institution and its ancillary bodies as charades undeserving of the task of overseeing the preservation of human rights across the continent. The AU's inability, perhaps even lethargy, in discerning between the self-interest of Africa's political leaders, and the marginalized African majority, has never been as evident and deeply worrisome. The AU's embarrassing failure in Gambia's ongoing political quagmire is only a microcosm of its broader moral bankruptcy. In many ways, the AU's detachment from critical national issues and its lack of diligence may have prompted the emergence of civil unrest across the continent. The corruption, human rights violations, and massive economic pillage, on one hand, and the abject poverty of the African people, on the other, are in constant conflict, and this tension has caused African countries to slide into permanent states of civil unrest. This is the hallmark of the toxic political situation in the Gambia, where the smoldering bitterness over the state-sanctioned killings, executions, mass incarceration, and tribal bigotry combine to make the Gambia Africa's worst human rights violator. Even as horrendous crimes occur with impunity in Gambia under the nose of the ACHPR, the rights organization's deafening silence is an incomprehensible dereliction of responsibilities.

Furthermore, the banal ad hominem attacks on Gambia's dissidents in US, UK, Germany, and Scandinavia, have further stained Yahya Jammeh's character and diminished the Gambia's standing in the west. Apart from his periodical murderous sprees, Yahya Jammeh's unapologetic tribal divisions are more likely to cause the two decades of simmering resentment to manifest in a bitter political and cultural realignment in the event of political change.

The inability of the AU and the ACHPR to enforce adherence to a human rights agenda goes far beyond the borders of the Gambia. The drowning of young, able-bodied African immigrants who desperately seek to escape poverty, dearth of opportunities and political tyranny, on one hand, and the murders and torture of Africa throughout North Africa and the Middle East, has shed light on the AU's criminal indifference to the welfare of Africa's long-suffering people. The failure of AU and its ancillary bodies is rooted in African leader's greed, which has given rise to political chaos and economic cannibalism that continues to ravage Africa.

The lack of patriotism and sense of African nationalism, as opposed to the individualism of its leaders, is at the heart of so many of the continent's political and economic grievances. Yet, even as a few African leaders attempt to change the social compact and political paradigm, for the good, more of its citizens continue to languish in political despair even with the ACHPR headquarters located in the Gambia.

The AFPRC's response to the murders, executions, mass incarceration, and tribalism in the Gambia is endless meetings, which yield only anemic reactions and soaring rhetoric memorialized in meaningless resolutions. Unless ACHPR ignites a sense of fidelity to justice, a country like Gambia, where the organization is based, will most likely lurch toward civil unrest, all because there was absolutely no one to put Yahya Jammeh in check and hold him to account.

IN PRAISE OF ECOWAS LEADERS MACKY SALL, MUHAMMED BUHARI, AND JOHN MAGUFUL

It is a historic failure of epic proportions, which began gradually and steadily, metastasized into an abominable culture. Africa, after half a century, continues to agonize over its painful inability to shake off the vile image of the continent as the cesspool of incompetence and obscene corruption. The universal perception of Africa as a dark continent stuck in an undeniably pathology of moral and ethical bankruptcy has reached the pinnacle of absurdity, with disastrous results. In spite of Africa's vast resources, investors with excess capital to plow back into Africa's economy largely declined to touch the continent with a ten-foot pole. Africa's prodigious corruption and administrative incompetence are only a part of its fatal failure of leadership. In political terms, too many of Africa's leaders would rather change their constitutions than give up political power, which spawned the rise of military rule and plunged the continent in darkness for decades. From South Africa to the edge of the Sahara, and from Madagascar to the Cape Verde Islands, the haunting laments of the African people persistently echo, growing louder and more desperate as the political and economic failures become more entrenched, and the manipulations of the political processes is rewarded with periodic sham elections. Nowhere are the muffled echoes of political and economic catastrophe as shrill and as persistent as in the Gambia, Angola, and Equatorial Guinea, where corruption supersedes the public interest. The notorious tyrants, Yahya Jammeh, Eduardo dos Santos, and Teodoro Obiang Nguema Mbasogo, have turned their countries into their personal fiefdoms and imposed autocracies where bloodletting and intolerable oppression have set them apart from the rest of civilized society. In all three countries, usurpation of political power and the absence of freedom are absolute, making their imperial presidencies unremarkable in African standards.

The sobering reality of Africa's tyrannies and the abuse of power in the face of the desperate need for political change bring into focus the evolution of African despots and the institutional challenges to bend the focus toward moral rectitude. The inability of these three African leeches to surrender political power fosters the reptilian cruelty that has become a hallmark of the continent's political barbarism. It is the manifestation of intellectual small-mindedness and moral deprivation, a cancer that afflicts so many African leaders. There is a nagging feeling of an Africa spiraling out of control and descending rapidly into political anarchy and economic ruin. And this is not too far from the collective mind of its poor people, yet that sense of hopelessness ignores the continent's multidimensional political discourse. Despite this predicament, images of the continent as representing a window to the mind of its people overlooks pockets of excellence, which deserve to be revered. This deliberate omission is steeped in narrow-mindedness, and the dark vein of racial bigotry. The portrait of African politicians as excessively greedy and power hungry, though largely true, has exceptions that invalidate sweeping generalization of the African political character as monolithic. Increasingly, a vocal minority of leaders is beginning to emerge from the shadows and, conscious of the steep climb to redemption, defy the stereotypical notions of Africa's incurable sycophancy. Africa's spectacular political and economic failures and dive into violent poverty, often punctuated by ruthlessness, form the basis for the bruising adversarial relationship between its ignorant demagogues leading the countries, and the poor moral majority.

Further, distrust between Africa's educated and its political oligarchs have come to a stalemate where relentless dissidents delegitimize regimes that spurn the concept of conceding power to the people. Africa's blunders are indeed plentiful, yet the spirit and the sage of Nelson Mandela, leader of South Africa's moral majority, lives on in some of Africa's new crop of leaders. For, just when the challenge is grave, and impediments to sane leadership seem insurmountable, the dynamism of change hardens the resolve and compels the moral consciences to display the true character of what it means to be an African. Africa's post history is replete with incompetent leaders whose criminality is made created the mayhem that still grips the continent. But this year, a level of discipline is scribed to some African politicians, which promises to change the culture of corruption by showing ways to responsible management devoid of administrative incompetence. And even as Africa's senile octogenarian political leaders make a complete mockery of politics, Senegal's President Macky Sall, Nigeria's President Muhammed Buhari, and Tanzania's President John Magufuli are championing radical changes to the character of Africa's tragic political systems. The combined impact of what the three laudatory leaders are exploring, in order to tackle the greed, corruption, and excessive state power, reflects the geography of the minds of true leaders in an age of political awakening and economic inclusiveness. Africa has long languished in the dark pits of political and economic corruption, but now the embodiments of change, Senegal's Macky Sall, Nigeria's Muhammed Buhari, and Tanzania's John Magufuli, are charting a new course and cultivating a new attitude for a continent full of promise, but also of political systems fraught with man-made calamities. For now, it looks like real change coming to Africa, one country at a time, and Africa salutes Macky Sall, Muhammed Buhari, and John Magufuli as they begin to unleash Africa's true potentials and carry forward Mandela's unquenchable torch of freedom and economic dignity.

THE CHANGING CHESS GAME IN WEST AFRICAN POLITICS

Former president of ECOWAS, James Victor Ghebo, was a catalyst in the dawning of West Africa's changing political culture. Not to be outdone, the African Union came out swinging with jaw-dropping reference to Africa's abominable political lethargy of the recent past. The AU daringly maintained that Africa's leaderships can no longer expect shelter behind the power and influence of their nondescript tyrannical regimes, nor hope that public resistance to their political impunities, a hallmark of Africa's cataclysmic rule, will continue to fall on deaf ears.

Africa's proverbial winds of change are blowing, but this time around, the shifting sands of political culture are neither fleeting adventure in the political grandstanding Africa has become accustomed to, or renewed manifestation of the numbing hypocritical indifference that has bedeviled the continent's political landscape. Nowhere does Africa's evolving political paradigm offer more promise than West Africa, where recent history boasts the unenviable brutal civil wars and collapse of civil society. The Ivory Coast, Liberia, Guinea, Sierra Leone, Guinea-Bissau, and Mali have all been mired in the nightmare of whimsical political leaderships and the vicissitudes of endemic corruption, bureaucratic paralysis, and political paternalism.

In Gambia too, an unorthodox political culture rules supreme, a place with a sad history of summary executions, forced disappearances, political intimidation, and a culture of nepotism and tribal bigotry. Years under Yahya Jammeh created a portrait of malignant political perils and turned the once fledgling democracy into a state of debauchery and human rights abuse. In past ECOWAS member countries, the common thread was the capriciousness of its clueless leadership and wayward bureaucracies. The objectification of African citizens, clear indication of politically motivated and selfishly tailored policies, lulled citizens into painful conditions of emasculation, helplessness and total subordination. But, by far the most poignant example of arbitrary use of brutal force in Africa is the Gambia, where the regime-compelled citizen apathy maligned a whole nation through the constant threat of force to suppress political dissent. For ECOWAS, the postelection fiasco in Ivory Coast and rejection of legitimizing Gambia's fraudulent presidential elections were the testing grounds for a new approach to confront Africa's political irrationality and indifference to the public welfare. The result is a groundbreaking coalition of ECOWAS's leaders around the long overdue sanitization of West Africa's corrupt politics.

In Senegal, Gambia, and Guinea-Bissau sub-region, the election of Macky Sall has instantaneously altered the embattled tristate region's political dynamics and ushered in an unexpected transmogrification of the most hated political pariahs of our time, Yahya Jammeh. If politics were a sport, Yahya Jammeh's surreptitious change of political trajectory after President Sall's elections can be described as a defeat, but he is left with no choice. Senegal's President Macky Sall came to Gambia hopefully to draw a line in the sand and dare Yahya Jammeh to cross it. But Yahya Jammeh will not court the wrath of Senegal the political dynamics there have changed with the defeat of the Senegal's senile President, Abdoulaye Wada. In the tripartite Senegal, Gambia, and Guinea-Bissau family, Yahya Jammeh will be relegated into political oblivion if he dares to jeopardize the region's stability with his customary meddling in the political affairs of Casamance and Guinea-Bissau. Yahya Jammeh's grandiose dreams of carving out a Jola hegemony in our region will forever remain buried inside the psychopathological delusions of the man who has visited so much grief to so many Gambians and non-Gambians alike. The promises of peace in Casamance and Guinea-Bissau are commitments Yahya Jammeh is obliged to concede to, yet that alone would not be enough to indemnify him of his regime's grotesque atrocities. Yahya Jammeh has become the metaphor for everything wrong with Africa, all because former President Abdoulaye Wada was impaired by age, which clouded his judgment. President Wada's failed sub-region and created a vacuum that allowed the Yahya Jammeh menace to thrive, but Senegal's new sub-regional policies will hopefully reshape the tripartite geopolitics by removing Yahya Jammeh's grip and influence in both Casamance and Guinea-Bissau.

But due largely to his prolonged meddling in the affairs of Casamance and Guinea-Bissau, Yahya Jammeh represents the tragic legacy of military ignominy that has crippled Africa for half a century. He is now on a short leash, and any misadventure in Casamance and Guinea-Bissau could possibly have consequences detrimental to his maligned regime. Yahya Jammeh's bravado and chest-beating days are over; there is a new sheriff in town. Senegal's President Macky Sall must be determined to end the senseless rebellion in Casamance, and give no time for Yahya Jammeh's mind games and public diatribes. Now that Yahya Jammeh has been obscured by the charismatic shadow of President Sall, he has no choice but to subordinate his authority to that of President Macky Sall. President Sall's recent visit to Banjul was a defining moment in sub-regional diplomacy, and his message to Yahya Jammeh, both succinct and unambiguous, conveys an element of serious political maneuvering and Yahya Jammeh understands it all too well. But Yahya Jammeh's proclivity to deceive and legendary violence for even the most benign and innocuous will come back to haunt him as Gambians increasingly shed the fear that has paralyzed them into total submission to Yahya Jammeh's power for the better part of two decades.

Today, as Yahya Jammeh's familiar public threats boomerang as result of the intense political activity going on in the sub-region, his stranglehold on power has weakened and rendered his regime vulnerable to civil disobedience. Just when it seemed that Yahya Jammeh had relegated the collective will of the Gambian people in a permanent state of fear, citizens are revisiting the pride and honor of past generations, to rediscover the common humanity lost to Yahya Jammeh's cruel parochialism. Fear, as a psychologically debilitating tool, was used by Yahya Jammeh to devastating effect, yet each year could have turned out as the year of his undoing. Across the world, Gambians are organizing, and as this critical mass grows to embolden others, the march to free Gambia, through the streets of Banjul, Serekunda, Brikama, Bakau, Basse, Farafenni, and Fatoto, and every town and village, becomes a likely proposition. If this nightmare is to end, Gambians have to take the lead. There is so much goodwill built for the Gambia's cause around the world, from the corridors of the African Union, to the hallways of ECOWAS and the marble columns of United States Congress. President Macky Sall's ascension has disciplined Yahya Jammeh to the extent he can no longer expect deafening silence from Senegal. The end of the Gambia's longest nightmare may be upon us. The writing is on the wall, but Gambians have to seize the moment and make that final push to liberate our country.

LESSONS OF MALI, BURKINA, AND
LESSONS FOR AFRICA

The return to multiparty democracy in Mali and Burkina Faso symbolize the new philosophical bend of two organizations, the African Union and ECOWAS. It's as though these two West African nations and ECOWAS members are playing catch-up with the popular political sentiments of Africa's vast dispirited population. But this is only the beginning, probably a microcosm of what the rest of Africa's dictatorships could potentially face. The transition to democracy in Mali and Burkina Faso is worth celebrating, but with cautious optimism. The moral fortitude, which the African union and ECOWAS have demonstrated since the Mali military coup, to restore democracy, is evidence of an unmistakable departure from the AU's predecessor, the OAU's revolting attachment to military regimes' ineptitude, and their distraction from Africa's miserable reality. The tethering of the defunct OAU, and ECOWAS to the imperial powers and moral bankruptcy of African leaders, which is an undeniable historical fact, has, for half a century, driven the continent to a tailspin into the dark depths of despair and pessimism. The characterization of Africa's reckless regimes as pathologically corrupt, and its leaders as greedy political cannibals, emerged out of the continent's long history of disastrous economic plunder and unchallenged human rights violations, a practice of moral insensitivity that has taken on a dimension of regularity in many African countries. Besides, the patronage of African leaders ignores the will of the people, surrenders absolute power to individual leaders, motivates the entrenchment of the greedy, and carves out imperial powers for leaders in their countries. This typically contradicts the democratic process that elevates leaders to positions of power, just as it devalues the civil rights of Africans to regularly change their government through free and fair electoral processes.

The atmosphere, in which African leaders operate with monarchical power and outside the boundary of constitutional authority, inhibits the emergence of legitimate political dissent and the foundation of robust civil society institutions that safeguard state sovereignty and citizen interest. African leaders very often foist the issue of constitutional amendments on unsuspecting citizens, designed to exclusively surrender to them legal and constitutional rights to guaranteed lifetime leadership, are in violation of their Constitution and citizenship rights to choose. Senegal's President Abdoulaye Wada, and now Burkina Faso's Blaise Campoare, efforts at Constitutional amendment to arrogate more power to them backfired and caused mass civil unrest, a clear rejection of arrogant presumption of ownership of the state. In Mali and Burkina Faso, where military authorities had no choice but yield to the continent's and international pressure, showcasing the breadth of AU and ECOWAS authority when these institutions flex their muscles to defer political power to the people, rather than to divisive, power hungry and corrupt leaders who lack the concept of republican constitutions. In 2012, AU and ECOWAS had the first real test of their authorities, moved swiftly in textbook fashion to delegitimize Mali's new military leaders, and paved the way for quick return to civilian rule. The rapidity with which the Mali military junta conceded authority and deferred power to civilian rule opened a new frontier in confronting African leaders to shed their pretentious divine authorities and restore the dignity of democracy and rule of law. If the recent events in Mali and Burkina Faso underscore AU and ECOWAS's commitment to reject the bigotry of low expectations assigned to an uninspired African population, the continent's journey to political and economic redemption could, like a phoenix, rise from the bowels of the earth.

The story of Mali's wildly successful political change is a refuge to African intellectuals and academics that salivate for political change as the way to open the continent's vast economic opportunities. And to the extent that AU and ECOWAS hold the cards, Burkina Faso, one of the continent's poorest, can hardly afford the devastating effects of politically destabilizing sanctions, and characterization as a regional political pariah. And repetition, in Burkina Faso, of the rapidity of Mali concession to the will of people, will be a significant political milestone in the long struggle to disentomb Africa from its self-inflicted political and economic misery. If the paradox of African poverty, as the mineral resources rich continent cursed with a population in abject poverty, does not begin to preoccupy bureaucrats in the AU and ECOWAS, and other regional institutions, failure of development in Africa can be blamed on the lack of imagination and total insensitivity to the crisis of poverty that consumes the continent. The challenge for the AU and ECOWAS is to create a bulwark against pervasive moral bankruptcy, economic cannibalization, in order to assure the integrity of governments in service of the African to supersede the narrow, selfish interest of African bureaucrats and political leaders. Nowhere is the complete rejection of Africa's institutions' authority more forcefully ignored with impunity, in full public display, as in Gambia, where the regime's disregard for ECOWAS court rulings has reduced that body to an unremarkable spectacle.

But Yahya Jammeh's antics include the invitation of Equatorial Guinea's mass murderer, President Teodoro Obiang Nguema Mbasogo to Gambia, arming rebels to destabilize the Casamance, and undeniable ownership of a large shipment of military weapons seized in Nigeria. Yet, through it all, ECOWAS and Senegal have been paralyzed by lack of commitment to regional peace, to confront Yahya Jammeh's ubiquitous show of contempt for international laws that govern peaceful coexistence. And in order to repel widespread perceptions of redundancy, both AU and ECOWAS must pressure leaders to commit to transparent governments, laws that advance the interest of citizens, and guarantee the sanctity of their inalienable rights. At this juncture, Mali must be the reference point, and hopefully Burkina Faso too will follow suit, but the challenges that lie ahead cannot be trivialized into wishful simplicity. True, the existence of bureaucracies and institutions in Africa as appendages of the ruling parties, and blurring of the lines between the parties in power and the public service, presents a unique, but not insurmountable challenge. Notable though, is that fact that when the political space offers possibilities for more parties to govern, bureaucrats and civil servants have an amazing ability to neutralize their political biases, and show remarkable resilience in adapting to the governing circumstances of any new party in power. But the founding of viable, rival political parties and civil society institutions, a tenet of democracy and rule of law, must prevail to ensure the sanctity of political and governing systems, deter the domination of government by single parties, and ensure regime change occurs regularly, through the democratic electoral process.

To date, regime change across Africa, through the ballot box, has remained a pathetic manifestation of greed and lust for power, exemplified by the continent's unapologetic and longest-serving leaders: Cameroon, Paul Biya, twenty-nine years; Equatorial Guinea, Teodoro Obiang, thirty-five years; Angola, Jose Eduardo Dos Santos, thirty-five years; Zimbabwe, Robert Mugabe, thirty-four years; Uganda, Yoweri Museveni, twenty-eight years; Sudan, Omar al Bashir, twenty-five years; Chad, Idrisa Deby, twenty-three years; Eritrea, Isaias Afwerki, twenty-three years; and Gambia's Yahya Jammeh, twenty years. In spite of their projections of power and invincibility, Burkina Faso strongman, Blaise Campoare, surreptitious flight to Ivory Coast, exposed the apparent and inherent vulnerabilities of power-hungry African kleptomaniac. Burkina Faso has now shown the way; the onus is for opponents of lifetime reigns to reassert their power and redefine politics in their countries. And in the life and death struggle for African political emancipation, neither the African Union nor ECOWAS can afford the luxury of receding into the comfort of neutrality and inaction. Imagine that Gambia's Yahya Jammeh and Equatorial Guinea's Teodoro Obiang own adjacent properties outside Washington, DC, in America's most plush real estate market, and if Zeinab Jammeh's shopping forays to New York are not offensive enough, the luxury, opulence, and wealth of the playboy son of Equatorial Guinea's president, Teodoro Obiang, will leave one speechless. At a time when dire poverty is eroding the dignity of citizens, both Gambia and Equatorial Guinea exemplify the ridiculous unworthiness of African leaders. The recent events in Burkina Faso certainly prove a glimmer of hope for a continent on the brink of change, from half a century of African neo-colonialism as Senegal's former president Maître Abdoulaye Wada soon found out. Now, Burkina Faso's murderous military strongman, Blaise Campoare, is finding out too. But are Africans ready to close this sad, immemorial chapter of deadly reigns of terror and devastating economic plunder?

OVERTHROWING YAHYA JAMMEH: THE WEAKNESS OF THE DICTATORSHIP

As a country, much of what shapes the politics we observe is not based on reality, but on the flawed ways our brains process information, what we see and observe. We draw conclusions that rely on limited information, which often results in a myopic representation of the reality. In my experience living in and learning about various totalitarian regimes, the one constant is their inherent weaknesses and fragility. And because dictatorial regimes use fear as an instrument of gaining control and compliance, they are able to create false senses of stability, strength, and invincibility. The truth, however, is far different from the perception, and the Gambia experience is no different from any other dictatorship, past and present. The more the terror that a regime like Yahya Jammeh's unleashes on its people, the more it is consumed by a morbid fear of its population. Dictatorships, therefore, survive only because they learn to create and manage the cloud of mutual suspicion and mistrust that they plant among the population. Different regimes use a variety of methods to achieve their objectives, but the end result is always the same—the establishment of police and military state as instruments of repression. Remaking of the Gambia into a police and military state has been a long time coming, but for all intents and purposes, it has arrived.

Having committed so many human rights atrocities over the years, this was perhaps a foregone conclusion, because the alternative would be a violent and brutal uprising that would put the life of Yahya

Jammeh and his enablers in danger. Today, because Yahya Jammeh cannot undo the past, nor placate the present, the only course of action available to his regime is to continue his brutal oppression. By leveraging the unconstitutional powers granted to Gambia's deadly National Intelligence Agency and military to plant fear and suspicion among the population, the regime has managed to prevent all criticism by the press and the public. Additionally, efforts by civil society organizations to present a united opposition front against the regime are preempted by the brutality of the regime's agents of repression. But so much has changed over the years that it is difficult to imagine how the Gambia got where it is. The fear of Yahya Jammeh is so pervasive that families, neighbors, and friends have been ripped apart as a result of the cloud of mutual suspicion that pervades all levels of our society. Political dissent can and does result in murders and forced disappearances, and criticism of and complaints about the regime's failures could result in forced disappearances. These draconian measures enable the regime to survive, but also present answers to the reality of the dictatorship.

Rather than represent the true face of stability and invincibility, the regime's oppression does more to expose its weaknesses and vulnerabilities. The show of strength and stability, expressed in the brutal and intolerant attitude toward citizen dissent, is actually a façade that masks its fear of the population. As is observed above, one of the misconceptions surrounding the Yahya Jammeh dictatorship is the perception and aura of invincibility. While a vast majority of the Gambian population shares hatred of the Yahya Jammeh regime, they remain so suspicious of one another that they are unwilling to confess their frustration and hatred of the regime to one another. In this constant grip of this fear, Gambians as a society have remained mute and unwilling victims of the regime's abuses and excesses. If only Gambians could read one another's minds, it would be easily possible to start a spontaneous revolt that would forcibly remove Yahya Jammeh from power. Today, even selective targeting of the regime's interests could shake it to its foundation, since it will project a regime in loss of control. At this juncture, it is imperative for every Gambian to understand that what the regime projects as a sign of strength is the psychological equivalent of staying calm even when one's body is numbed by paralyzing fear. Once Gambian's come to this realization, they will understand that only a handful of military and security officers are willing to fight to keep Yahya Jammeh in power.

In this matter tribe is not a factor, because Yahya Jammeh has hurt his own tribe, the Jolas more than other tribes. As for the Casamance and Guinea-Bissau Jolas, the bulk of Yahya Jammeh's support, the road to Casamance may prove to be a very long and hard one, in the event of a change of regime. But for now, as a country Gambians must realize that no one will come to save them, and as the saying goes, 'it is we the savior we have been waiting for all these years.' The time to begin organizing resistance is now. Such resistance must begin with a show of defiance that will include tearing down or defacing Yahya Jammeh posters around town. Once we start a campaign of defiance, it will be easy to observe how the regime will crumble like sandcastle, because despite Yahya Jammeh's frequent show of bravado, his shy smiles betray the reality of a man scared to death. The regime is unsure whether each day could be its last, as it can sense the writing on the wall. We must save our country from further disaster, because we are the real saviors we have been waiting for. Let us stand up to this challenge. We are tired of the dying, the arrests, the detentions, the torture, the brutality, the dysfunctional government, and the enslavement of our people. The time to begin mass resistance is long overdue. Yahya Jammeh's regime is unstable, despite its public display of bravado, and overthrowing it is much easier than it appears. Let Gambians begin to organize for the final push to liberty.

THE SOULLESSNESS OF AFRICA:
THE CURSE OF THE GAMBIA

Senile octogenarians, youthful maniacs, barbaric psychopaths, and crude nitwits all share the exact same idiosyncrasies: greed, moral decadence, ignorance, cruelty. They dress in leopard skin, popularize fashion trends, own bronze lion statues, sit on golden thrones, and one carries the Islamic Quran close to their chest.

They bear blame for Africa's lost generations, but leave the burden and the agony of poverty on the shoulders of its dispossessed population. They are loathed and reviled. They are the causes of the Africa continent's lurch toward the dark and dangerous side of politics. Today, sixty years after political independence, their tragic slippage from civilized society to crippling inhumanity continues to saddle Africa with the haunting images of abject poverty and insufferable brutality.

Since the dawn of independence, the African continent has been trapped in a state of permanent dysfunction. I was too young to understand how the deification of African political leaders started, but its continuation is written in the blood of its wretched and beleaguered population. It is a history that, in part, was perpetuated by international geopolitical interests, but that is a small piece of this mega African tragedy. African leaders' greed and fixation with political power is at the center of the failed politics that have brought devastation to a continent.

The early years of African independence were infused with heavy doses of hope and idealism, but disappointment soon set in as the hope began to fray. The euphoria surrounding independence began to slowly dissolve into nothingness, and utopia became exactly what it is—mere fantasy. Africa's pioneering heroes were trapped between two diametrically opposite forces: own up to the failed economic policies, or turn into monsters, an unacceptable human behavior.

In the political upheavals and savagery that followed, "men of consciences" emerged from the military barracks in countries drifting into inevitable chaos and anarchy. The rise of the militaries to power was a watershed moment that quickly accelerated Africa's downward spiral into political chaos and economic collapse. The history of greed, brutality, incompetence, and corruption, which the military regimes continued to live by, had come to stay.

Growing up, one pioneering independence movement leader, in

particular, captured my youthful imagination. I worshipped the grounds he walked on. I was full of teenage exuberance, but I was not naïve, or so I thought. I was a blank slate trying desperately to create my own identity. I was both ignorant and susceptible to intellectual manipulation. My mind was fertile ground for anyone to write their own script on. I fell for the adulation of other humans. I did not understand it, nor did I care to know. But I did. I became a follower. Kwame Nkrumah, Ghana's first radical president occupied much of the vacant space in my mind and influenced my early political consciousness. He was my pied piper. But a handful of other political characters too played significant roles in casting their long shadows on my political and intellectual development, and helped shape my worldview.

Kwame Nkrumah was larger than life. In hindsight, Osajeyfo, or Savior, the name of endearment Ghanaians gave him after independence, may have started African political leaders infatuation with empty titles and meaningless accolades.

My gradual maturation into the world of politics came at a price. I disowned the people I once adored. At first, I was in a state of denial, but in the end, evidence prevailed over fantasy, and helped free my mind of the terrible stigma of socialism. The dogma that socialism personified was utopian and inherently intransigent. Put simply; the ideals of socialism were the flight of fancy. Led by Dr. Kwame Nkrumah, African leaders who had begun to dabble in a failed political ideology—Tanzania, Ghana, Guinea-Conakry, Congo—began bankrupting their counties and bringing mounting poverty to the dusty streets of their beleaguered countries. The risks of socialism were great; the benefits, negligible and dangerous.

At the other end of the political spectrum, indoctrination of Africa's young minds in Marxist ideology was as fashionable as Timothy Leary's popularizing LSD on college campuses around US. In another sort of way, Africa's young were first drawn to the intoxicating social and political rebellion that Soviet socialism represented. But, political doctrine, spread by violence and maintained by political tyranny, was the perfect antidote to the freedom of the mind. African leaders of the period frothed over their good fortunes. This political nightmare spawned a culture of massive brain drain, which gave rise to Africa's characterization as the epitome of utter failure and absolute incompetence.

In many African countries, the post-independence political ideologies were founded on premises hostile to Western values, as exemplified by Ghana. Kwame Nkrumah's drift toward Soviet-style political tyranny meant the complete state domination, and people's forfeiture of their civil rights. The poster boy for anti-Western imperialism and post-independence voice of a continent, the larger-than-life Kwame Nkrumah soon became the trailblazer who lost his way in the fog of his extraordinary ambition, and helped doom Africa for decades to come.

Inarguably, the center of the continent's political and cultural activity, Ghana offered the good and the bad—successes, but also failures. Ghana, more specifically, Osajeyfo Dr. Kwame Nkrumah, was the archetypal African paradox, the brilliant political strategist who brought both hope and ruin to a continent he sought to lead. His noble idea of a great Africa, unified by necessity, would have to wait. In Ghana, his star was beginning to dim, sending his regime into a tailspin. Not even he could foresee his fall from grace, and sudden loss of power.

Africa's military coups, political repression, silencing of political dissent, incarceration, economic mismanagement, and the phenomenon of the one-party state, so popular in the early years of African independence, were the brainchild of Osajeyfo Dr. Kwame Nkrumah. Today, the Nkrumah effect continues to color African politics—the addiction to power, the economic stagnation, deterioration of citizen welfare, lack of human rights, and the pugilistic political atmosphere. The terror of African leaders in allowing robust dissent as constitutionally guaranteed is still anathema, as it was when Kwame Nkrumah ruled.

And back when it took news weeks to reach Africa from America, much of what happened politically around the globe was almost a mystery, unknown around the world. The idea of human rights was not on the international radar; the championing of economic transparency was decades away, snail mail was still in vogue, and African leaders routinely got away with murder.

Much like Ghana under Kwame Nkrumah, Africa is riddled with political paranoia induced by debilitating fear of losing power. But understanding the mind-set of African leaders, sixty years after the end of colonialism, is critical in getting a grasp of their incomprehensible voracity for political power. Even in an era of ubiquitous cell phone, cameras, and instantaneous news broadcasting, the crimes against African citizens seem more prevalent now than in years gone by.

In West Africa, Gambia, more than any other country epitomizes everything morally wrong and intellectually dishonest African politics. Simply put; Gambia is a microcosm of the ugly, vicious, and inhuman African politics. The executions, state-sanctioned murders, endemic corruption, tribalism, exploitation of resources for personal benefit, and the daily doses Yahya Jammeh's fury combine to make Gambia a living hell. Yahya Jammeh's political demagoguery, a relic of Guinea's Sekou Toure's rambling anti-Western tirades, makes him look like a schoolyard bully, yet he has succeeded, beyond imagination, to make the Gambia completely subservient to his will.

It is hard to talk about the Gambia without getting caught up in tribal issues; however, most Gambians, regardless of tribal affiliation, have made conscious decisions not to be drawn into Yahya Jammeh's bigoted public policy issues. If there is one place where the Stockholm syndrome has found firm footing, it would be in Gambia. Today, Gambians in the diaspora have made a habit of predicting how long a new appointee to Yahya Jammeh's regime will take to fall from grace, and they are right most of the time.

Whether Gambians are motivated to stay silent by paralyzing fear or by the acceptance of the pain of mental servitude, it is hard not feel pity for them. It is as though Gambians have become zombies, without voices and without opinions. The kind of control Yahya Jammeh has over his Gambian subjects is imperial in nature and has nothing, whatsoever, to do with elected constitutional democracy, as the Gambia is supposed to be.

On a trip to Benin in 1989, I was stuck by the level of fear Mathieu Kereku's regime had brought on his people. What I witnessed seemed absolutely surreal. I noticed how our irritated guide reacted when I pointed toward the presidential palace. The reminders of Mathieu Kereku were ubiquitous, but above all, as in the Gambia today; the people of Benin dared not mention the ruler's name in public. And like Benin, it is as though Yahya Jammeh has reached the sky, a deity of some sorts, with power over life and death. On returning to Gambia at Yundum Airport, I was overcome with an indescribable rush of emotions—happiness and pride of being in a free Gambian.

But not even Mathieu Kereku wielded the level of power, authority, and control Yahya Jammeh holds over the Gambian people. The constant fear of arrest, incarceration, and death is an incessant reminder of the tragedy of Yahya Jammeh's reign of terror and the paralyzing fear he has planted in the Gambia.

Yahya Jammeh has learned the African way of politicking. He has perfected it in his own way, and it has served him well for two decades. And like the old and senile, wide-eyed African ignoramuses and greedy kleptomaniacs, Yahya Jammeh has mastered the science of political longevity, in spite of the chaos, murder, and mayhem his regime has brought to Gambia. The Gambians constantly draw hope from long gone monstrous African characters who eventually fell from grace, and out of power; Jose Eduardo Dos Santos, but like Kwame Nkrumah, Sekou Toure, Mobutu Sese Sehou, Jean-Bédel Bokassa, and Ethiopia's Mengistu Haile Mariam.

This is the story of the African paradox, a continent with resources like no other place on earth, but with the poorest people on this planet. It is also the story of elected and unelected leaders who, time and again, morphed from high school teachers into brutal rulers, who amassed wealth, usurped power, and, on top of all that, are worshipped as deities by people reduced to objects to abuse and neglect.

The legacy of African leaders is a story of pitiful ignorance but also of pervasive corruption on a continent drenched in the blood of people who dared to have voices. Africa is a place where the sweep of history has left its mark of fear, poverty and leaders who live large at the expense of Africa's impoverished populations.

As for me, I am going back to do what I always do—continue my quest to understand the soul of Africa's leaders, and what turns them into monsters that kept the African continent still dark, still stuck in despair, and still oblivious of the changing world around them. But for now, I digress.

OPEN LETTER TO THE UNITED NATIONS SECRETARY GENERAL

Hon. Ban Ki-Moon
Monday, January 2015
Secretary General, United Nations
760 United Nations Plaza
New York, New York 10017

Dear Hon. Ban Ki-moon,

Allow us the opportunity to elaborate on the genesis of the Gambia's ongoing civil strife, a strife marked by devastating human rights violations and the impossible task of changing our government through the normal democratic electoral process. May we first remind you that educating the international community about the Gambia's deteriorating political situation began twenty years ago. And although Gambians recognized the steep hill they have to climb to put a small West African nation, without natural resources, on the radar of the international community, they have never stopped trying to and never stopped hoping. Along with two respected international organizations, Amnesty International (AI) UK and Media Foundation for West Africa (MFWA) Ghana, the

Gambia's growing dissident movement never missed an opportunity to call the attention of the international to the deadly human rights violations in the Gambia. Sir, Gambians first began to inform and educate the United Nations in an open letter addressed to that body early in the 2000s. Since then, the Gambia's overseas dissident movement has continued its efforts to inform the United Nations, European Union, the Commonwealth, as well as the governments of the United States and the United Kingdom about the Gambia's frequent flares of unprecedented state-sanctioned violence against citizens. Most notable, among the barbarities committed by the Gambian state, these episodes of mind-numbing brutality stand out to attract attention to the despair in the Gambia:

1. November 1994, the extrajudicial executions of ten military officers
2. June 1995, murder and burning of Finance Minister Koro Ceesay's body
3. April 2000, massacre by security forces of sixteen demonstrating students
4. December 2004, assassination of Deida Hydara, president, Gambia Press Union
5. July 2005, execution of forty-four Ghanaians and ten other ECOWAS nationals
6. April 2006, execution of eight military and security personnel
7. August 2006, forced disappearances of twenty civilians
8. November 2006, mysterious deaths of witnesses of forty-five Ghanaians' massacre
9. March 2009, rounding up of over one thousand elderly, and death of ten in witch hunting
10. June 2009, rounding up and detention of a dozen journalists/media personnel
11. August 2012, execution of nine Mile 2 Prison prisoners

12. April 2013, abduction and disappearance of Gambian dissidents from Senegal
13. December 2014, rounding up and parading of gays on national television

Sir, between these notable atrocious human rights violations, the Gambia's Yahya Jammeh has sanctioned the murders of hundreds more innocent citizens and non-citizens alike, caused the deaths of nearly three hundred prisoners at the notorious Mile 2 Prison, and the fleeing of thousands more to the west and across the West African sub-region, notably Senegal, Ghana, and Mali. Sir, the recent efforts to restore democratic civilian rule in the Gambia in December 2014 were conceived against the background of the glaring indifference by the international community to the atrocities in the Gambia. It is an ongoing effort approved by the suffering Gambian people. Sir, December 30, 2014, was prompted by the deadly Gambian tyranny and the inability of Gambians to change their government through the democratic electoral process. The collective Gambian population and the dissident military forces, faced with doing what is not legally right but morally just, chose the latter, in an effort to restore sanity in the country, prevent further senseless loss of life, and seek justice for hundreds of the Gambians who faced extrajudicial executions, forced disappearances, and incarceration in the Gambia's notorious gulag, Mile 2 Prison.

Sir, for a brief period on the night of December, 30, 2014, Gambians across the globe once again sensed a glimmer of hope for their country. It all started back in 1994, when the newly installed military regime commissioned the drafting of a new constitution. After the Constitutional Commission completed its work, the two-term limit recommended by the commission was promptly stripped out of the draft constitution without the approval of either the Drafting Commission or the Gambian people. By all accounts, this is what spelled Gambia's ongoing political catastrophe. It was the genesis of the Gambia's current political predicament and the inability to change the ruthless military

regime through the electoral process. This inability to effect peacefully
political change through free and fair elections, reinforced by the parallel
tragedy of reptilian human right violations—for instance, the murder
and burning of the body of the former civilian finance minister, Koro
Ceesay, and the multiple rape of a Senegalese national, Ms. Tabara
Samba, before her execution by a military firing squad, among other
cases—combined to factor in the decision to effect regime change by
military action on December 2014.

Sir, in 2006, the former ECOWAS president, Hon. James Victor
Gbeho, after a fact-finding mission, determined the presidential
elections in Gambia would not be free and fair and, therefore, declined
to send ECOWAS electoral monitors to an election whose results were
predetermined by the regime. The Gambia's Yahya Jammeh is renowned
for a combination of three strategies that have kept his regime alive
and in power for so long: dangerous tribal divide, bribery of regional
organizations and the indifference to Gambians' egregious human right
violations by the international community.

As we speak, Gambia's Yahya Jammeh is salivating over an
opportunity to waste more human lives in human sacrifice rituals amid
the confusion prevailing in the country. In light of this, Gambians across
the world commend the United Nations for promptly sending envoy
Mohamed Chambas to Gambia. Hopefully, the UN envoy can prevent
the summary executions of both the accused persons and those falsely
implicated and rounded up across the country in the December 2014
coup effort. Sir, Gambians prefer and will always prevent unnecessary
loss of life, but without international assistance to enable peaceful
change of government, Gambian dissidents, working in tandem with
members of the dissident military and security forces, reserve the right
to use any means necessary to stop the ongoing carnage and bloodletting
being perpetrated by a callous military regime. Gambians ask your
indulgence in permitting and facilitating meetings with Your Excellency,
or your representatives, to allow us the opportunity to further elaborate
on the Gambia's human rights crisis. Sir, we also seek your indulgence

in authorizing the relevant United Nation bodies to interview former members of the regime who have horrendous stories of human sacrifice of newborns, the mentally sick, and many heart-wrenching human rights abuse cases. Return mailing information has been provided to facilitate communications. The Gambian people hope the United Nations will understand their position, stuck between a rock and a hard place, and look forward to having the opportunity to open dialogue with Your Excellency and or your representatives, in order to more fully elaborate on the Gambia's sickening and desperate human rights situation. Thank you.

CC
President, European Union
President, African Union
President, ECOWAS
US, Secretary of State
Foreign Minister, United Kingdom
Foreign Minister, Republic of Senegal
Sgd: The Gambia's Dissident Movement-Madison WI

WHY ECOWAS SHOULD REVISIT THE TERM-LIMITS ISSUE AND WHY IT MATTERS

The anticipation was both joyous and infectious, but so also was the ambivalence and skepticism. If the recent proposal to establish presidential term limits for ECOWAS member states was a hopeful sign, its failure was incomprehensible and emotionally devastating. After four decades of existence, hundreds of millions of dollars wasted, thousands of meetings and conferences, and 350 million citizens waiting for even a single moment of glory, ECOWAS, some argue, has done little to justify its existence.

And nothing crystallizes this more than the recently torpedoed democratic process, designed to return power to citizens to exercise their constitutional right to periodically change their governments. And equally distressing was the ease with which the two least eminent countries, the Gambia and Togo, steamrolled the remaining fourteen member nations into shelving the idea of institutionalizing the celebrated presidential term-limit proposal.

This was one of the purest tests of one of the cardinal tenets of democracy, majority rule, but ECOWAS flunked it spectacularly and, in doing so, set itself up for public scorn and ridicule. The speed with which ECOWAS allowed the term-limits proposal to come crashing down in total failure was an embarrassment that questions the loyalty of the body to its 350 million citizens. But, the term-limits proposal, down in defeat, also proves ECOWAS's puzzling lack of appreciation of the interconnectedness of Africans, in particular, the educated African diaspora and its support for ECOWAS's term-limits proposal.

An irrefutable but largely unknown fact is how, over two decades, Africans across the United States, Europe, and beyond have built institutions of common interest that transcend the artificial divides by tribe, national origin, and social and economic status. In so many significant ways, the African diaspora is far ahead of the AU and other regional organizations like ECOWAS, and this was loudly demonstrated during South Africa's mob massacre of African immigrants, despite the fact that countries like the Gambia took in so many South African refugees during the years of apartheid rule.

The African diaspora has created multiple oases of institutional unity that will make the African Union and ECOWAS's efforts at continental and regional unity seem like child's play. The significance of the African diaspora's one-Africa mind-set concept, at the heart of the Byzantine diaspora political and cultural linkages, is in facilitating support for issues like the ECOWAS's term-limits idea, for which Africans roundly condemn ECOWAS's stunning failure to implement its proposal. The growing exchanges of ideas and opinions among Africa's diaspora will make the concept of artificial boundaries seem obsolete, and the protestation over the failure of ECOWAS to implement its proposed term limits proves it.

Further, and even more significantly, the limitations of people's ideas and opinions to diaspora's countries of origin are inconsistent with the spirit of the internet media platform as a platform where the international community can meet in unity. And Africans without regard to nationality, are increasingly outspoken in matters affecting the interests of other Africans all across the continent. Gone are the days when most Africans focused their attention and criticisms exclusively on the governments and regimes in their country of origin.

The internet is a force of nature that has given voice to Africa's hitherto politically powerless and with no avenue to participate in their political process. A magic of the internet and social media has enabled the 350 million ECOWAS bloc citizens to coalesce around the common interests of establishing term limits in countries under the tyranny of imperial rule. The unremarkable way in which the ECOWAS term-limits idea has crumpled without pushback by the majority says more about its leaders' failure to fully grasp how regimes like the Gambia have consistently and willfully defied established republican constitutions. This speaks to both the democratic organization of the state and the triangular decentralization of administrative power into three co-equal branches. The collapse of ECOWAS's term-limit proposal, a mechanism of facilitating and promoting good governance and empowering ECOWAS citizens held down by the ruthless arms of political tyranny, further solidifies the perception of the West African body as a hegemony of its leaders, not its opposed to it citizens.

In the unsuccessful term-limits issue brought up by ECOWAS, Senegalese citizens, like Gambians, lament its failure, just as the issue was bemoaned by such nationals as Nigerians, Ghanaians, Sierra Leoneans, Malians, Guinea-Conakry, and elsewhere in Africa. This proves that the growing interconnectedness of Africans in this new century is more than just symbolic; it is substantive and the core belief system of Africans, especially among the highly educated minority. Importantly, ECOWAS leaders have failed once again to give consideration to the Gambia's dire political situation, because the regional body is not attuned to the emerging political paradigm that informs the politics of the twenty-first century.

ECOWAS, it appears, still operates on the basis of the old United Nations doctrine of noninterference in other countries' internal affairs, a doctrine that has since been overtaken by the broadening of democratic values, in the ever-changing and ever-maturing global democracy project.

The new United Nations doctrine of "responsibility to protect" or "R2P," still largely alien to African countries with long histories of paternalistic systems of political and social organizations, mandates the use of force, if necessary, in order to wrest power from rogue regimes and restore order in countries burdened by the cruel overreach of state power.

The inability of Gambians to actuate constitutional change of power, in part due to Senegal's firm denial of Gambian dissident's military activity within its borders, has hamstrung Gambians' efforts and severely limited their ability to force political change in their country. This is all the more why, despite ECOWAS's recent blunder, the need to revisit the term-limits issue is underscored by desperate need for peace and stability through political change.

The Gambian people's desire for change is sparked in part by state violence and its collision with Gambia's laws and constitution. It is why Gambians continue the relentless call to institute the presidential two term limits in ECOWAS's sphere of influence in order to restore peace, security, good governance in the sub-region.

HIJABS, BURQAS, AND THE CULTURAL CONSTRUCT OF FORCED ISLAMIZATION OF A SECULAR STATE

The needless executions in 2012, of nine prisoners where more than five hundred prisoner deaths have been reported, since 1994, Gambia's notorious Mile 2 Central Prison, reinforces the belief that Yahya Jammeh has reached the peak of insanity. The startling executions in 2012, preceded by five mass murder incidences, dating back to the November 1994 executions of nine military officers, exemplify the uthlessness of Yahya Jammeh and his military henchmen. But, notwithstanding the past tragedies, the Gambian people recently woke up to a different kind of reality—a craziness that embodies the essence of Yahya Jammeh's unapologetic cold-bloodedness.

The dark vein of tribal bigotry that runs through the past two decades of Yahya Jammeh's monarchical rule is not his predictable psychosis, but the depth to which he is willing to descend, to confound the public interest and his self-interest. Only two weeks after his unilateral and illegal declaration of the Gambia as an Islamic state, in contradiction to its secular republican constitution, Yahya Jammeh began his jihad against the Gambia's animist majority and Christian minority.

And last week, in a widely publicized state directive, female in the Gambian civil service were obliged to dress in Arabic hijabs and burqas, in a mass social engineering that has already proven to be an aberration that disparages Gambian culture, undermines the freedom of choice, and subverts individual dignity. Yahya Jammeh's adventure of folly in the futile effort to sabotage Gambian society and culture has no precedence in Africa and ECOWAS member states, and even by General Idi Amin Dada's low standards of ethics and morality, Yahya Jammeh's forced Islamization and his radical directives range in from extreme to downright idiotic. Paradoxically, in true African tradition, Yahya Jammeh's superstitions and voodoo and shamanism rituals make his stand on Islam, at best, spurious and, at worst, deceptive and mere showboating.

As opposed to organized religion, voodoo rituals and shamanism practices are intricately woven in the fabric of Gambian society, among both Christians and Muslims, but are punishable by beheading under Islamic state's strict Sharia law. Thus, the Gambia's Islamization is the epitome of contradictions, which challenges the Islamic declaration as a comical exercise in futility.

Gambia's Islamization decree is compelled not by a sense of religiosity but by the ongoing, debilitating economic downturn that has forced Yahya Jammeh to turn to the schmucks in the Middle East to finance his corrupt and extravagant lifestyle. The worsening economic situation in Gambia is impelled by the terrible human rights record, which compelled Africa's cash cows, the United States and European Union to withhold funding and, by extension, push Gambia's economy toward free fall and bankruptcy.

The issue of forced Islamizing of the Gambia is a tough sell, largely due to the cultural barriers on its path. And increasingly, for the highly educated minority, religion is, at best, the transfer of alien cultures, and, at worst, represents primitive superstitions. In the face of these insurmountable obstacles, Yahya Jammeh's dream of forcibly Islamizing Gambia, if only in the superficial context, is driven by slavish subservience to his Arab masters and, in the process, is using the Gambian people as pawns in his sinister and corrupt conspiracy to deceive Arabs to fund his regime.

Besides the fact that true faith resides in the hearts and minds, and recognizing that inconsequential changes to female civil servants' dress codes doesn't make them Muslims, Yahya Jammeh has a steep hill to climb in order to accomplish his infamous religious quest. Islamization necessarily requires deep social and cultural transformation in the Gambia, which will put the legal as well as some sectors of the thriving economy in jeopardy—European tourism, Banjul Breweries, the unregulated Jola alcoholic palm-wine tapping, equally unregulated Manjago zum-zum brewing, the raising of swine for food, and the beachside food service for the tourists industry, among others.

For workers who lack education and marketable skills, and are dependent on the unregulated economy—in particular, Jolas and Manjagoes—Islamization will be devastating to their livelihoods. Besides, the pervasive practice voodoo in the Gambia, in conflict with Islam, and punishable by beheading in the Middle East, is a thriving multimillion-dalasi, unregulated industry in the West African region.

But a close scrutiny reveals the dirty con game Yahya Jammeh is playing on his Arab benefactors, using the Gambians people as his pawns. In Gambia, more people believe in primitive worship of jinn, witches, and witchcraft than the concept of monotheism, which Islam adapted from the Hebrew Old Testament.

And under Sharia law doctrine, a product of Islamization, Yahya Jammeh, who surrounds himself with voodoo priests practicing pre-Islamic African religions and Islamic clerics, is an atypical Muslim, in particular, due to his well-known animist beliefs, which conflict with Islam. The YouTube media platform is replete with video clips that show Yahya Jammeh in voodoo rituals "curing" HIV Aids, infertility, high blood pressure, and diabetes. But even more relevant than the superficial hijab and burqas dress codes, Islamization is a stand-alone legal system that requires abolishing the Gambia's common law, or relegating it to an obscure role in the Gambia's legal system.

The complexities of Islamization are many and varied and must include the reconfiguration of the banking and educational sectors to conform to the hadiths of truly Islamic state. But what is transpiring in the Gambia, over the last three weeks, is a vivid example of the endless fall from civility and besmirching of the country, as a function of one man's greed and lust for power, exposing Yahya Jammeh as the charlatan, and a quintessential sellout, lacking virtue and morality.

In the final analysis, it comes down to the criminal inaction by the Gambian judiciary and National Assembly in enforcing fidelity to the Gambian Constitution. In the face of Yahya Jammeh's abuse of power and overstepping the boundary of authority as defined by the Constitution, these branches of government have the constitutional responsibility to act as the bulwarks in preventing the executive's legal, administrative, and unconstitutional overreach. And in their fearful silence and complete lack of moral fortitude, the judiciary and National Assembly are as good as dead, to the Gambia's suffering population.

CONTINENT-WIDE INSTITUTIONAL FAILURES
IMPAIR A CONTINENT IN CRISIS

Precedence to the Africa Union's shameful failure to assist in ending Burundi's gradual descent into bloody civil war and avert the unfolding bloodbath was bred in Abuja, Nigeria, in late 2015; well sort of. As in Abuja, arguments for military intervention in Burundi to help end the carnage from spiraling into total anarchy, and bring that country back from the brink of disaster, was advocated by some of the same opponents of ECOWAS's two-term-limits proposal last year. But the relative ease with which the Gambia's mass-murdering tyrant, Yahya Jammeh was able to exert disproportionate influence, and compel AU to abandon the Burundi people, was shocking, to say the least. Yahya Jammeh's opposition to the proposed ECOWAS two-term limit was as much a reflection of the regional institution's weaknesses, and its crippling lack of a defined mandate as its guiding principle. And by replicating the ECOWAS blunder in which Gambia's Yahya Jammeh and Togo's Faure Gnassingbé were able to easily override the policy objectives of the sixteen-nation member body, the African Union is also exposing the fatal flaws, which border on gutlessness and a complete lack of direction, in the face Burundi's growing civil unrest.

The African Union's demonstrated institutional failure in Burundi's political crisis showcases an unflattering moral failure, which crystallizes why, after half a century of independence, Africa, the wealthiest continent on the face of the planet, still chokes on its own vomit of incompetence, corruption, financial looting, and economic plunder. The ignorance, patronage, and paternalism that are dominant in African institutions' management styles, at the national, regional, and continental levels are absolutely both disastrous and detrimental to the continent's political and economic development. The AU's failure to dispatch intervention forces to a member nation in distress and on the verge of collapsing into a state of bloody civil strife and bloodbath brings back the haunting memories of Rwanda. And given the potential catastrophic consequences of the Burundi unrest, it is inconceivable that the Gambia's Yahya

Jammeh, a monster who has executed and murdered hundreds of Gambians and non-Gambians, would easily pressure the African Union into rescind its Burundi military intervention project. As in the case of ECOWAS, it says more about the AU as an institution than about Yahya Jammeh, who, acting out of fear, is fighting to maintain the status quo. By succumbing to pressure and deferring to the banal antics of Africa's bloodsucking political leaders, the AU has effectively reaffirmed the existence of the nauseating culture of patronage, which continues to stifle progress and deter economic development across Africa.

Denying the African people their right as the center of power and shifting it to Africa's greedy kleptomaniac leaders and corrupt psychopathic politicians, the AU has established that the body has learned very little since the failed days of the defunct OAU. The African Union's, Africa's regional institutions', and African governments' chronic failures of leaderships continue to have broad implications for Africa and its people. Over the past decade alone, thousands of young African men and women have perished in the Sahara Desert and the Mediterranean Sea, murdered across North Africa, from Egypt to Morocco and across the Middle East, but through all this barbarity, the African Union has largely remained unconcerned and disinterested. But the murder of Africans citizens is not limited to distant Arab lands. In southern Africa, in particular, Angola and South Africa, and Gambia in West Africa, the rampant murder of African immigrants has a chilling effect, and above all, no one has yet been held accountable for these crimes. The barbarism that African immigrants encounter, in the continent itself, particularly in Angola, Libya, and elsewhere across the Arab world, is absolutely unworthy of civilized human behavior. The documented evidence of young African men and women being tortured, murdered, and hanged across the Arab Middle East is incredibly shocking, yet through it all, the African Union remains silent, distant, and uncaring about the blatant atrocities committed daily against Africans. As a continent, the absence of altruism and a sense of African nationalism ensure that, as a people, Africans will remain malleable, subjugated, and backward, for a long time.

CHAPTER 5

HUMAN RIGHTS VIOLATIONS

REMEMBERING THE APRIL 10, 2000, STUDENT MASSACRE

Exactly fourteen years ago this week, sixteen young Gambian students' lives were cut short by the crackle of machine-gun fire. The morning began uneventfully as citizens went about their normal business. In downtown Serekunda, the hustle and bustle that gave notoriety to the Gambia's largest metropolis, lived up to its image of confusion and disorder. Two miles to the east of Serekunda, where the Kairaba Avenue, Birkama Highway, and the Serekunda/Banjul highway converge, and the spectacular display of human activity spoke loudly of hope, but also of subdued desperation, no one could predict the tragedy that was about to happen. On that morning of April 10, 2000, when Claesco Pierra woke up in her London Corner home, she was bubbly and full of life. She had just finished eating breakfast of porridge and sugar-laced skim milk and could not wait to get to school. She longed to meet her four best friends and do what they did best, small talk about teachers and whatever else adolescent girls talked about. By now, the time was 7:30 a.m and everywhere one looked, in all directions, schoolchildren walked singly or in groups toward St. Theresa's School. Close to Westfield clinic, as a little boy with a running nose ran to catch up with his older siblings, his left hand tightly clutching his loose shorts, a ragged white Toyota van suddenly veered off the street to avoid hitting him.

Around 7:45 a.m., the Kanifing/Serekunda/Talinding Kunda junction was teeming with young lives as boys and girls walked gingerly toward school, with a future so full of promise ahead of them. Standing on the edge of the street near the former Maroun's store, where Kairaba Avenue and Banjul/Serekunda highways intersect in an eternal embrace, Jonfolo Ceesay, Ngone Jobe, Elizabeth Jatta, and Ndungu Jallow giggled and made sounds that mockingly mimicked one of their female teachers, as they anxiously awaited their friend to appear. As the four girl-friends turned to look at a group of boys their age on the other side of Kairaba Avenue close to St. Theresa's Church, their friend Claesco Pierra sneaked up on them. "Surprise!" she shouted as she wrapped her arms around her four friends. The five exchanged greetings and walked toward school and stood for a moment on the sidewalk with arms locked together as they always did when they crossed a street. That morning, there was not enough time for the five to spend together under the usual mango tree at the far end of the schoolyard. As soon as the five friends entered the schoolyard, they parted company and went each to their separate classrooms. But prior to entering the schoolyard, they once again renewed their friendship vows, and promised to remain friends for the rest of their lives. They vowed to never allow other girls or boys to get in between them and ruin their friendship.

At eight o'clock sharp, the school bell rang as the school Principal William Kujabi emerged from his office, his menacing hulk crowned with his stern but harmless face. As if on cue, the remaining students who stood outside in the schoolyard bolted and ran helter-skelter in all directions toward their classrooms. Mr. Kujabi surveyed the school grounds one more time to make sure no student remained loitering on the school grounds or around the school perimeter fence. Meanwhile, in a secluded block of classrooms facing away from the rest of the school, the senior school students were meeting to discuss the events of the day. A few minutes earlier, Claesco Pierra, one of the school seniors, was motioned to join other senior students at the meeting. There was unanimous agreement among the gathered students to actively participate in the students' demonstration against the death of Ebrima Barry, in police custody and the rape of a fifteen-year-old girl slated for later that morning. It was agreed that only the senior students would be permitted to participate in the morning's demonstration along the Brikama/Banjul highway. The school head boy Bola Roberts sought permission from Principal Kujabi. The mildly warm day looked like every other school day. When the school bell rang at exactly nine o'clock, students from the three senior classes gathered in the schoolyard in front of the principal's office.

At exactly 9.15 am, led by the school head boy, Bola Roberts, the adolescent students exited the schoolyard, poured into Kairaba Avenue sidewalk, and turned south toward the Westfield junction. Already, the busy Serekunda Banjul Brikama junction was full beyond capacity with students from area schools. The excitement was palpable. The senior students from all the area schools gathered at the tri-street convergent point to create a carnival atmosphere, egged on by admiring adults proud of their teenage sons and daughters. Five miles to the north, at the Bakau Army Camp, unbeknown to the mass of gathered students, military personnel in riot gear sped toward the Kanifing junction, even as more reinforcements deployed from Yundum and Denton Bridge military barracks also sped toward the direction of the peaceful student march. Before long, the whole area was saturated with armed military men in riot gear. It looked as though they had come ready to do battle with defenseless students rather than control the gathering of unarmed young students whose peaceful march had assumed a fun, carnival-like atmosphere. But even with the festive mood of the protest, to the hundreds of gathered students, the protest was no joke. The murder of Ebrima Barry and the rape of a young student by the regime's thugs was no laughing matter.

As students continued their peaceful march, the security forces were bracing for a fight, threateningly showing off their AK-47 machine guns. Soon tensions were high on both sides of the divide. Exchanges of insults between the protesting students and some security forces intensified, yet despite that, the least the students expected was what happened next. Unprovoked and in a deliberate show of brute force, security personnel opened fire on the crowd of peaceful, unarmed students. When the crackle of machine-gun fire fell silent after five minutes of frightening machine-gun fire, small groups of students hovered over the bodies of the dead and dying. It was utter mayhem and pandemonium. One of the students who lay dying was a beautiful female student in St. Theresa's school uniform. She lay sprawled on the ground close to the old Cooperative Union complex where she stumbled and fell, trying to escape. A bullet entered the back of her head and exited her forehead above her right eye. She twittered violently one more time and fell silent. Claesco Pierra was dead. The beautiful young girl with so much to live for was no more. Back at St. Theresa's School, Jonfolo Ceesay, Ngone Jobe, Elizabeth Jatta, and Ndungu Jallow, her four best friends, had no idea what had just happened. When it was over, sixteen lifeless bodies lay dead or bleeding profusely on the streets of Kanifing.

That April 10, 2000, so long ago became the most tragic day in Gambia's history. It was the day Gambia lost its innocence. This year, like previous years, the innocent students massacred fourteen years ago are remembered and honored as martyrs of freedom for Gambians at home and abroad. The mourning of their deaths and the celebration of their short lives will become an annual ritual that will grow bigger as more Gambians become aware of the historical significance of that day of notoriety. This year, Gambians and Gambians' civil society organizations around the world are calling everyone to join in commemorating the freedom they stood for, and celebrate the short lives they lived. For their legacy of bravery will forever be etched in stone and inscribed on the mural of Gambian history. Like all the murders perpetrated on the orders of Yahya Jammeh and Isatou Njie-Saidy—from the assassination of Ousman Koro Ceesay, the cruel murder of Deida Hydara, the broad-daylight shooting at the Royal Albert Market of Sergeant Dumbuya, the strangulation of Sergeant Illo Jallow, the executions of the nine Mile 2 prisoners, and every murder and execution in between—the perpetrators of the student massacre have never been brought to face justice. As the murdered students are remembered, Gambians once again send messages to Yahya Jammeh and his brutal regime: the spirits of Gambia's dead will never die from the consciousness of the people. For, in our hearts, they reside until their troubled souls see justice.

1. Reginald Carroll
2. Karamo Barrow
3. Lamin Bojang
4. Ousman Sabally
5. Sainey Nyabally
6. Ousman Sembene
7. Bakary Njie
8. Claesco Pierra
9. Momodou Lamin Njie
10. Ebrima Barry
11. Wuyea Foday Mansareh
12. Bamba Jobarteh
13. Momodou Lamin Chune
14. Abdoulie Sanyang
15. Babucarr Badjie
16. Omar Barrow (journalist and Red Cross volunteer)

BAI LOWE, WITNESS TO EXTRAJUDICIAL EXECUTIONS

Bai Lowe's confession was delirious and breathtaking, his narrative about the executions of Gambians and Ghanaians, gruesome and grisly. Just listening to the former military officer, Bai Lowe, confess his role and involvement in Yahya Jammeh's mass killings at times felt surreal, like the mesmerizing chronicle of an out-of-body experience that numbed the soul and enraged the heart. Out of the blue, last week, an obscure former warrant officer in the Gambia's military regime, Bai Lowe, became the object of headline news in the Gambia's vibrant online media and blogosphere circuit. Bai Lowe's debut into the public square, last week, was preceded by debriefings in Dakar, Senegal, and his confessions, recorded and archived for posterity, will preface one of the saddest chapters of the Gambia's most recent but still largely unwritten storybook. An ex-warrant officer, Bai Lowe's animated, if not guilt-ridden, tear-jerking, and incriminating narrative of the true story of Yahya Jammeh's military regime was a spellbinding revelation whose time had come. Bai Lowe's jaw-dropping encyclopedic knowledge of the landmark events that captured the litany of murders and executions, his enumeration of the brutality and violence of the Yahya Jammeh regime, and his uncovering of the casualness and easy calm with which Dictator Yahya Jammeh brutally and remorselessly dispatched innocent Gambians and non-Gambians to their ugly, shocking, and awful deaths left Gambians flabbergasted and utterly devastated with disbelief.

Bai Lowe's revelations are horrendous, even nauseating and ghastly, but his sickening narrative is not entirely new; in fact, it is a mere confirmation that puts in proper context the ruthlessness and savagery of Gambia's last eighteen-year history. And, not unlike every country that has suffered the indignities of political tyranny, the truth of Yahya Jammeh's mayhem will come out sooner or later, and for the Gambia, the time is right now. It is a high order of patriotism to unveil the grim realities that have swathed the Gambia's military regime and police state in a fog enigma and mysterious ambiguity. Today, after eighteen long years of the fear and terror that has paralyzed Gambians across the political spectrum, the moment of truth is upon us. The unraveling of the Yahya Jammeh military regime has begun in earnest as the Ton Ton Macoute chambers of death, hidden behind dictator Yahya Jammeh's fake fury, the torture dungeons that mask the silent complacency of

Ousman Sonko's demonic ambition, and the unknown grave sites that challenge the morality of Isatou Njie-Saidy's tortuous, dry, and wrecked smile have brought the worst out of fellow countrymen and women. The devaluation of human life has epitomized the Gambia's eighteen long horrific years of death and dying, of murders and executions, of kidnappings and forced disappearances, of arrests and unlawful detentions, and of kangaroo trials and the wholesale incarcerations of innocent citizens and noncitizens alike.

To date, Yahya Jammeh's regime's panacea for the Gambia's underlying crisis of political unrest, the subterranean social disquiet, and the biting economic blight, like many dictatorships before him, has been to resort to harsh punitive underhandedness. But Bai Lowe is only one of many exiled Gambians with direct involvement in the Yahya Jammeh atrocities who has remorselessly crossed the line from the regime's insanity to reecho the horrendous transgressions that have shrouded the Gambia in a cloud of hopeless despair. The revelations of the indiscipline of Yahya Jammeh military and security apparatus, the frightening details that typify the barbarism of the Yahya Jammeh regime, and the moments of rare truthfulness that are setting former regime operatives apart from the rest will continue the slow drip of information until a full accounting of dictator Yahya Jammeh's military regime and the police state's atrocities see the sunshine of the day. Bai Lowe's spectacular and heartbreaking testimony opened the floodgates to doom the paternal reverence for Yahya Jammeh and condemn Gambians' cavalier tolerance of the atrocities of the regime. We have marveled at Jali Nyama Suso's soulful ballads of love and betrayal; our feet twitched to the nostalgic anthems of Yusuma Gigane; and our womenfolk danced to the melodious lyrics of Jaliba Kuyateh, but it is now time to marvel with disgust at the horrific carols of eyewitness accounts of the genocide by Gambia's military and security officers sworn to protect Gambians and uphold the Constitution.

NINE MILE 2 PRISON EXECUTIONS

The oldest inmate, Lamin Darboe, had his death sentence commuted to a life in prison years earlier by the former president Dawda K Jawara. The youngest, Buba Yarboe, of Busumbala village, was suffering severe mental illness and was incapable of making rational decisions, much less having the capacity to understand his predicament. And beautiful Tabara Samba, the only female in the group, with little children at home, tried and sentenced for murder in an apparent manslaughter case, was first gang-raped by her captors, and her breasts were cut off in human sacrifice rituals. This is not a preamble to the opening chapter of an Agatha Christie crime novel; it is real, and it happened in the Gambia. What all three individuals had in common was their cruel, mind-numbing execution at Mile 2 Prison on orders of Yahya Jammeh, an act of brutality so unimaginable it left an entire nation numbed by utter disbelief. On that fateful August night two years ago, when nine inmates were led out of their concrete-walled and steel-door cells and executed in cold blood with willful disregard for human life, the Gambia descended further into new depths of mindless barbarity. But this time around, Yahya Jammeh's fate will not be determined by primitive superstitions and devil worship, which have hitherto dictated the way he ruled the Gambia with bewildering ignorance. Moving forward, his life will rest in the hands of the Gambian people. For the first time in twenty years, Gambians both at home and abroad cry out their deadly rage with a determination never before seen in two decades of tyranny and political madness.

For the past twenty years, Yahya Jammeh ruled Gambia with extraordinary cruelty and mean-spiritedness, in the process, turning himself into an object of hate and scorn, but it is his vexing detachment from reality that has locked him into a perpetual state of delusion and illusions of grandiosity. Today, the relationship between Yahya Jammeh and Gambians is a marriage that has never worked well; consequently, the time for it to end came and went with each extraordinary abuse of power, which has included the frequent murders of fellow citizens. But the recent execution of as many as twenty-six helpless prisoners was the straw that broke the camel's back and sealed Yahya Jammeh's fate for the rest of time. The executions in Mile 2 Prison of so many innocent Gambian prisoners is more than anyone can imagine, and if Yahya Jammeh thinks this egregious act of violence will be unremembered a year from now, he is underestimating Gambians' resolve to keep the memory of the executed alive. More baffling still, while the regime admitted to the execution of nine inmates, the real number of executions on Yahya Jammeh's orders could be as many as twenty-six people, and unless the regime can produce evidence to the contrary, Gambians and the international community will continue to assume that twenty-six, not nine, inmates were executed. This case is similar to the Ghanaians' massacre a decade ago when the regime admitted to eight murders instead of the real number of forty-four executed according to eyewitnesses. But to make matters even worse, rumors are rife of the use of the victims' body parts in ritual human sacrifice and devil worship.

The fact is; Yahya Jammeh's extreme dependence on primitive African belief systems makes the rumors not all that far-fetched. If the ritual sacrifice rumors are revealed to be true, it will further aggravate the Gambian people and animate an even more violent outrage among Gambians and the international community. Two years after the execution of as many as twenty-six Gambians and Senegalese, lost in the conversation is the issue of burial of the dead. So far, families of the executed have not received the bodies of their loved ones in order to give them decent burials according to local customs and Islamic tradition. The relatives of the dead are urged to never give up demanding the remains of the dead relative in order give them the decent burials they deserve. In the same vein, the Gambian public is urged to support the quest by family members to retrieve the dead bodies of their relatives from Yahya Jammeh, no matter how long it takes. In the same vein, the Senegalese community in Gambia should also demand the surrender of the remains of Tabara Samba and Gibbi Bah for repatriation to their villages in Senegal for burial. This effort should be supported by the Senegalese government, yet it remains a mystery why President Macky Sall has still not demanded the return of the remains of his citizens to accord them the proper burials according to their Islamic religion and African traditions. Yahya Jammeh has no authority under any law to continue to detain the remains of his victims executed under a false pretext. Family members of the nine executed have the rights to demand the return of their dead relatives without letting the irrational fear of Yahya Jammeh force them to abandon their obligation to their deceased relatives.

And this week, Gambians across the globe will express outrage on radio programs that bring back to life that sad day two years ago. While the Senegalese violently demonstrated the execution of their compatriots, on Gambian soil, the stark contrast in the Gambia, where even the media appeared timid to report the executions, was so glaring. But it was the tepid protest letter by the group of six political parties that many found aggravating and incredulous. And more puzzling still, the group of six's letter to Yahya Jammeh, arguing the legal basis for the executions, was completely misguided, out of line, and irrelevant to the situation. The illegality of the executions is an established fact; besides, Yahya Jammeh does not respond to the Gambia's Constitution or simple common sense. Time and again, he has shown his unwillingness to respect the Constitution and the laws of the land, and the scores of letters from politicians over the years have been ignored with recklessness for the laws of the land. The time for the politicians to overcome their fears of Yahya Jammeh is now, and what Gambians expect from Ousainou Darboe and the politicians is to call the country out in a massive show of dislike for the regime. Today, hundreds if not thousands of diaspora Gambians are ready and willing to join nationwide anti-regime demonstrations seeking the forced removal of Yahya Jammeh. We can no longer afford to be held back by fear, and besides, if such blatant acts of violence, such as the Mile 2 Prison execution of nine known and probable twenty-six inmates, do not embolden our collective resolve, it will mean the acceptance of the devaluation of Gambian life. Enough Gambians and non-Gambians have been killed already. It's time to force change. Meanwhile, let us remember the nine to twenty-six prisoners Yahya Jammeh has executed.

THE CATASTROPHE OF THE PRISON CULTURE AND THE NUMBING INCARCERATION CRISIS

An indignant headline in the *Daily News* casting the godless Gambian judiciary and kangaroo court as the unbearable embodiments of Yahya Jammeh's imperial regime may to some seem pietistic, or it may even seem as an ostentatious political grandstanding, yet no one will equate it to dogmatic ecclesiastical pontification. The paper's unequivocal indictment of the growing culture of incarceration of young, productive Gambian men is a challenge for political introspection that goes far beyond narrow political self-righteousness. The sweeping criminalization of Gambian society for even the most innocuous and trivial, emanating from the mean-spiritedness of a clueless regime, deserves our collective condemnation, a sentiment that was recently echoed by more harrowing news of more incarceration news. Under Yahya Jammeh, the acculturation of a prison industrial system as a panacea and the convenient cop-out for the regime's pungent administrative failure effectively demonstrates the tentativeness of a political system ardently blinded to its own ideological waywardness and rank criminality.

The most recent victim of this Orwellian gulag, Lawyer Lamin Mboge, whose letter castigating the Gambia Bar Association could have been written by a Medina Sering Mass primary six student, did not endear himself to the broader Gambian population. In a futile effort to appease Yahya Jammeh, Mr. Mboge, the cantankerous epitome of the truly hopeless and demoralized society, brilliantly displayed a less than lawyerly betrayal of a cause Gambians are demonstrably invested in. Yet even his cowardly exposition of inglorious self-preservation could not save him from the cruel excesses of Yahya Jammeh's political apostasy and peerless shiftiness. The hapless Lawyer Mboge, whose pharisaical subordination to the avatar of boundless political power, Yahya Jammeh, now stands as the newest guest of the notoriously oppressive Mile 2 Prison. The regime's lethargy to even the most innocuous criticism is a clear manifestation of the jarring incarceration epidemic, which is now on the cusp of mindless absurdity. In addition, *Daily News* again lamented that the further deterioration of the regime's apocalyptic political power exercise has reached a new milestone with the arrests of innocent citizens whose crime was failing to salute Yahya Jammeh's speeding militarized convoys.

With an unprecedented number of citizens and noncitizens incarcerated than ever in the Gambia's history, the political abuse in the country has reached a crisis level and headed toward a breaking point. Mass incarceration as an instrument of political control is a willful violation of citizens' rights, which demonstrates both insensitivity and stupidity unmatched in modern African politics. The total lack of accountability for the regime's succession of egregious crimes, which range from extrajudicial executions to witch-hunting deaths, and now the arrest of citizens who fail to salute Yahya Jammeh's convoys, is a pattern of abuse that has progressively worsened and emboldened Yahya Jammeh to push the boundaries of unacceptable behaviors to new intolerable levels. The recent spate of citizen arrests for not saluting Yahya Jammeh's speeding motorcades is indicative of the senseless relinquishing of infinite power in the hands of a single individual. And with the docile political opposition disengaged amidst such an oppressive political climate, Yahya Jammeh has all the latitude he desires to expand the broad reach of his power, posing an even greater danger to the future stability of the country. This dangerous descent into political chaos and anarchy continues to seep into the consciousness of a people who are cognizant of the unforgiving transgressions of this ruthless regime. The *Point News* also recently carried ten court case stories, all poignant reminders of a dysfunctional regime that has perfected a tradition steeped in the art of juxtaposing political intimidation and platitudes designed purely to shift attention away from his unbelievable criminality.

And now, buoyed by the results of the fraudulent November elections, and consumed by a need to demonstrate the burdensome arbitrariness of power, Yahya Jammeh's capacity for injustice easily comes through especially with the recent establishment of a tax commission that excludes his vast local and international holdings. Yahya Jammeh's arrogant display of absolute power knows no boundary, and the extremely asinine nature with which he has thrown his weight around is further indicative of a regime left to perpetuate the social and economic injustice that has plunged Gambia in a miasma of political quandary. But there is always a glimmer of hope, and the recently concluded weeklong TANGO celebration of the Gambia's charitable organizations offers possibilities for political rights hitherto withheld by the regime and hindered stability of the country. TANGO's resolution to inject issues of human rights into its broader agenda is a natural progression of the need to tie economic empowerment and political freedoms, and could not have come a moment too soon. Late Kanjiba Kanyi, a former Catholic Relief Service employee, and Omar Barrow, formerly of the Gambia Red Cross Society, both arrested and disappeared in 2005, have largely been forgotten not only by the Gambia's media, but even by the nonprofit community they so admirably served.

And with the parliamentary election fast approaching, and the Independent Electoral Commission lukewarm to the idea of electoral reform, it is conceivable that the opposition is down to a most humiliating defeat that could easily reduce Gambia to a single-party rule under the AFPRC military regime. The opposition parties, which should serve as a bulwark against the overreach of the military regime, have largely been incapable of subsuming their political interests for the greater Gambian good. Typically, the level of sacrifice these demands would be a no-brainer in the civilized Western world, but Gambians lack the sense of national good, consumed instead by the individualism that has given rise to the banal overreach of a regime slowly choking on its own vermin.

Clearly, Yahya Jammeh is expanding political capital he does not deserve by dint of the fraudulent elections corrupted by an elaborate scheme of intimidation, coercion, and vote buying. The outrageously impossible results that Yahya Jammeh is shamelessly boasting about are not atypical in dictatorships around the world; in fact, they are the norm. Yet there is a revelation of hope in this perennial political quagmire, and it is that even Saddam Hussein was voted back into office by 99 percent of his subjects before they turned and hanged him. Saddam Hussein, Muammar Gaddafi, and Syria's Bashar al-Assad are metaphors of how not to rule. Yahya Jammeh could have learned from the error of their ways, especially from his mentor, Col. Gaddafi. It is too late now. As for what fate awaits Yahya Jammeh, only time will tell. But with so much pent-up anger and rage among Gambians, his end will likely be ugly. Yahya Jammeh has no easy escape from the tragedy waiting for him. You can take that to the bank.

KIDNAPPINGS, ABDUCTIONS, TORTURE, AND POLITICAL VIOLENCE IN GAMBIA

It looks like the plot in a masterpiece Agatha Christie novel or a scene scripted for a Hollywood movie. Imagine a CIA abduction of Edward Snowden from the heart of Moscow; only this one is real and far smaller in its political profile. Yet it does not diminish the grave degeneration of Gambia's human rights abuses into the apocalyptic state that has gripped the country in recent times. But first, Gambia is a country that has not known peace over the last two decades; the arrests, detentions, and incarcerations, which have become a constant feature of life, have sapped the energy and the will to live from a once free and vibrant population. Today, the fear of even the mention of Yahya Jammeh's name in public, except in glorifying him, the constant nervousness of the wide-eyed population, the dreaded midnight knock by agents of the National Intelligence Agency, the shadowing of unsuspecting citizens, and the regularity in which disfavor of Yahya Jammeh courts never failed to push the Gambia toward the dangerous edge of a pariah nation. Gambians have been blindsided by many unilateral decisions Yahya Jammeh has made on their behalf and without their consent, but it is the recent spate of kidnappings and abductions that have caused disbelief and consternation among Gambians and non-Gambians alike. By all accounts, the Gambia is unsafe for visitors, regardless of nationality. The attempted kidnapping of a white child on a tourist visit to Gambia, four years ago, began the dangerous descent into a new dimension of human rights abuses. That attempted kidnapping of a British child for the purpose of human sacrifice was the first sign of the devolving nature of human rights abuses in the Gambia into something truly sinister. Since that failed abduction, the Gambia has emerged as the most dangerous place to live in West Africa.

The state of the Gambia's military regime's ruthlessness is crystalized in so many ways, not the least of which is the massive exodus of young men and women drawn toward the challenges of the perilous Mediterranean Sea, where so many African youths have perished, the huge Gambia refugee population in Senegal and around West Africa, the forced disappearances, and the state-sanctioned murders of citizens that know no end. To further compound the egregious acts of violence and discontent, the regime resurfaced its campaign of kidnapping. In April 2013, Gambian businessman Saul Ndow and politician Mahawa Cham, both based in Dakar, Senegal, were abducted and have never been seen again. This was crushing news for the families of both men and a punch in the guts to Gambia's dissident movement, and it somehow reflected Senegal's tolerant attitude toward Yahya Jammeh's destabilizing nature and capacity to operate in Senegal with criminal disregard for the territorial integrity and sovereignty of Senegal. Gambia's human rights abuses have, with these kidnappings in Senegal, a country thought to be a safe haven for Gambians fleeing the butchery in their own country, driven some dissidents underground and left others worrying about the long arm of Gambia's regime and its capacity to flaunt international law by abducting political dissidents under Senegalese protection. And the following year, February 2014, Alhaji Mamut Ceesay and Ebou Jobe, two naturalized US citizens visiting the Gambia, were abducted and have never been heard from since. The circumstances surrounding this particular case seem like a blast from Latin America's past, when abductions and kidnappings were the policies by many military regimes. But nothing frustrates Gambians more than the inability of the United States and its Banjul Embassy to force Yahya Jammeh to unconditionally free these US citizens.

But, what continues to make headlines throughout Gambia's vibrant online media is the recent kidnapping, torture, and incarceration of children whose military father was said to be involved in the attempt to restore democracy and the rule of law in the Gambia, in December 2014. Not surprising, Yahya Jammeh's caveman mentality has resulted in child sacrifices and kidnapping of others over many years. Yusupha Lowe, a thirteen-year-old, and Pa Alieu Lowe, a seventeen-year-old teenager, both son and brother of exiled Warrant Officer Baboucar 'Bai' Lowe of the Gambia Armed Forces, have been under illegal incommunicado detention for nearly four months. Yahya Jammeh's willful ignorance and brazen flaunting of the laws of the land know no bounds, and not even the scathing criticisms of his crassness have had an effect in awakening him to the dangerous consequences of his insipid acts of cruelty and savagery. The multiplicity of his violent acts and complete contempt of the rule of law have more than adequately illustrated Yahya Jammeh's philosophical indisposition to truly change the nature and character of Gambian society. After years of citizens' murders, any attempt to mitigate his senseless crimes will collide with the reality of the depth and gravity of his actions. The visible surface calm and deafening silence in Gambia, hides a dangerous reality—the insidious rage, blinding desire for revenge, and the sadistic impulse for payback that awaits Yahya Jammeh. Nothing Yahya Jammeh does will any longer shock the conscience of a nation, especially knowing his morbid fear of the consequences of losing power. John Minto, the spokesperson for Global Peace and Justice, poignantly captured the essence of the Gambia's pathetic lawlessness in a celebrated article titled "Peace is not the absence of war, but the presence of justice." This is embodied in Yahya Jammeh's revenge detention of an innocent child, Yusupha Lowe.

THE NEW MIND OF A PEOPLE AND THE COLOR OF BETRAYAL

To digress from the nastiness of politics for a moment, this article focuses on human nature in the Gambia as a powerful component of the changes in Gambia's cultural landscape. This daring plunge into complex human nature puts in context the enormous lapses in judgment to which many Gambians have become unwilling victims and participants. This anecdotal observation does not in any way reference theoretical psychology; rather, it is based on experiences that respond to our moral groundings, experiences embodied in society's norms and distinguish our capacity to rationalize as humans from other creatures in nature. At one critical level, our countrymen and women have deliberately or unwittingly fallen into the traps of the promises of power and prestige, not an insignificant motivator in the economics of self-preservation. In short, acceptance to work under Yahya Jammeh's dictatorship is an issue of self-preservation, combined with the need for power and self-protection. Over the past eighteen years, our concept of Gambian society has been devalued, but more significantly, our perception of our countrymen and women is the study of the contradictions in moral obligation and the primordial survival instincts. The most recent castigation campaign and moral marginalization of Nana Gray-Johnson typify the stark division among Gambians, a division explainable by the surroundings where Nana Gray-Johnson lives. Throughout the initial harsh criticisms of Nana Gray-Johnson, there has always been an awareness of how dire economic conditions at home provide a powerful incentive for malleability and indifference to moral rationality.

Nana Gray-Johnson deserved criticism for failing the moral test fro taking up employment under Yahya Jammeh, but with that story behind us, he is not unmindful that he is stuck between the dangerous company of Yahya Jammeh and the unforgiving indignation of the vocal Gambian majority. The issue of Nana Gray-Johnson reminds us that Gambia is in the grip of an intellectual degradation unlike anything Africa has ever seen since the seventies. The regularity with which Gambians fall victims to Yahya Jammeh's authority, and the lure of economics and political power are objects of debate among Gambians, and the list of case studies that provide the empirical evidence to facilitate the understanding of the cruelty of Gambian politics includes, but is not limited to Sarjo Jallow, Nene Macdolle, Fatoumata Tambajang, Nana Gray-Johnson, Bala Garba-Jahumpa, and Mbemba Tambedou, all of who constitute only a small slice of the nearly hundred cabinet appointments and dismissals under Yahya Jammeh. But, the failure of moral and ethical obligation in the Gambia has a religious dimension, further complicating the enormous challenges of moral rectitude. The fact that many Gambians have chosen to disregard Yahya Jammeh's leadership failure for so long is stunning, but for so many to endure the indignities of arrests, tortures, and recycling back into the system is mind-blowing. Even today, Gambians continue to take positions in different capacities in the military regime, while others continue to be murdered, disappeared, or reduced to their ambitions and limited in their freedoms.

Intellectual prowess dictates the assumption of moral superiority, but the utter failure to fulfill this ideal compels Nana Gray-Johnson and others to endure the cloud of bitterness likely to hang over their heads for a long time to come. The collapse of Gambians' moral moorings, more than seeming so tantalizing, is slowly reconfiguring the Gambian psyche and changing the value system inherited from our noble past. As of now, Gambians will disappear, the murders still continue, prison, once an anathema is now almost like a rite of passage, executions in the darkness of night with still terrorize, and the terror of Gambians speaks loudly in its eloquent silence. And despite everything else, Gambians seem unbothered by the regime's criminality and most specifically,

Yahya Jammeh's absolute power over life and death. The unflattering nature of the regime's crimes typifies the loss of credibility that borders on illegitimacy. The subjugation of an entire society into a permanent underclass has tasked Gambians' endurance, and the highlighted the inevitable need for political change. But whether Yahya Jammeh will leave office by his own free will or whether he is forced out is another matter. The Gambia people have time on their side; for even the longest nightmare has its day of hope, and the Gambia is not an exception to that rule. As it is now, Gambians lack the basic tenets of ethics and morality, and Nana Gray-Johnson, like all the others who served Yahya Jammeh, clearly speaks to the color of betrayal and serious moral and ethical deficits.

DEATH PENALTY AMENDMENT, SHARIA LAW, AND THE DANGEROUS DESCENT INTO LAWLESSNESS

It almost seems surreal, like the incantation of a funerarial ballad that shows the Gambia slowly morphing into the Third Reich reborn, methodically transforming itself into an archetypical anarchist society. The constitutional parameters that limit and inhibit the excesses of state power in the Gambia have crumbled and dissolved into nothingness. Gambia's Constitution, a revered social and political organizing document, long ago lost its moralizing force, victim of Yahya Jammeh's systemic subversion and determination to decree who lives and dies in the Gambia. Yahya Jammeh has totally usurped the authority of the judiciary to determine the legal fate of Gambians, and to insert the death penalty language into the Constitution will essentially legalize the indiscriminate and needless killing of more Gambians. For the second time in five years, Yahya Jammeh's fixation with amending the Death Penalty looks suspicious and total lacks of legal justification. The Death Penalty Article itself has a storied history. The 1970 Republican Constitution permitted its legal basis for the felony crimes of murder and treason, but in 1993, former president Sir Dawda Jawara's government amended the Constitution and abolished the death penalty. In 1995, however, the new military regime repealed the Constitution and reinstated the Death Penalty. In 2010, Yahya Jammeh's human sacrifice blood lust and overarching need to conceal his connections to South American drug kingpins, ordered former justice minister and attorney general Edward Gomez to introduce a Constitutional amendment in the National Assembly, which added drug possession and sale as death-penalty-eligible crimes. This addition of the death penalty crimes was, however, severely constrained by Section 18 (2) of the 1997 Constitution, and in 2011, it was repealed in short order, without much fanfare. But a year later, in the summer of 2012, Yahya Jammeh ordered the executions of nine Mile 2 Prison inmates, even before the legal appeals of some were exhausted. Two and half years after those executions were heard around the world, Yahya Jammeh again intends to amend Gambian's Constitution in order to broaden the death-penalty-eligible crimes.

By now it has become all too apparent that Yahya Jammeh is not driven by the same emotional forces that haunt the conscience, and steer the mind toward compassion and altruism. In a rather comical statement that reveals the absurdity of the idea and deviousness of the constitutional amendment proposal, the motion to amend reads like a scary line from an J.R.R. Tolkien novel: "the amendment seeks to amend the 1997 Constitution of The Gambia to provide for the application of the death penalty in circumstances other than where there is actual violence or administration of toxic substance resulting in death." What Yahya Jammeh wants in this ridiculous amendment motion is additional death-penalty-eligible crimes, which will open Gambia to Yahya Jammeh's characteristic brutality, with the sole purpose of planting more fear, foil citizens' verbalization of their grievances and prolong his hold on political power. One of the inherent dangers posed by this Death Penalty amendment is that it will give Yahya Jammeh, through his puppet judges, extraordinary latitude to adjudge who lives and dies. Without sounding cynical, the politicization of the judiciary will fulfill

Yahya Jammeh's objectives of establishing Sharia law in Gambia. For Yahya Jammeh, the expansion of the death-penalty-eligible crimes will serve three purposes: satisfy the human sacrifice blood needs for his oracles, eliminate real and imagined political opponents, and attract financial support from wealthy Sharia law–compliant Middle East nations. Several years ago, the heavy blowback from Yahya Jammeh's dabbling with the concept of introducing Sharia law was spontaneous and intense, leading to the demise of that idea. Besides, adding more crimes to the Death Penalty crime roster runs counter to the African Union's intent of completely abolishing the Death Penalty in member nations. As late as April 2015, in the Fifty-Sixth Ordinary Session, the African Commission on Human and Peoples Rights (ACHPR) put abolishing the Death Penalty at the heart of its debates, and adopted a draft treaty to help African Union member states move away from capital punishment. An official panel discussion on capital punishment in Africa took place at the ACHPR session in April 2015. For the AU, it's time to close this chapter of Africa's political barbarism, even as the Gambia seeks to broaden it.

In the 2010 death penalty constitutional amendment, what most stood out as a signpost of hope, became a poignant reminder of the cruel political underpinning surrounding the very concept of expanding the Death Penalty eligible crimes. Then Attorney General and Justice Minister, Edu Gomez, unwittingly admitted to the international community of the draconian nature of the amendment, which made drug possession and sale eligible for the Death Penalty. The contradiction between what is legal and what is draconian was a compelling enough reason to provide the grounds to again reverse the Death Penalty Clause. The issue is to challenge why Yahya Jammeh is bent on making state-sanctioned killings easier, not harder. With the mass Mile 2 Prison executions seared in Gambians' collective memory, the lingering question is whether Gambia's rubber stamp National Assembly will have the fortitude to withstand the bruising test to Yahya Jammeh's spiteful retribution. Certainly, there is no historical evidence to support the independence of the National Assembly; on the contrary, digressing from Yahya Jammeh's stated goals, in 2006, led to the expulsion of the entire retinue of AFPRC National Assembly representatives. Even without making it official, Gambians are living under the constant state of martial law, and the creeping lawlessness of amending the Death Penalty will further aggravate the dominance of the regime over the people. The bottom line is this: the National Assembly has completely surrendered to Yahya Jammeh's messianic pretensions and latched onto his every command as a divine order. The way in which the National Assembly has deferred to Yahya Jammeh's arrogance and alienated the Gambian population, violates their solemn contract with the electorate, and National Assembly members need reminding that the arm of justice is long. And as we go to press, Yahya Jammeh's deception has again come back to center stage as he supposedly pardons some Mile 2 prisoners. Lama Jallow, whose name was read on national television as pardoned died last week in that death trap called Mile 2 Central Prison. This brings the death toll at Mile 2 Central Prison to nearly five hundred, and still Yahya Jammeh wants more incarcerations in that hellhole, not fewer. I have no plea to make or advice to give the National Assembly. The Assembly has a choice between doing what is right for Gambia, and what is convenient for Yahya Jammeh. That's the bottom line.

THE CASE OF NORTH KOREA IN THE HEART OF WEST AFRICA

In more ways than one, the similarities are just as striking as they are notorious. Even the subtle differences are mind-blowing and bear diabolical resemblances. Behind its total isolation and unmatched secretiveness, this self-absorbed political juggernaut champions a visionless political maxim characterized by brutal lethargy to social and economic justice. It is a regime stigmatized by a legacy reminiscent of a long-gone era, a regime with a history mercilessly excoriated for its mindless cruelty. It is a nation guided by antediluvian axioms so traumatizing, they etched a permanent mark of guilt and shame on the global conscience. Importantly, it is a place where even time seems to stand still, and the people, beaten and battered by neglect and unbelievable abuse, seem to have lost the will to live. In this country, on the far eastern rim of the Asian continent, this epitome of a pariah nation north of the dreadful Korean DMZ, the darkness of primitive ignorance still lives on, the rivers of blood still flow senselessly on hallowed grounds, and a longing for life as human beings still haunts a terrified people silenced by the unforgiving power of state terror. In this country, even after many generations, the merciless projection of political tyranny is exercised beyond the forceful use of words.

Anyone ever had the urge to reach up a library shelf to grab a book, journal, or magazine exposé of North Korea? No? Then, ready, set, go. What you will find is the depressing reminder, not of the rebirth of the demons of Adolf Hitler but a frightening memorial to unrivalled cruelty that effortlessly vexes the unflappable voices of conscience and offends the sensibilities of human compassion. It exemplifies the nauseating capacities for reptilian cruelty imposed by a privileged few who sit in judgment of a barbarized nation, a vicious cabal that stands in the way of people's liberty and economic justice. If this Asian nation exists anywhere else on this planet, it has to be in Africa—West Africa, to be precise. North Korea and Gambia, two nations separated by wide expanses of paradoxically harsh, yet awe-strikingly beautiful; rugged mountains, mighty blue oceans, and vast expanses of rolling African savannah, in more ways than one share, haunting resemblances. And it's not North Korea's awesome sunrises, or the alluring beauty of Gambia's magical sunsets that obsess the deep sense of anguish of the collective human conscience. As the international community, saddled with guilt and utter shame, continues to look the other way, the barbarism of North Korea continues, the dysfunction of the government is undeniable, and its people, silenced by the unbelievable cruelty remain silent and faceless, living on the edge of Armageddon.

In North Korea, decades of tyranny and global indifference have forced the people to cede their inalienable rights to the state, with devastating consequences. The senseless subordination to state authority has effectively reduced its people to objects of sympathy and hopelessness. But this is also the story of the Gambia. The insensitivity with which Gambia is disorientated toward a culture of individualism, selfishness, and state barbarism is a clear departure from the country's long history of peaceful tribal coexistence. It is as if Yahya Jammeh has drawn lessons from Kim Il Sung's playbook or ripped a chapter right out of Nicollo Machiavelli's tragic political thesis, *The Prince*. Yahya Jammeh has proven every bit as cruel and narcissistic as North Korea's Kim Jong un would want, and Machiavelli would celebrate. However, Yahya Jammeh has added to the Kim Jong un script by his ignorant introduction of tribal bigotry and social Darwinism in Gambia society. But, Yahya Jammeh is fighting a losing battle for the survival of his doomed Jola hegemony, which was planned to extend from Casamance in Senegal, to the depth of Guinea-Bissau. In the same vein, the extraordinary capriciousness with which Yahya Jammeh executed twenty-six prisoners bears an uncanny resemblance to North Korea and generated a firestorm of visceral reactions from around the globe.

The past several years of political tyranny and butchery of Gambians have emboldened the proliferation of an inordinate number of diaspora human rights organizations, a phenomenon inspired by the new social media and sustained by a deep commitment to the rule of law and the return to democracy in Gambia. But, with diverse viewpoints in the diaspora, disagreements among organizations often materialize, but these are vastly outweighed by the profound need for change and a burning hatred for Yahya Jammeh and his regime. Since the cataclysmic and brutal Mile 2 Prison state sanctioned massacre elevated Yahya Jammeh's standing as an international pariah, the senselessness of his actions will come back to bite him. Yahya Jammeh is inconsolably aware of the nagging feeling that the curtains of his leadership may soon come down, that the bright lights will dim, the perpetual glitz and glamour of unchecked power may soon fade into distant memory, and a nation

held hostage for so long will again breathe free. Gambians growing
determination to end the barbarity and senseless killings has infused
a new dose of commitment to the Gambia's liberation struggle. And
as the countdown to Yahya Jammeh's inevitable demise ticks on, the
eventuality of his end days will bring out his worst reptilian character.
Yet the world watches and waits for his inevitable downfall. Africa needs
it. ECOWAS wants it. The Gambian people deserve it.

THE GAMBIA: AFRICA'S LAST REPRESSIVE REGIMES

Much of the news the *Point* and the *Daily Observer* newspapers churned
out told stories of economic mismanagement, but occasionally, some
glimmer of hope bursts out like rare desert flower, radiating like a
breath of fresh air. July 22, 1994, was no exception, but it was different
in so many ways. Later in the day, as a sign of relief replaced confusion
and consternation, many people were just happy the uncertainty was
over. When the dust settled, what seemed unlikely happened. The most
politically stable government in Africa was toppled. Former, Sir Dawda
K Jawara and some of his cabinet ministers, somewhere in the open sea
between Barra and Banjul, were refugees on a US frigate. An era had
ended. But the mood in the country was not one of universal approval, as
the merits and demerits of a coup became the center of focus everywhere.
That evening's news was reassuring for many fence-sitters across the
country. Not me. I had previously experienced military dictatorship up
close, and as recently as 1989. In General Franco's Spain, many African
nationals were routinely rounded up and thrown in prisons, because
the Guanches, the North African tribe who originally inhabited the
Canary Islands, were still actively resisting colonization and demanding
independence from Spain. And most recently in military strongman,
Sani Abacha's Nigeria and, of course, Benin's Mathieu Kereku, a place
where staring at the presidential palace could potentially land someone
in jail. Nonetheless, on that evening in 1994, the refrain of the news

broadcast was 'soldiers with a difference' and like skeptics, I bought into the military's image marking hype. A big mistake!

At first, little was known about the coup makers. But within a few months, the unstable peace was shattered by allegations of a countercoup in November, followed by the executions of several military officers. The cohesiveness of the coupists suffered its first casualties, with the arrests of Sana Sabally and Sadibou Hydara. The two were hastily tried and sent to prison. It has been a downhill slide ever since. When the infighting subsided and the struggle for political power ended, an intellectually challenged and little-known high school graduate emerged as the leader of the eclectic group of coupists. In the struggle for domination, Yahya Jammeh went through a baptism of fire, yet the real work had only begun. The political journey that lay ahead was fraught with unknowns, and the future was daunting. Abandoned by Western democracies, the AFPRC regime used religion as a tool of diplomacy, turning to Libya and the Islamic Middle East for much-needed moral and financial support. It was a match made in hell. Repressive Middle East nations, hardly paragons of virtue themselves, should have been the last from who the confused AFPRC military officers could get an education in good governance. It would not take long before Yahya Jammeh would prove this theory right. The gruesome assassination of Finance Minister Koro Ceesay became the clearest sign that the so-called political revolution in Gambia was derailed; the train left and was headed for the cliffs. As a shocked nation mourned Koro Ceesay's violent death and the new military regime nervously sized up the bewildered population, the gruesome murder put the country on edge. But this was only a harbinger of things to come. Yahya Jammeh had learned a lesson in political survival. His newfound dictator friends willingly tutored him on how to desensitize from the cruelty he inflicted. His worst animal instincts kicked in. Yahya Jammeh's desensitization was complete, and the delusional coup leader successfully transformed into a freak of nature. This once friend, brother, classmate, and neighbor had turned into a stranger that Gambians no longer knew, a monster they could no longer recognize.

As the metamorphosis of Yahya Jammeh was taking shape, the preface of the coup was becoming increasingly obscured by events that contradicted the spirit and the letter of Yahya Jawara's overthrow. The coup leader, Yahya Jammeh, put his sight on entrenching his rule, and his self-absorbed goal overrode the important task of bringing the failing economy back from the brink. Not that he knew how to do it, but at least someone expected him to try something—anything. He did not. Without realizing it, Yahya Jammeh had begun to write the first chapter of his legacy. For many Gambians, the AFPRC movie script provided a familiar sense of where our country was heading, and it was not a place of peace. Put in proper perspective, Gambia was turning into yet another post-colonial dictatorship. Yahya Jammeh had taken a page out of Muammar Gaddafi's playbook—or shall we say Robert Mugabe's unfinished script. The miseducation of Yahya Jammeh was taking a terrible toll on Gambians, as economic mismanagement was worsening, and the murders, tortures, arrest and detention, and disappearances of citizens, once unheard of in Gambia, were becoming fearful and routine. The pain that Gambians began to experience was too great, the agony pervasive, and the trauma too deep.

And it all seemed to have happened too soon, too fast and too furiously. Yahya Jammeh had his tentacles in every aspect of Gambian life by usurping power. The summary executions, students massacre, the torture centers around the country, the ubiquitous police stations cropping up around the country, the security roadblocks, Yahya Jammeh's posters displayed on telephone and electrical poles, business interests within every money making venture, and the appropriation of properties from their rightful owners, all became symptoms of political overreach. Yahya Jammeh declared war on business entrepreneurs and often ordered them arrested, and falsely accused of law breaking. This added to the daily hiring and firing, and the tribalism that had begun to take its toll on Gambians. It is in the fog of this confusion that Yahya

Jammeh, through terror, achieved the supreme power he had killed and maimed for. It seemed nothing could stop him. Yet, as his power grew, so did the hatred. Several attempts to topple his barbarous regime ended in failure. But Gambians were as determined to get rid of him, just as he was determined to stay in power. In the end, Yahya Jammeh will realize, rather belatedly, that the people are the sole repositories of political power, not him. For most citizens, there is no ambivalence about which direction they want the country to go. And it is with anyone else but Yahya Jammeh. The idealism and pragmatism that drove Yahya Jammeh and his clique to topple the Sir Dawda government became a sad story of epic failure. And Yahya Jammeh's last stand was to retreat from the promise to perdition, and in so doing, he became the curse of a nation. Our nation!

MASS INCARCERATION, SUMMARY EXECUTION, AND HUMAN SACRIFICE

The 'Smiling Coast of West Africa' is the first welcoming characterization on the headline news and on every tourist brochure—the intersection of happy, cheerful and sun-drenched sandy beaches that snake the mighty Atlantic Ocean coastline as far as the eye can see. This was Gambia then. The Gambia today is almost like a journey back in time to the mysterious Aztec civilization, and back again to the chilling, fearful silence on Pyongyang's empty boulevards. Despite the significant time lapse, there is subtle similarity between the Gambia and the Aztec's human sacrifice and North Korea's murderous political intimidation. In Gambia, human sacrifice ritual, murder, and summary execution, combine to link the country to the Aztec's dark past and North Korea's contemporary stories of mass executions and citizen incarcerations. Yet this week, as Gambia's twentieth attorney general in as many years, continues a long tradition of denial of human rights violations, before the United Nations Universal Periodic Review Working Group, in Geneva, still shrouded in mystery is that little-known dark side of Yahya

Jammeh's military rule. The ancient Aztec's human sacrifice rituals as hard as it is for westerners to believe is being practiced in the Gambia, and has been, since Yahya Jammeh's military regime ascension to power in 1994. Gambian journalists, for the most part, have deliberately been ambivalent about reporting the regime's child sacrifice for fear of looking ridiculous to Western partner organizations and governments or being victims themselves.

As the UN Universal Periodic Review and the UN special rapporteurs work to piece together Gambia's stories of extrajudicial summary executions, murders, mass incarceration, intimidation, fear, rape, forced disappearances, and the exodus of citizens to seek safe havens in foreign countries, over the past two decades, it is fitting to revisit Yahya Jammeh's bizarre child/human sacrifice practice. It may or may not come as a surprise to Gambia's Western partners that child and human sacrifice has been used in modern African societies to achieve success. Child and human sacrifice is used by highly educated Africans to amass financial wealth, secure coveted positions in governments and international institutions, win in elections, fend off evil spirits, and heal physical ailments. Needless to say that in Africa, superstition and shamanism is a billion-dollar business, but human sacrifice practices prescribed by African witch doctors are prevalent among African tribes with lethargic attachment to Christianity and Islam. Tyrant Yahya Jammeh comes from this primitive superstitious and idol worship traditions, with a belief system predicated on spilling animal or human blood as an offering to the spirits.

Yahya Jammeh uses child and human sacrifice to amass wealth and prevent toppling of his military regime. Of the many children killed by Yahya Jammeh's motorcades, he never once apologized to the parents of any of the dead children, and the parents are too scared to report these deaths to the authorities. It has also since come to light that many children are missing from populated centers in the Kombos and Foni regions. Western scepticism to the stories of child sacrifice may seem far-fetched to Westerners, which comes as no surprise given the incredulity of the act, but what this skepticism confirms is how little the West knows about the dark side of African cultural practices. In most African societies, both Christianity and Islam are heavily infused with traditional idol practices, as exemplified by the ubiquitous and pervasive jujus or magical amulets believed to ward off evil spirits. Among some African tribes, Islamic Friday prayers and Christian Sunday Mass services also means offering animal blood to idols, represented in objects such as rocks placed in dark corners of living rooms.

The child and human sacrifices aside, in 2009, Yahya Jammeh hired three Guinea Fula witch doctors to purge Gambia of witches. This led to three agonizing months of relentless witch-hunting around the country in which elder citizens were routinely forced to drink hallucinogen concoctions to expel witches. It resulted in more than a dozen deaths, the hospitalization of many, and sustaining permanent physical and mental injuries for most. And Importantly, Yahya Jammeh's Islamic religiosity is mere farce designed to hoodwink wealthy Middle Easters to reward him with financial assistance. Like the collapsed Taiwan dollar diplomacy, the Middle East has for many years provided support to Yahya Jammeh, in effect engaging in religious diplomacy for the purpose of introducing Sharia Law in secular Gambia. Another feature of Yahya Jammeh's military regime is summary executions, some of which have been heard around the world, while circumstances surrounding others still largely remain unknown. There were six major executions carried out by the regime since 1994, with the latest occurring in late 2012.

1. In November 1994, a dozen military officers, including Basiru Barrow, Dot Faal, and others, were summarily executed without trial for an alleged attempt to topple Yahya Jammeh's new military regime.

2. In April 2000, eighteen secondary and high school students were summarily gunned down execution style for the peaceful protest of the rape of a schoolgirl and the murder of a schoolboy at the hands of the police in the city of Brikama.

3. In 2005, forty-four Ghanaian migrants to Las Palmas, Spain, were apprehended in Gambian waters, forced to land, and executed.

4. In September 2012, nine Mile 2 Prison prisoners (some believe the number is three times higher) were executed before their legal options were exhausted.

5. In 2012, two elderly brothers opposed to Yahya Jammeh's tribal divisions were arrested and executed in cold blood in the outskirts of their village.

6. In 2010, former national security chief Daba Marenah and more than dozen others were executed for allegedly failing to disclose a plot to topple the military regime.

Every one of these extrajudicial executions was a tactical effort to instill fear and preempt Yahya Jammeh's removal from power. Curiously, none of the bodies of these victims' was ever received by family members to give them decent burials according to religious protocols.

The Gambia's child and human sacrifice, and the summary executions are triangulated by an equally bizarre forced disappearance of innocent citizens. The list of known Gambian forced disappearances, after their arrest by the National Intelligence Agency (NIA), is believed to be much higher than what is reported. Forced disappearances, in particular among Yahya Jammeh's own Jola tribe, in the Foni region, are rampant. The number of forced disappearances in the Fonis still remains a mystery, and this is in part because the media and opposition politicians are banned from that part of the country, which is fiercely loyal to Yahya Jammeh. This list of forced disappearances in Gambia since Yahya Jammeh took power includes a journalist, an international aid worker, local politicians, and community leaders. Each of the names listed has never been seen alive after eyewitnesses saw the notorious security service agents arrest them in broad daylight.

1. Ebrima (Chief) Manneh, arrested July 2006
2. Kanyiba Kanyi, arrested September 2006
3. Haruna Jammeh, arrested in 2005
4. Marcie Jammeh, arrested in 2005
5. Alfusainey Jammeh, arrested in 2005

6. Momodou Lamin Nyassi, arrested in 2005
7. Ndongo M'boob, arrested in 2006
8. Buba Sanyang, arrested in 2006
9. Alieu Lowe, arrested in March 2006
10. Sgt. Sam Kambai, arrested in 2006
11. Kebba Secka, arrested in 2007
12. Ebrima Dibba, arrested in May 2008
13. Ebrima Kunchi Jammeh, arrested in May 2008

And, between the forced disappearances, summary executions, and human sacrifices, close to three hundred Gambians have died, and others developed mental illnesses behind the walls of the notorious Mile 2 Central Prison walls, and other secret detention centers spread like spider web around the country. The deaths in prisons and detention centers occur as a result of malnutrition, sickness, torture, deplorable living conditions, and lack of treatment for health conditions.

It is ironic that the main thrust of the opposition to military regime in the Gambia is led by exiled citizens. In exile, the dissident movement gradually built a robust media and civil society infrastructure which spearheads the movement to remove Yahya Jammeh's military regime, and replace it with democracy and rule of law. The number of Gambians who fled the country in a massive exodus is staggering—from former vice president and finance minister B B Dabo, Dr. Sedat Jobe, Gambia's former external affairs minister, and ex UNESCO director, to the most recent, Dr. Gumbo Touray, former director of international affairs, University of the Gambia, and director of Lands. In between are thousands of Gambians of all tribal and professional stripes—journalists, diplomats, former senior government bureaucrats, academics, disgruntled former senior military officers, lawyers, and more—who fled the country. Gambian exiles founded fifteen known civil society organizations and twelve online newspapers and radios across the globe to head a sustained campaign to return the Gambia to its democratic foundation. Like the poisoning deaths of former regime collaborators back in the late 1990s and early 2000, there was a spate of recent abductions of Gambian dissidents from the streets of Dakar, Senegal, without Senegal's President Macky Sall government demanding their return. Dissident politician Mahawa Cham and businessman Saul Ndow, both kidnapped in Senegal, have never been heard from in years. In addition, two more Gambian-born naturalized US citizens, Alhaji Mamut Ceesay and Ebou Jobe, on holiday in Gambia, vanished in thin air. Their disappearance has since been linked to the regime.

Finally, it is understood but still to be verified that the regime is building a state-of-the-art prison complex in Basse, Upper River Division, in the eastern part of the country. With the prisons and detention centers around the country filled to capacity, the construction of another prison to continue mass incarceration was a foregone conclusion. Mass incarceration to silence citizens is the regime's way of dealing with its monumental economic failure. Like all dictatorships past and present, what is known by Gambian opponents of the military regime and the international community, in terms of the egregious of human rights violations, is only a tip of the iceberg. But as the UN human rights rapporteurs prepare to visit Gambia on a fact-finding mission about the decades of human rights violations, they should be mindful of the fear of citizens to freely volunteer information. But, luckily, also helpful to the human rights rapporteurs in their investigations are exiled former military and security officers who stand ready to provide useful information. With assistance from the international community, Gambians would welcome the end of impunity and the rapid restoration of democracy and the rule of law in a country once described as the smiling coast of West Africa.

CHAPTER 6

POLITICAL
DEFIANCE

WINNING THE SMALL BATTLES; LOSING THE WAR

It was not quite like the notorious Röhm-Putsch of 1934, yet Yahya Jammeh's malicious Faustian denunciations of his political opponents and self-righteous, hypocritical pontificating about the immorality of tribal politics, in a strange way, bear remarkable, if not an unsettling resemblance to the Night of the Long Knives. Like Adolf Hitler before him, Yahya Jammeh deviously orchestrated a stunning political takeover that could inaugurate a desperate era of one-party rule in the Gambia. This nauseating political development is an absolute obstruction of the emerging global political culture of our time. Reluctantly, Gambia, under Yahya Jammeh's military regime, has entered into an era of unrepentant Machiavellian politics, an era of rationalizing and moralizing corrupt bureaucratic systems whose dominance is unequal to its constitutional powers. Today, social activism around the globe has consolidated and ossified around the theme of social justice, a necessary counter-weight to the political impunity that for long dominated African politics. This has rendered obsolete the malevolent forces that gave rise and drive Yahya Jammeh's insidious political agenda. Ten days after the nightmare of the'

November execution of nine innocent Mile 2 prisoners, Yahya Jammeh's esoteric political victory rings hollow, and his standing in the world is irreparably damaged by his malicious disregard for human life.

How Gambia arrived at this point of debauchery and antagonistic political posturing is hardly a mystery. Yahya Jammeh's use of fear, intimidation, and terror as a tool of governance has totally undermined the will of the Gambian people to defend their own rights, effectively forcing them to surrender to the intimidation, which in the space of a decade has turned Gambia into a pariah nation. Gambia is sneered at by neighbors, loathed far and wide by people who value democracy and the rule of law, and grudgingly abandoned by some of its most illustrious sons and daughters. Consequently, the Gambia's descent into the depth of helplessness emotionally haunted and paralyzed by devastating politically motivated pogrom, precludes holding the recently ended presidential elections, which ECOWAS deems intolerable mockery of the democratic electoral process. ECOWAS's principled refusal to consecrate an electoral process that stands out as epitome of subversion of the will of the people was a heart-stopping departure from the norm, inspiring in its boldness and infectious in its courageous empathy with the maligned people of the Gambia.

Ten days after the fraudulent and polarizing presidential elections, a funeral-like atmosphere that pervaded the postelections, is turning into a burst of energy, propelled by the challenges of a new chapter in the perennial struggle for the soul of the country. And if the drumbeat for justice emanating from United Democratic Party's Ousainou Darboe, and the National Reconciliation Party's Hamat Bah offer a modicum of hope, it is that the prodigious subversion of the voices of Gambians will no longer go unchallenged. Yahya Jammeh's bullying and threats have served him well, but this is a new day, and Gambians at home and abroad are impelled by the rise of organic social justice movements to summon the moral courage to go out of character and for once, stand up to Yahya Jammeh's destructive overreach and sadistic perversion of the Constitution and laws of the Gambia. As the election results recently crystallized, Gambia has been held captive to the destructive force of a mindless tyrant whose delusional egomania and pugilistic disposition have not endeared him to those Gambians and non-Gambians who operate with the fullness of their mental faculties.

Nonetheless, a requiem for the Gambia is not a choice, for our country is worth rescuing from a man whose unflattering disregard for the values of human life and social order are legendary. For a country entangled in a political morass for nearly two decades, it would be an understatement to say that the crushing weight of tyranny has incapacitated Gambians and reduced them to mere shadows of their former selves. For now, elections of 2011 have renewed the determination to seek justice for our people, because the painful history of the past is mortifying in its cruelty and mind-numbing in its barbarity. Gambian people have long subordinated themselves to a regime that is proven to lack decency and reverence for human life. A look at the way Yahya Jammeh is maliciously dragging our judicial luminaries before his mercenary judges is revealing, to the extent he is avenging the Gambia Bar Association's challenge to his authority over magistrate the Moses Richards's case. The time to jettison our irrational fear of Yahya Jammeh is now, because if lawyers can be intimidated, then no one else is safe. As we begin to turn a chapter in the fight to save the country, the support and recognition the cause attracts will ensure that while Yahya Jammeh may win the small battles, the hatred generated for his military regime will ensure that, in the end, he will lose the bigger war.

OF PHANTOM HEROES AND DEGENERATE JOURNALISTS

In Gambia, nowadays, the Orwellian dystopia is no longer that anticipated vision of impending doom. It is already here, it's real, and it's surreal and mind-numbing, not just because Gambians let it fester, but also because a whole nation has allowed the dignity and pride of its citizens to be subservient to Yahya Jammeh's malicious and unforgiving narrowmindedness. Any level of qualifying the despondence in Gambia under Yahya Jammeh will be an understated. As another election season dawns on the country and the political echo chambers churn out false senses of outrage and fake fury, the political debate is being framed for complete failure, and no one is impressed. It is painfully obvious that the opposition People's Democratic Organization for Independence and Socialism party (PDOIS) has still not learned from simple mathematics that under Yahya Jammeh, its success or failure is inextricably tied to the success or failure of the United Democratic Party (UDP), and not the other way around. The past three election cycles saw the formation of alliances of political parties marketed as panacea for the opposition's past failures, which will write the last chapter of Yahya Jammeh's inglorious reign and the Armed Forces Provisional Ruling Council (AFPRC) postmortem. I beg to differ, even though I too have oscillated from a coalition advocate to an impersonal but scurrilous critic of UDP's leader Hon Ousainou Darboe's failure to recognize not only the existential threat UDP poses to Yahya Jammeh's reign, but also to his party's seeming inability to leverage the obvious threat UDP's power and prestige poses to Yahya Jammeh's rule, and UDP's incapability to turn political advantage into electoral success.

The absence of political coalition notwithstanding, the UDP has the potential to grow into a formidable political war machine that could overcome any barrier created by Yahya Jammeh's infinite state power. Even this close to elections, the UDP's ground game appears to lack the sense of urgency that Gambians attach to ending the political tyranny and economic nightmare that has turned Gambia into an Orwellian oasis in the middle of West Africa. Consequently, this make or break election season has yet to assume any broader significance to the general electorate, not necessarily out of political apathy, but, in my view, out of the opposition's faulty political theme and irrelevant messages. This reality was encapsulated in two recent editorials on the pages of both the *Point* and *Foroyaa* newspapers. Once again, impelled by dogma and fixated on scoring cheap political points, PDOIS set the Gambian blogosphere ablaze with its moral grandiosity and delusional political brinkmanship—all to no effect.

But what drives PDOIS's veneer of messianic sanctimony and sense of its mystical aura, also drives the inflated sense of its political stature, which clouds its sense of objective reasoning. By its divine-like pontifications, PDOIS seized the opportunity to gleefully frame the political debate entirely around painting UDP as godless straitjackets. But the reverse is the reality. My point is this; PDOIS's demagoguery and holier-than-thou approach to the formation of a coalition has a disingenuous textbook Darwinian quality to it. PDOIS must recognize that in spite of the make believe image the party projects of itself for public consumption, it is UDP that should drive the united opposition agenda, not PDOIS. PDOIS owes it highest loyalty to itself, and its storybook in the Gambia's political landscape has been a marketing strategy whose aim is to articulate the brilliance of an ideal, its dogmatic socialist ideal, with the hope of attaining political power by whatever means necessary, through its highly suspect and superficial political brinkmanship.

PDOIS's trite approach to the formation of a coalition is predicated on its nebulous, ad nauseum subliminal attacks on the United Democratic Party. But the UDP does not answer to PDOIS's agenda, nor is the party obliged to fulfill what the PDOIS leadership seems to characterize as precondition to coalition formation. For a coalition to come into fruition, PDOIS must subordinate its authority to UDP without attempting to dictate the political agenda. Only then will the party's hope for elevation to national and international prominence come close to being reality. And in the same vein, the *Point* newspaper's attempt to sanctify Yahya Jammeh's image and that of his AFPRC party, whether done deliberately or inadvertently, underscores the paper's lost glory, and its lack of purpose and direction. In its editorial, the paper admonished UDP opposition leader Ousainou Darboe to hone in on issues relating to agriculture, education, and health, but failed to make any reference to the corruption and gross human rights violations that include murder and extrajudicial killings, which are uppermost in the minds of Gambians.

The *Point* newspaper's effort to define the political talking points for the opposition is not only mischievous, but appears self-serving, and veers beyond self-censorship, to currying favor with the military regime. The *Point* newspaper's visionary founder, the late Deida Hydara, must be turning in his grave that the media house he built and in whose name he was mercilessly assassinated by agents of the Gambia's regime is a shadow of its former glory. Both PDOIS and the *Point* newspaper need to come back to message again. The unfettered national interest must be the dominating political principle that drives the debate, not any parochial precepts that have no loyalty, whatsoever, to the larger Gambian interest. And until PDOIS can come down from its Trojan horse, and *Point* newspaper can resuscitate its long lost pride, both will respectively remain phantom heroes, with degenerate journalists.

SELECTIVE AMNESIA OR INTELLECTUAL QUANDARY

His decision to challenge the status quo was a courageous act of political defiance, if not a daring assault on sixteen years of state impunity and uncaring nonchalance. But still, Dr. Amadou Scattred Janneh was under no illusion about the wall of resistance that loomed menacingly ahead of his aspirations for the Gambia. The paradigm shifts evolving from Tunisia, Egypt, and elsewhere in North Africa and the Middle East provided Gambians a blueprint, an impetus, and moral obligation to take control of the country from a military regime that continues to manifest its deadly contempt for its people. After a long hiatus from reality, Gambians can no longer continue the unsustainable paradox of luxuriating in political amnesia, as the country continues its degeneration into economic blight and social and cultural morass. While the sickening and hopeless sense of collective apathy and defeatism have permeated every aspect of Gambians' lives, and made it difficult to extricate the country from the overpowering political quandary that has devalued the self-esteem and bankrupted Gambians' sense of moral rectitude, much of the blame for the subjective views of politics in Gambia rests on our collective puerile naivety and callous indifference to what's happening in the country.

With the Gambia held captive in a vortex of social, economic, and political degeneration, the pathway to Gambia's political liberty rests on a determination that values its humanity and self-worth. Still, as the banality of paralyzing fear of Yahya Jammeh's absolute power continues to hamper the ability to rationalize the national interests, the degeneration into lawlessness and anarchy is increasingly exemplified by an emerging national psyche devoid of morality and empathy. The duty to ourselves, children, and future generations must remain the cornerstone that inspires and motivates citizens to stand and defend against the ruthless machination by a regime that is numbed to reason, and sanguinary in its exercise of authority. The predilection to take Yahya Jammeh's gross power abuses, lying down, has predictably worsened the chances of freeing Gambia from political bondage, which prompted Dr. Amadou Scattred Janneh to deliver lectures that radiated the need for freedom and liberty for the downtrodden. Increasingly, the friendly international community has focused attention on Yahya Jammeh's cruel dictatorship, and needless to say, sooner or later, his sadistic disregard for human life and morbid obsession with absolute power will be his undoing. Nothing in recent memory has perplexed Gambians and the international community as the arrest and detention of Dr. Amadou S Janneh and CCG members, whose brush with the regime showcases Yahya Jammeh's lethargy to free speech and his regime's free fall from grace.

Dr. Amadou Janneh's arrest and detention exposes the new dimension of the cruel underbelly of Gambian politics, but also the abominable contortion of facts by some online papers over the past three weeks, which is both disgustingly surreal and sickeningly mischievous. The ad hominem attacks on Dr. Amadou Janneh, for his service as Information Minister, under Yahya Jammeh, so pitifully devoid of reasoning, say more about the superficial sanctimony and provincial mentality of his nemesis, than of Dr. Janneh. The viciousness and ham-handed approach with which Dr. Janneh's arrest and detention were received by a scornfully misguided few will never stain the integrity of an honorable man who decided to stand tall, so Gambians may follow his example out of the dungeon of political servitude. If anything, the ignorant intransigence will backfire miserably on those whose motives and off the wall attacks are typically spawned by lack of objectivity. For a man who dared to do what most of us can only think, Dr. Amadou Janneh sits in prison, a victim of the dithering stupidity of a paranoid regime easily agitated into acts of vengeance against perceived threats to its existence. Any malicious efforts to aggregate the pain of Dr. Janneh's needless incarceration by a regime that has proven time and again it lacks legitimacy and credibility in the view of a plurality of Gambians, will fail, hands-down. And the parochial mentality exhibited by a handful of Gambians, in Dr. Janneh's arrest and detention, while the vast majority of Gambians and the international community rally behind the person who had the fortitude and guts to represent what every Gambian only dared think, is grossly underwhelming, to say the least.

Equally important, Yahya Jammeh's political subterfuge designed to mask the reality of his less than noble intentions has become an all too familiar fact of life in Gambia. As Dr. Janneh and his co-defendant's saga, the latest in the never-ending stream of arrests and detentions, shows Yahya Jammeh will stop at nothing in his attempts to silence voices that have political views contrary to his tribalist agenda. Dr. Amadou Janneh, by dint of his outspokenness about the restoration of democracy in a country wallowing in social, political, and economic misery, has become the latest victim of a regime that is maddeningly intolerant to the most innocuous political dissent. This is the daunting issue facing Gambians, an issue critical to freedom and liberty, and so challenging to Gambians' sensibilities as to wake citizens up from selective amnesia and intellectual quandary, which corrupts their sense of objective reasoning. Together, Gambians must collectively rally around a common interest, rather than allow themselves to be drawn into the dangerous depths of narrow, self-serving prejudices.

Like it or not, Dr. Amadou Scattred Janneh has become one of the symbols of resistance to the dictatorship in Gambia, not unlike Lui Xiaobo of China. The nonviolent struggle for fundamental human rights in the Gambia has the undivided attention of the regional and international communities, and Gambians must never rest until the murders, disappearances, tortures, intimidations, and mind-numbing plunder of Gambia's financial wealth and national resources ends, and Gambia once again joins the community of free, democratic nations. Gambians must commit to nothing less than a country that is free of tyranny, a country where the values of caring, sharing, and empathy, which we hold so dear, are again restored in their lives. That is what Dr. Amadou Scattred Janneh fought for, for our beloved country—nothing more and nothing less.

THE CHALLENGES OF A STRUGGLE AND THE PROMISE OF THE REBIRTH OF A NATION

This is not another heart-wrenching narrative about the barbarity that the AFPRC military regime foisted on the Gambia for the past twenty years. Far from it! It is a narrative about a struggle in much need of unanimity in action and a clear sense of direction. What brought Gambians around to this level of political discourse is a long, painful journey fraught with daunting pitfalls and seemingly intractable obstacles, often unanticipated and invisible, and sometimes deliberate and man-made. It is a learning process in which the cries of agony and the voices of acrimony constantly echo in the valley of despair. The severe psychological trauma arising from Gambia's shocking lack of political freedom is absolutely devastating, yet through all the pain and agony, a modicum of hope always remained tethered to the realization of the inevitability that this dark chapter of the Gambia's cheerless history and festering economic decrepitude will be reversed by unity in action for the liberation of the Gambia. Yet for now, in spite of the regularity with which the regime makes deadly policy decisions, the unravelling economy and the bigotry of willful tribal divisions, exacerbated by barriers to political freedom, the Gambian people have consistently failed the practical challenges of good citizenship, which motivates the creation of a unified dissident in opposition to the nightmare tearing Gambia apart at the seams. And for all the Gambian organizations engaged in the struggle for political liberty, similarities of objectives present a unique opportunity to interface action plans and work in tandem to eject a craven regime that is rapidly consumed by the trappings of imperial power.

As the arrogant arbitrariness that has created the pariah state continues to steer Gambia toward crushing economic calamity and hostile diplomatic isolation, the triviality and pettiness that also challenge the struggle, pales in comparison. The existential threat posed by the regime's asinine mind-set, pivotal in spawning the islands of independent voices and broad diversity of opinions, crystallizes the challenges that necessitate the coalescing of Gambian dissident movement for the push towards political liberty. If Gambians formed heterogeneous institutions of political struggle, they remain united by the vibrancy of the innate will to be free. The lingering differences in tactic and strategy, however profound, are not ossified around irreconcilable ideological obstinacy, but rather underscore the need and necessity for a common ground that maintains the broader national interest as the centerpiece of the political liberation's effort. The infrequent waves of trivial and inconsequential conflicts and rare lack of diaspora consensus often color the struggle, yet eruptions of unnecessary flares of friction are moments of opportunity for reflection and learning, notwithstanding the intensities of the divisive rancor that often obscures the dissident agenda in a cloud of animosity. The struggle to remove Yahya Jammeh, weighed down by self-interest and the lack of objective reasoning, is, nonetheless, supported by a broad swath of the Gambian population, for whom the sanguinary nature of the regime fundamentally disagrees with the true character of the Gambian people.

Despite the overwhelming indignities of tyranny, a majority of Gambians remain faithful to the values of our common humanity and selflessness. Clearly, instances of disagreements occasionally manifest in differences in strategy, yet this can serve the struggle positively if embraced as educational moments, rather than to further foment discord. Today, the Gambian liberation struggle is riding a wave of international support, but difficulties in centralizing messages and action plans often diverts attention from the challenges of the struggle, rather than its promise and opportunity. The spitefulness, which totally lacks relevance to the onerous task of restoring democracy and the rule of law in the Gambia, ought not dominate the political debate or subvert the struggle's intentions by irrelevant distractions. The baseless characterization of activists, in the media, apart from showcasing patently malicious intent, demonstrates a far less clear underpinning than the agenda for the removal of Yahya Jammeh from his celestial perch. Certainly, no one expects the intersection of the multiplicity of strategies to flow seamlessly without the perils of forceful disagreements, yet familiarity with similar situations, offer glimmers of hope that a struggle by Gambians of broad intellectual appeal and moral fortitude has a chance at success. The struggle to restore sanity in Gambia, once so full of determination and energy, cannot now be allowed to simply wither away for lack of passion and enthusiasm. Now more than ever, the stakes are high and Gambians must rise up to the challenge. The time is now.

BALANGBAA POPULAR UPRISING NECESSARY—EVEN INEVITABLE

The swanky private jet, with the distinctive Gambian flag festooned conspicuously on its sun-scourged sides stood idly in a secluded corner of the Ronald Reagan International Airport in Washington, DC. As its primary occupant, accompanied by a large entourage of bodyguards and other human accessories, made her way in a convoy of limousines to a plush and opulent hotel in a seedy part of suburban DC, the country she left behind three thousand miles away on the miserable continent of Africa was crumbling under the weight of her husband's repressive regime. And this was only one of Mrs. Zaineb Jammeh and her children's many shopping forays to the US. But this time it was different. Mrs. Zaineb Jammeh, for all intents and purposes, this time around came for the kill; to purchase a big-ticket item worth over a million dollars. And the magnificent house she bought was an investment she and husband, Yahya Jammeh, hope to hedge against his inevitable downfall.

Mrs. Zaineb Suma Jammeh, the quintessential Imelda Marcus, seemingly heartless, had done it again. But all this was last year. This year, far to the north of Gambia, where the golden sun scourges the rugged landscape across the northern edges of the African continent, and the tip of the Atlas Mountains soars high above the ominous clouds, the political geography of a continent was fast changing. The harsh and unforgiving twins, the Atlas Mountains and the Sahara Desert, at once serene and violent, are witnessing one of the greatest political upheavals of the past several decades. The Maghreb region of Northern Africa, with a history as old as human existence, is undergoing a bold political transformation that is making the spontaneous revolutionary groundswells and violent collapses of Eastern Europe's socialist regimes look like picnic. And as history repeats itself in the Arab world, the striking political and economic parallels between Eastern Europe then and the Maghreb and the Middle East now is glaringly and evident. But evident also are the similarities between the dictatorial regimes of North Africa and the Middle East, and Gambia, where Yahya Jammeh's absolute power is akin to the obsolete kingdoms and outdated feudal systems of long ago. The compendium of excesses that have defined Yahya Jammeh's regime over the past decade are unequaled both in depths of gravity and broad reach, to the Arab world tyrannies.

By far, Yahya Jammeh greatest and inarguably most serious criminality against Gambians is the litany of executions, murders, and forced disappearances of citizens and noncitizens alike. Anecdotal evidence shows that the frequency and regularity with which the murders, executions, and disappearances occur has reduced, but it does not make the crimes less grave. Between January and February of this year alone, two civilians deaths under police custody were reported, and a third, the high-profile murder of my nephew Sgt. Illo Jallow, the former chief bodyguard of Mrs. Zaineb Jammeh, left Gambians bewildered and demanding answers. But as usual, Yahya Jammeh has remained mute and appears unburdened by his criminal responsibility for the serious crimes against our people. To date, more than a hundred known deaths by execution and murder at the hands of agents of the regime have been recorded, and still sixteen more forced disappearances at the hands of the feared National Intelligence Agency remain unaccounted for since 2005.

The deaths and disappearances are serious moral and criminal aberrations. but they represent only a fraction of Yahya Jammeh's overall record of abusive behavior and denigration of Gambian society. As of now, Gambia's descent into chaos in governance and the disintegration of its social and political fabric have combined to put the country on edge as thousands of its citizens flee, and a million more who stay at home remain powerless; held captive to Yahya Jammeh's regime as they call for mass popular political uprising. The reasons, motivations, and the need for regime change in Gambia are many and varied, yet they all stand on a strong and credible foundation, based not on mere political hyperbole, but on objective facts and lived reality. Before the proliferation of the Gambia's overseas online media, the regime's executions, murders, and disappearances were blatant and frequent, but that has since changed as the vigilant diaspora online media, to a significant degree, forced the regime to alter its behavior in an impactful ways.

Notwithstanding these significant developments, crimes against our people has remained a constant feature that has instigated widespread hatred for Yahya Jammeh and his cabal of rapists, drug dealers, violent robbers, and extortionists. Evidence of citizen intimidation is bad enough and compared only to the endemic and institutionalized government corruption, which has risen to a crisis level. The social and economic degeneration that has developed over the past decade and a half has left a lasting and traumatizing, imprint on Gambians' minds. In his effort to build a defensive wall of intrigue and mysticism around him, Yahya Jammeh has, instead, succeeded in reducing himself to a buffoon as evidenced by the bizarre witch-hunting exercise around the country in 2009.

The statistics surrounding those random incidences of terrorism primarily directed at the elderly remains unknown, but a rough estimate puts the death toll to a dozen elderly men and women, excluding three dozen who were hospitalized for prolonged periods of time and whose health conditions are unknown at this point in time. But if these examples of tyranny and moral bankruptcy are not enough, the narrative about the country's welfare points to a gloomy scenario. Unemployment, especially among the youth is as high as 70 percent, and this is a growing trend, particularly due to the 30 percent decline in tourist arrivals, which began a decade ago and is not projected to get better anytime soon. But even that is only a part of the story of how Yahya Jammeh, with the willing collaboration of some elements of the military and security forces, has instilled paralyzing fear and hopelessness across the country, and this is evidenced by how some citizens and other selfish elements in the military and security forces support Yahya Jammeh's subjugation of the Gambian people and the denial of opportunities to select tribes that Yahya Jammeh categorizes as an enemy, and so marginalized.

One only has to look at the bureaucrats in senior positions in every agency, department and government ministry, starting with the military to every agency of government to determine that that level of bigotry is untenable and insupportable. In government agencies and institutions where the heads are not Yahya Jammeh's preferred tribe, a senior assistant or a junior employee in one of Yahya Jammeh's chosen tribes, are agents reporting directly to Yahya Jammeh, and mandated to exercise power and control over every government institution. But tribalism is only a part of the story of how Yahya Jammeh is running the affairs of the country into a ditch. In the business sector, Yahya Jammeh is involved in a variety of business endeavors—import and export, bakery, food distribution, construction, public transportation, entertainment, sand mining, agriculture, meat processing, supply and distribution of general goods, and port handling, among many other business enterprises.

Yahya Jammeh's involvement in business was illegal and undermined the entrepreneurial spirit in the country largely due to the disadvantage other business enterprises are put in. For one thing, Yahya Jammeh and his chosen few do not pay the customs and excise, labor, and import taxes, which other businesses are subject to; consequently, other businesses cannot compete in the marketplace with goods imported by Yahya Jammeh and his cabal of corrupt tax cheats, who undercut the market price of goods and commodities. In other areas, one of the most intriguing aspects of Yahya Jammeh's reign is the question of where he gets the billions of dalasi he uses to buy loyalty, bribe, and give away to people and groups who do not deserve to have it. Recently, Yahya Jammeh put aside more than two million dalasi as prizes for the Quran recital competition.

This is not only discriminatory in a multi-religious society; it was totally unbecoming of a government in a secular state to sponsor religious activities of any nature. The separation of religion and politics must be absolute and unambiguous. The government's primary responsibility is to the physical and mental well-being of its citizens, not their spiritual sanctity; consequently, funding religious activity of any nature falls behind the parameters of what is legally acceptable. But one of the most disturbing aspects of Yahya Jammeh's military rule is the quality of its public servants most of whose competence and qualifications are called into question. Yahya Jammeh's war on the educated class has significantly reduced the quality of government performance and rendered the civil service to a skeleton of its former self.

If anyone knows anything about management and administration, it is that there is a huge logistics cost involved in the frequent hiring and firing of civil servants, regardless of their positions in the bureaucratic hierarchy. To look at this in another way, the implications of hiring and firing means that no one stays in any particular job long enough to acquire competence and knowledge developed on the job. In other words, no one remains employed in a particular position long enough to develop professional expertise in their field of work. There is a calculable drain on the state's meager resources, which is more than just the financial component, but includes other indexes that measure national security as well as the quality of citizens. For now, suffice it to say that Gambia has a dysfunctional government bureaucracy, which will take a lot of work to rebuild into a fully functioning and efficient state apparatus. The challenges that lie ahead for Gambia, post–Yahya Jammeh are many and daunting but not insurmountable. Gambians have the capacity to successfully give citizens a government they deserve, after nearly half a century of unbridled corruption, nepotism, tribalism, and political patronage. The youth and future generations deserve nothing less, but as long as Yahya Jammeh remains in control of every aspect of Gambia lives, the country will continue its downward spiral and descent into political anarchy and bureaucratic dysfunction. The obligation to save Gambia from this eventuality means that a popular uprising à la Libya, Tunisia, and Egypt, is not only necessary, but perhaps even inevitable.

POLITICAL COALITION AND GAMBIANS' CRIME OF APATHY AND INDIFFERENCE

It was the nexus of patriotism and the recognition of the constitutional rights of Gambia's political parties, a seminal moment driven by sheer sense of urgency and necessity. The crippling fear and pitiful surrender to Yahya Jammeh's lawlessness, which has haunted the Gambia for so long, finally hit the ceiling as Gambians coalesce around the compelling need for political change. Last week's joint UDP, PPP, NRP and GMC communiqué, an unprecedented rejection of Yahya Jammeh's smudging of the character and integrity of Gambia's long-standing benefactors—Great Britain, United States, European Union, and the Commonwealth—was a remarkable departure from the norm. It was a breath of fresh air in a country where fear and mindless terror have long trumped the moral compulsion to question the state-sanctioned terrorism, murders, disappearances, kidnappings, incarcerations of countless innocent Gambians. In the less than flattering Commonwealth pullout debacle last month, Yahya Jammeh's vexing unilateralism took the Gambia by surprise, unsupported by the broad Gambian community, both at home and abroad. The sweeping rejection of Yahya Jammeh's revolting fulmination was swift and unequivocal. Yahya Jammeh's singular decision to vacate the Commonwealth of Nations is significant, pointing specifically to the fact that Gambia is ruled as an unmistakable criminal enterprise of lawlessness with murderers, terrorists, rapists, body part snatchers, drug dealers, and economic plunderers. As speechless as the Gambians were over the inexpedient Commonwealth pullout, opposition parties' decision and the implacable diaspora rejection of the notion of the Gambia outside the Commonwealth, were enough to reassure the Gambian people that as a nation, the country remains a partner of the Commonwealth, regardless of Yahya Jammeh. And more, Gambia's relations with Great Britain, the US, and the EU can never be changed by the stupor and thoughtlessness of one man; Yahya Jammeh.

But even more surprising than the Gambia's unilateral withdrawal from the Commonwealth, throughout this catastrophic saga, Gambia's pusillanimous rubber stamp National Assembly, the unmistakable embodiment of everything that went so wrong in the Gambia, offered no resistance to the incredible folly of unilateral Commonwealth withdrawal decision. In customary fashion, the cowardly National Assembly rolled over and capitulated to Yahya Jammeh's nescient singlehanded decision. Gambian oligarchy under Yahya Jammeh challenged by an unintimidated diaspora that is witness to the most gruesome state-sanctioned crimes, can no longer expect the luxury of an ominously silent population. The child sacrifices, neck breakings, female breast amputations, abductions, executions by firing squad, dumping corpses in infested wells, and severing of limbs—the cruel legacies of Yahya Jammeh combine to smear Gambia's character around the world. Yahya Jammeh and his AFPRC regime's monikers are so shocking as to veer from normal human behavior to defy the imagination. The depth and breadth of Yahya Jammeh's crimes against Gambians and non-Gambians is truly out of this world in sheer depravity. But with the curtains closing on, on West Africa's most ruthless regime, Yahya Jammeh compounded the demise of his regime with his blistering attack on the Mandinkas, in effect fermenting the ugly flames of tribalism. And nothing has encapsulated Gambians' rejection of the singling the Mandinkas out in ways that insult the intelligence of the Gambia's entire population. Gambians completely support the combined opposition in repudiating Yahya Jammeh's dangerous tribal bigotry against the Mandinkas.

But worth noting is that Yahya Jammeh's cheap attack of the Mandinka tribe was met with the stiff resistance of the combined forces of the Gambia's opposition establishment, UDP, PPP, NRP, and GMC. The condemnation the political parties issued in addressing Yahya Jammeh's infatuation with the Mandinka majority also marked the historic beginning of a new chapter in Gambia's political history. With support from the consequential Gambian diaspora, the political establishment must seek to regain its voice, preordained with constitutional rights to dissent loudly when Gambians are reduced to objects of indiscriminate human rights abuse, expressed in the wanton killings, dissent when Gambians are illegally fired from their jobs, dissent when the Gambian judiciary is occupied by mercenary judges who lack commitment to the Gambia, dissent when prisons become a pipeline for Gambians marginalized for possessing views that counter the regime, dissent when Gambians are forced to flee to the safety and security of foreign lands, and dissent when Yahya Jammeh's tribe, the Jola minority, is singled out for opportunity in a mult-itribe society. Yahya Jammeh's inordinate hold on power is accentuated by blind subservience, and the absence of dissent; the highest form of patriotism. With the Gambia run as a one-man enterprise, and with the countless state-sanctioned murders, executions, forced disappearances, and exodus from the Gambia, Yahya Jammeh could never have survived this long in many other countries. But Yahya Jammeh is his worst enemy, and history has discounted him as a lynchpin of how not to govern. Today, with opposition political unanimity assured, the crime of apathy and indifference may soon be history as Gambians across the board finally come to grips with the political reality.

RECONCILIATION, NO; INDEMNIFYING, HELL NO

It does not come without huge costs. It's an extremely traumatic experience that robs citizens of their moral grounding by consciously downgrading their humanity and elevating their materiality. It poses an existential threat to the fact of human existence. For a system that desensitizes citizens to devalue their own humanity, no extreme is far enough in debasing society. The catastrophic impact of the Gambia's tyranny is undeniable and characteristically showcases emotional scars far worse than physical traumas human beings can sustain; it's brutal and psychologically destructive. In a large number of homes throughout the moon-crater streets of metropolitan Sere-Kunda, innumerable wives have lost husbands, and their kids lost fathers to two decades of state-sanctioned murders, executions, and political mayhem. In the Kombo Saint Mary's area, far too many mothers and fathers lost daughters, husbands, sons, and wives; disappeared by Gambia's notorious National Intelligence Agency. Throughout the length and breadth of Senegambia, in deep dry wells and shallow graves, in unmarked tombs and animal-desecrated burial sites, in dense forests and the open sea, Gambian and non-Gambian families have lost sons, daughters, fathers, uncles, friends, and neighbors to the cold, cruel hands of a regime completely oblivious of the pain and agony of a nation. In Gambia's gulag prison system and secret detention centers, innocent citizens and noncitizens alike are warehoused to languish in dark, dingy cells, where so many died behind steel doors and tall concrete walls, far from public view.

The Gambia is a country whose history, over the last twenty years, is written in the blood of its citizens by a regime whose savagery continues to stun a civilized world. It is a history etched in stone—undeniable, unacceptable, and unforgivable.

What has occurred in Gambia since the military regime seized power in 1994 is a travesty of justice that defies imagination, and challenges the conscience of a nation—extrajudicial executions, murders, forced disappearances, and mass incarceration. The end result of twenty long years of pernicious human rights abuse is the unparalleled savagery, aggravated by the collective reticence of citizens to challenge the state's cruelty and moral bankruptcy. This state sanctioned terrorism and citizens' aversion to standing up to state ruthlessness has engendered a vicious tyranny that has robbed Gambians of their dignities. Even more striking still is the ability of an insignificant number of citizens to derogate the extreme savagery in Gambia as immaterial in a nation deeply scarred by abuse and neglect. The lack of political reconciliation in the Gambia exacerbates the suffering of citizens who lost loved ones to the diabolical depravity and ruthlessness of a regime, which long ago lost the moral authority to shape the course of the nation. In spite of the shocking disregard for human life as demonstrated by the regime, some Gambians are driven by self-interest to advance a dubious reconciliation agenda that does not support accountability or penalize the perpetrators of the Gambia's decades old crippling criminality. It is preposterous to think Gambia will just return to politics as usual, without adequately addressing the catastrophe and burdens of nearly two decades of brutal and bloody human rights abuses. The rabidity with which few Gambians have pursued a deeply flawed reconciliation effort completely negates altruism as the driving force behind the strategy, and validates the hypocritical superficiality of their efforts. On his own freewill, Yahya Jammeh initiated, organized, and funded a reconciliation attempt with the dissident diaspora movement and sponsored the willing few to travel to Gambia for what was labelled the diaspora summit.

In the end, it was a complete failure that has since receded into obscurity and irrelevance. But what is scarier than attempts to reconcile with Yahya Jammeh is what transpired in Gambia since that craven reconciliation effort in 2011. Before the ink of reconciliation effort dried up, Yahya Jammeh had fallen back an old, familiar habit of disregarding human life, resulting in the execution of nine Mile 2 Prison inmates, abduction and murder of Foni brothers, Wuyeh and Enor Colley, abduction of businessman Saul Ndow and politician Mahawa Cham, and the abduction and disappearance of two US citizens of Gambian descent. It comes as no surprise that nearly fifty more Gambians and non-Gambians have since been executed, fled the country, are languishing in Mile 2 Prison, or abducted in a forced disappearance from the face of the earth. In exhibiting an uncommon level of cruelty, Yahya Jammeh displayed his diabolical character, making it impossible to give weight to his words or rely on his goodwill. The strident anti-reconciliation blowback is less a reflection on Gambians' incapacity to agree than on Yahya Jammeh's untrustworthiness. Reconciliation, in any way it is looked at, only means throwing in the towel and capitulating to a killer who has shown an inability to rationalize. It is inconsiderate to the pain Gambians are feeling and surrenders to a character of international disrepute, Yahya Jammeh. Gambians are about delivering justice for all the dead, disappeared, and languishing in prisons, not stroking Yahya Jammeh's ego. If Yahya Jammeh resigns, unconditionally frees political prisoners and returns his looted wealth, Gambians may reconsider his reconciliation. This a decision only citizens can make, not a random purely political motivated interest. Until then, Gambians maintain no reconciliation and indemnifying a killer regime.

DIASPORANS REJECT YAHYA JAMMEH'S AMNESTY AS RIDICULOUS.......STOP

A big part of the miracle of change occurs through the forces of nature, sometimes with human influence but more often, not. It is dynamic, imperceptible, and mostly irreversible, with an innate capacity to draw the human instinct to respond to changing circumstances. In political terms, Gambia and Gambians have reached a level of alienation that nature can only balance out with a corresponding decline of the fortunes of the Gambian regime. This week, Gambians' emotions were on a roller coaster, with a few stragglers unsure of how to respond to Yahya Jammeh's chronic detachment from reality. But for a majority of the Gambian diaspora dissidents, Yahya Jammeh's amnesty offer is absurd and borderline insane to give consideration. International pressure and the convergence of politically disastrous events, at home and abroad, forced Yahya Jammeh's precipitous course reversal, which for many Gambians is rather too little, too late. Yahya Jammeh's pathetic amnesty to diaspora dissidents is a comical expression of insanity, unequivocally rejected by a defiant Gambian diaspora as absolutely laughable. The echoes of diaspora voices from around the globe are expressions of unmistakable calls for political change as the only acceptable compromise for reconciliation. The recent release of prisoners, political or otherwise, who did not deserve to be locked up in the first place, confirms Yahya Jammeh's insensitivity to locking up children, politicians, women, farmers, businessmen/women, students, and foreign tourists alike. Gambians have long been convinced that Yahya Jammeh is a bloodthirsty maniac and retarded carpetbagger, someone blinded by fantasies of grandeur. Yahya Jammeh's efforts to insult Gambians' intelligence with an amnesty offer, and prisoner release, is the manifestation of his own intellectual myopia. The dissident diaspora movement rejects Yahya Jammeh's amnesty as unnecessary distraction since they committed no crime. Their only crime is defending Gambia's traumatized citizens from Yahya Jammeh's criminal regime. Compound Gambians' legitimate grievances, Yahya Jammeh recently characterized the dysfunctional political system at home as a zero sum game, calling politics a 'dirty game' as the headline of one article screamed out loud. This is the closest Yahya Jammeh has ever come to first confessing, and then justifying the murders, executions, mass incarceration, tortures, and disappearances of Gambians and non-Gambians.

This week, as Chad's former military ruler, Hissein Habre, was forcibly lifted up and manhandled by personnel of the Senegalese paramilitary in a Dakar courtroom, what stood out was his helplessness and the angry, deafening jeers of relatives of his victims raw expressions of rage. Across the border, in the Gambia, Yahya Jammeh must be watching the unfolding trial of a brutal tyrant, Hussein Habra, as possibly exemplifying his own end days. But if Yahya Jammeh is not moved by the tragedy of Hussien Habre, perhaps the brutal end of his mentor, Col. Muammar Gaddafi, was a watershed moment in his life. The story of Col. Gaddafi, more than any contemporary tyrant, debunks the illusion of invincibility dictators use to foil dissent, instill fear, and conceal their own weaknesses. In the Dakar courtroom this week, the fear of the Chadian people was unmasked to reveal the depth of anger and pain that, until now, was obscured behind the nervous looks on the hallowed faces of the battered Chadian people. The parallels between Chad and Gambia are astonishing in so many ways, but particularly the lesson that no matter how long it takes, the long arm of justice has the capacity to stretch into the future, until justice is served. That Yahya Jammeh is an exact replica of Col Gaddafi in both temperament and political attitude goes without saying, and his dramatization of the trivial and downplaying his crimes against Gambians is signature Gaddafi.

Like Col. Gaddafi, his luck will run out, sooner or later, and the Gambian people will have the last laugh. If Yahya Jammeh thinks he can wipe out his long slate of serious criminal infractions against Gambians by being patronizing or because he thinks his word is law, he is in for a rude awakening. The fact is; most Gambians live by their own laws and could care less what Yahya Jammeh thinks his words weigh. For now, the concession Yahya jammeh made with the amnesty and prisoner releases do not come close to meeting the demands for Yahya Jammeh to not contest elections and to offer his resignation. Additionally, the Gambian dissident movement will never betray the memories of their dead and the missing comrades by consenting to Yahya Jammeh's reconciliation gimmick and act like the last two decades never happened. Inasmuch we all Gambian dissidents long to kiss the ground of our homeland and feel the sounds, smells, and sights of their homeland, Gambians are tasked with carrying the legacies of the victims and demand answers as to why they had to die. Gambians owe it to the victims to bring them home one last time so that they can receive honorable burials. For, they too were warriors in the battle against tyranny in the Gambia.

THOSE WHO LIVE BY THE GUN
WILL DIE BY THE GUN

It was an accident of history, one of those things that would make someone pinch themselves and ask how in the world it could ever happen. It came out of nowhere, but it was not an act of God; rather, it was the doing of five clueless and naïve young men who acquiesced to ignorance. The selection of Yahya Jammeh as head of the five coup makers in July 1994 will live in infamy in Gambian history. The notoriety of that moment is perhaps the only thing parallel to Pearl Harbor, yet the lessons that can be learned from it are plenty. As is characteristic in many countries around Africa, a man came into Gambians' lives who's being head of state in the Gambia was inconceivable, but for the actions of the coup makers who agreed to crown him leader by dint of his age. It is evident that without the coup, chances of Yahya Jammeh becoming a president of Gambia would be remote to impossible. Yet as fate and circumstance would have it, Yahya Jammeh did wake to find the future of an entire nation in his hands. It marked the beginning of Gambia's long political and social nightmare, a reminder of African where the consolidation of political power has resulted in massive social dislocations, political apathy, and a level of indifference that borders on condoning and abetting the abuse of power.

Today, the fabric of social life in Gambia is corrosive and the degenerating political conditions are only exacerbating the suffering and the discontent in a once peaceful country. Slowly, but surely, Yahya

Jammeh is learning how a one-man government functions, and is exploiting the fear induced indifference of Gambians. The accidental president has come a long way from the early days of the regime's self-doubt, and anxiousness steeped in insecurity. On the surface Yahya Jammeh seems to be taking things in stride, but his mind is telling him something altogether different. Every person around the world who has ruled the way Yahya Jammeh is doing, has met a violent and merciless end. In the final analysis, when push comes to shove, the mercenaries Yahya Jammeh has hired from Iran, Cuba, Casamance, and elsewhere will not save him from the retribution of the long-suffering Gambian people. And while we are at it, we hope that Sana B. Sabally, Edward Singhateh, and the other living members of the coup maker's wake up each morning to pinch themselves and ask why and how they unleashed a monster in our midst. Now that the genie is out of the bottle, the nagging question for Gambians is how they can put the genie back in the bottle. Gambia needs rescuing from the hands of clueless idiots who see no value in human life with the propensity to use violence as a weapon of achieving political and social compliance. My advice to Yahya Jammeh is to be afraid. Remember the proverb "what goes around comes around." As the Gospel of St. Matthew rightly admonished, "those who live by the sword will die by the sword." That is plain, simple common sense.

YAHYA JAMMEH AND THE STATE OF THE NATION

To many Gambians at home, it looked like another propaganda coup, one similar to many others over the last year alone: the releases of Dr. Amadou S Janneh, Tamsir Jassey, lawyer Moses Richard, lawyer Lamin Mboge, hiring Nana Grey-Johnson, and now the recycling of Fatou Camara, who was recently unceremoniously fired again. In some of these instances, the one constant was the dubious, demeaning, and insulting praises about Yahya Jammeh's benevolence these victims were coerced into uttering on live national television. More telling still, for those who became victims of Gambia's unprecedented incarceration and abduction crisis, the opportunity to reecho Yahya Jammeh's benevolence in public was a concession worth the price of their freedoms. On Friday last week, the newly released from five months of illegal abduction and incarceration, Kanifing Imam Baba Leigh, surrounded by Banjul Imam Cherno Kah and State House Imam Abdoulie Fatty, fell into this familiar trap of being part of repeating the history of praising Yahya Jammeh for abducting and holding him prisoner. Imam Baba Leigh's repentance on national television was clearly forced. Still more baffling than the release of Imam Baba Leigh are revelations by US-based *American Street News* online paper of Alieu Mboge's involvement in Imam Baba Leigh's abduction and illegal incarceration.

But Yahya Jammeh's propaganda coup in releasing Imam Leigh seemed so rare that it almost seemed miraculous when it occurred. The story behind Yahya Jammeh's infrequent bursts of reconciliatory magnanimity has a tint of political undercurrents with international dimensions that threaten the regime's existence. The British and US governments were unequivocal in their unwavering positions on Kanifing Imam Baba Leigh, calling for his unconditional release. The addition of their powerful voices to the deadly human rights violations in Gambia, which the European Union and Amnesty International relentlessly criticized, succeeded to push the regime to the edge. Their combined political pressure forced the military regime into releasing Imam Baba Leigh. Beyond that, Baba Leigh's incarceration five months ago, illustrates the preponderance of the contempt for Yahya Jammeh's vexing, and deadly human rights violations. The international community and the Gambian people care more about the politics and policies that have had severe consequences in the Gambia since the ascension of the AFPRC military regime to power in 1994.

Clearly, for more than a decade and a half now, sweeping criminalization of even the most innocuous activities and utterances have transformed Gambian society into a massive gulag, unforgiving and as deadly as the starvation camps of North Korea. In Gambia, consequences of free expression, which our neighbors, the Senegalese, take for granted, are often characteristically merciless and deadly. But even as Yahya Jammeh is applauded by a sliver of Gambians both at home and abroad, for releasing Imam Leigh from prison, one fact still remains—he so often tries unsuccessfully to distract Gambians from what really matters, in his efforts to focus them on trivia and the politically inconsequential. More significantly, Yahya Jammeh is married to a superfluous logical fallacy. The exploitation of journalists, recently appointed Information Minister, Nana Grey-Johnson, and Fatou Camara, to help cushion him from the perils of the wrath of the national and international community, clearly manifests his miscalculations of Gambians who are not swayed by his unethical political paternalism. Nana Grey-Johnson and Fatou Camara will have absolutely no effect, whatsoever, on the online media's resistance, and for Yahya Jammeh to think differently, is the height of folly and absurdity.

Let me put it this way. The ability for Nana Grey-Johnson and Fatou Camara to bend the will of the diaspora online media is predicated on their divine powers to resurrect journalist Deida Hydara, bring Chief Ebrima Manneh safely back to his grieving family, and resurrect Omar Barrow and hundreds of murdered Gambians and non-Gambians back to life. This is Yahya Jammeh's saving grace—not Nana, not Fatou, or anyone else. A scrutiny of the position Yahya Jammeh espouses and his intermittent parodies and ridiculing of the Gambian online media insults their selfless sacrifice and patriotic dedication to the Gambian liberation cause. Yahya Jammeh's hatred of Gambia's diaspora media demonstrates how he lost the moral high ground in standing up as a model of politician. At home and abroad, the new Gambian mind is colored by a national crisis of monumental propositions, with international implications. Gambia's diaspora media whose power and influence holds sway at home and abroad, and endangers the existence of the Yahya Jammeh regime, will never succumb to Nana Grey Johnson's persuasion or Fatou Camara's magnetism. Gambians will never be sidetracked to lose focus of the issues of material significance to our people.

Today, through every lens one looks at it, Yahya Jammeh will go down in history as the worst thing to ever happen to the Gambia. And, woven in the fabric of his mind is the belief that he can inject spurious ideas into the collective mind of Gambians to detract their attention from his bedrock Machiavellian idealism. Years of deaths, forced disappearance, and exiling of Gambians has, as in troubled North Africa, created a moment of rupture that led to a new outbursts of imagination. There is universal realization that our country has to change, and no event in recent history epitomizes that more than this week's Raleigh, North Carolina, where the convergence of Gambians with determination to restore democracy and the rule of law in their country, will forge a common ground in achieving this goal. There may be numbing repetitiveness of Yahya Jammeh's public executions, disappearances, murders, and the prevalent climate of fear, but in the end, what Raleigh will represent is a gathering of Gambians determined to bring political sanity back to Gambia. There will be the juxtaposing of politics and camaraderie, and humbling and sobering realization that many in the Raleigh crowd are barred from returning to the country of their birth. But even as the Raleigh conference is partly colored in mundane Gambian politics, of overarching concern to the Raleigh Conference is the deadly seriousness the Gambian regime represents. Murders, incarcerations, forced disappearances, exiling of citizens, and continuous harassment of Gambians has gone on for too long. The state of our nation is tedious. That is unacceptable. It needs to change.

THE PRIMITIVENESS OF YAHYA JAMMEH'S IDIOSYNCRASIES

In George Orwell's *Animal Farm*, the two main characters, Napoleon and Squealer, ostracized Napoleon's partner Snowball, and drove him from the farm by making false allegations of impropriety and economic sabotage against him. The duo then proceeded to consolidate power and enrich themselves; looting and imposing an unbearable tyranny over the rest of the animal kingdom. *Animal Farm*'s storied narrative is a timeless melodrama that symbolizes human greed and humankind's capacity for evil deeds. This tragic Orwellian characterization of his times may be a work of fiction that could have easily have been written by William Shakespeare six centuries earlier, or crafted into a tragic theatre play by Sophocles twenty-three centuries ago, but the substance of the story is predictably relevant in our times. If the harrowing rancor that bedeviled relations between Napoleon and Squealer, and the governed kingdom animals spells the genius of Orwell, perhaps it is worth adding the gift of clairvoyance to Orwell's deserved collection of accomplishments and accolades.

Animal Farm captures the moral bankruptcy that is so characteristic of the Machiavellian school of thought, the acquisition and retention of absolute power, wealth, and privilege at any cost, which is symptomatic of every dictatorship in history. One would think *Animal Farm* was written with today's rulers in mind, for its narrative suddenly comes alive again in the stories of tyranny and dictatorship prevalent on the African continent. Close to home, Gambia's own *Animal Farm* story showcases a compelling narrative of the boundless lunacy, greed, and cruelty. Each day that passes, the *Animal Farm*'s main evil character, Napoleon, looks like many Napoleons from different eras in human history, now alive and well in the Gambia. The horror stories, known and unknown, of Gambia's recent past history under Jammeh's burdensome and unbearable tyranny, bear that out. Like dictators past, Yahya Jammeh embraced Niccolò Machiavelli's theories of leadership, lock, stock, and barrel, without moral reservation.

Yahya Jammeh continues to adapt to the times, not for the better, but for the worst, never deviating from the core Machiavellian doctrine, which has defined his sixteen-year reign of terror. The executions and murders of innocent citizens and noncitizens alike may account for the greatest stains on the regime's unflattering resume, but other bizarre behaviors that courted public attention, and deservedly so, point to a level of desperation that has compelled Yahya Jammeh to outdo himself in the severity of the agents and mechanisms of terror that he employs to secure compliance from a servile people. In a society so malleable to psychological manipulation, Yahya Jammeh's mystification of himself and declaration of having supernatural powers that enable him to perform cures of terminal diseases, left the scientific world and prestigious medical research institutions gasping with dizzying incredulity. Effects of herbal cures and devil worship on the Gambia's vulnerable and superstitious is yet unknown, but that has not stopped Yahya Jammeh giving false hopes to the poor and desperately sick.

But if this alone is not strange enough, the witch-hunting exercise around the country in 2009 makes the Salem, Massachusetts witch hunt in 1692 look like child's play. The desperation of the victims of the witch-hunting, the old and weak, created such a sense of despondency around the country that some people were willing to do anything to save the country of the monstrous and demonic behavior, even if meant losing their own lives in the process. Yahya Jammeh habituated to creating social disruptions with far-reaching psychological impacts, often severely traumatic to his victims, graduated to a new dimension of craziness that is leaving families worried that loved ones may fall victims of the overbearing behavior of the witch-hunting chaos. And three weeks ago, Yahya Jammeh's arrested family members of politician Mai Fatty, and last week, a former young Gambian military officer exiled in Senegal, Musa Drammeh, bore the brunt of Yahya Jammeh's cruel vengeance when his family was arrested and detained without cause.

This is a new departure from the norm for Yahya Jammeh, and it is bound to cause consternation among Gambians vulnerable to Yahya Jammeh's intimidation. Gambians must raise their voices and refuse to be silenced, and if the cases of Musa Drammeh and Mai Fatty's families are anything to go by, we might be in for a long night. One thing is certain. Yahya Jammeh's maltreatment of the innocent is the cruel epitome of the primitiveness of his psychopathological idiosyncrasies. This demented new chapter thrust before Gambians' discriminating consciences is greatly concerning. The famous and timeless German pastor and poet's quote is as follows: "At first they came for the Jews and I did not speak out because I was not a Jew. Then they came for the Communists and I did not speak out because I was not a Communist. Then they came for the trade unionists and I did not speak out because I was not a trade unionist. Then they came for me and there was no one left to speak out for me" (Pastor Martin Niemöller, 1946).

YAHYA JAMMEH'S SICKENING UNILATERALISM AND SINKING OF THE ECONOMY

The performance of the Gambian economy has been lackluster at best in spite of the glowing and often misleading reports by the World Bank and IMF. The World Bank and IMF often prepare glowing reports on the performance of the Gambian economy, but contradictory views are apparent looking at so many incontestable indicators, not the least of which is increased poverty, capital flight, lack of skilled manpower, a declining agricultural sector, which have all resulted in a marked drop of the GDP, and others. The defective appraisal methodologies the World Bank and IMF utilize to measure the performance of the Gambian economy are prone to conclusions that have absolutely no bearing on reality, primarily because the data provided by the regime is based on fudged and manufactured numbers and false and deceptive accounting practices and procedures. Most of the reports the World Bank and IMF prepare on the Gambia's economy are disproportionately rosy, and clearly, contradictions to their reports are manifest in the lack of improvements in the quality of life of most Gambians. Moreover, marginal gains registered have primarily benefited an insignificant percentage of the population, most of who either have direct access to foreign aid funds, by virtue of their positions in the regime, or can easily access government-administered funds through the pervasive crony culture. In spite of the World Bank and IMF reports, the Gambia has accrued a massive international debt of over $1.6 billion with a debt service of 25 percent of the GDP, which is stifling economic development.

The Gambian economy is burdened with illegal practices in the financial and banking sectors, exacerbated by ubiquitous corruption, chronic lack of accountability, money laundering, and recurrent budget deficits. But another key failure of the Gambian economy is its dependence on foreign aid, rather than investment, as the engine for economic growth.

In addition, the existing multitude of financial institutions are not set up to provide investment capital, either because of lack of liquidity or the institutions are designed to suit small savings and micro lending, hardly enough to spur economic growth. The necessity to overhaul Gambia's banking and financial institutions is overwhelming for several reasons, but mainly to exclude banking institutions that lack capital to lend for investment and economic expansion. Second, to protect Gambian consumers from losses that could be incurred in the likelihood of bank failures. Banks and fictitious financial institutions set up primarily to launder illegal drug money, counterfeit currency, other illegally monies, or for the purpose of generating quick profits at the expense of Gambians, must be excluded from participation in the nation's economic activity, due to the likelihood of failure they pose. The mere presence of such illegal financial activities is devastating to the economy and Gambians who entrust these banks with their life savings. However, one of the most contentious issues facing Gambia is Yahya Jammeh's multiple business interests, which across Gambia's economy—including meat processing, transportation, communications, construction, food distribution, agriculture, import export, manufacturing, food processing, and property development. Businesses under the Kanilai Group International, KGI, entirely owned by Yahya Jammeh, not only stifle competition, but also monopolize state resources and the state apparatus to expand business ventures of his company and created unfair disadvantages for competitors. This dampens business morale, discourages investment, discourages entrepreneurship, and creates monopoly that adversely affects the entire business sector, to the detriment of the overall national economy growth.

Despite the positive spin the World Bank and IMF reports have put on the performance of the Gambian economy over the years, the GDP has contracted significantly every year since 1975. The annual working capital, or the budget, if you will, is still heavily dependent on foreign aid, principally from Britain and the US. The Gambia's GDP is insufficient to generate adequate revenue from taxation and revenue from exports to finance public projects, make civil service payroll, invest in education, build roads and infrastructure, provide adequate health-care and security for the Gambian people. To date, Gambia's debt forgiveness, or debt relief, amounts to billions of dollars, and the regime is in part reliant on an existing debt-forgiveness regime to stave off bankruptcy. Gambia's productivity decline can be measured by a drop from $378 per capita GDP in 1985 to $353 in 2000. And agricultural production, which previously accounted for 75 percent of the Gambia's GDP two decades ago, now accounts for a paltry 22 percent, and employs 74 percent of the Gambia's labor force. The service industry, communications, energy, tourism, and hospitality now account for 64 percent of the GDP yet employ a mere 15 percent of the labor force and produces two-thirds of the GDP. This anomaly can best be explained in simpler terms as resulting in 60 percent unemployed and underemployment of Gambia's young productive labor force. And significantly, Gambia's export earnings have dropped from $.044 billion in 1975 to $.019 billion in 2000, a massive deficit of $.025 billion. In short, the Gambia now produces far less for export, both for the international and regional markets. Additionally, the rural population, self-sufficient in food production two decades ago, is for the first time completely reliant on imported food for their daily sustenance.

Over the past two decades, an increasing number of farmers have abandoned farming life and the rural countryside to migrate to the metropolitan centers in the Kombo region, in a massive rural urban drift that completely changed the character of the Gambian economy forever. Clearly, there is no longer an incentive to farm, due primarily to the lack of market outlets. And farmers across the country are owed money for products relinquished to private merchants and traders acting on behalf of the state, but they have been unable to recover their hard-earned money, some for several years. The result is a new cross-border trade war, at a great loss to the Gambia's economy. Justification of the natural pull toward new market sources is found in a theory of market economy, "capital, inherently growth generating, yet constantly limited by the market in which it has grown, has historically attempted by all means—including conquest, banditry and piracy—to push the frontiers of its market." This analogy explains the phenomenon of Gambian farmers abandoning the inadequate market outlets in Gambia for alternative markets sources across the border in Senegal. Yahya Jammeh's regime will be hard-pressed to show where the $1.6 billion or 48 billion dalasi of external debt was spent in Gambia. With schools in a terrible state of repair and lacking teachers, the healthcare sector understaffed and lacking supplies, roads in metropolitan centers and around the country in very poor state of repair, the economic deterioration is evident for all to see. What Yahya Jammeh is heading is in Gambia is not a government, but a cartel of drug dealers and shady financial bandits. The Gambia's future with Yahya Jammeh at its head looks bleak, but Gambians cannot lose hope. Somehow the Gambia will persevere and emerge from this political inertia as a better country. But as long as Yahya Jammeh continues his arbitrary and unilateral dictation of our fiscal and monetary policies, the Gambian economy will continue its downward slide to an inevitable meltdown and complete collapse.

CHAPTER 7

POLITICIZING RELIGION

ISLAMIC STATE OR YAHYA JAMMEH'S DESCENT INTO MADNESS

There were no rumors, no discussions, and not even official clues as to what was about to happen to the Gambia. Last week, when Yahya Jammeh said, at a Brufut meeting in a coastal town sixteen miles south of the capital city, Banjul, that "Gambia will become an Islamic state," his ambiguity was obvious, but reactions to him were swift and scathing. Listening to Yahya Jammeh speak, the sense is that his statement was more an aspiration than an actual declaration of Gambia as an Islamic state, but it did not prevent the media onslaught from sensationalizing and internationalizing his statement, adding to its confusion and ambiguity. Literally, Yahya Jammeh's Brufut statement, "Gambia will become an Islamic state" is not an unequivocal declaration. This misinterpretation is circulating around the globe as fact, causing a blotch on Gambia's once pristine character, and further disdain for Yahya Jammeh from the Gambia's highly educated Christian community and Gambia's animist majority in the country. In complete disagreement with Yahya Jammeh, Muslims are not the majority in the Gambia, and to make that allegation is to ignore the prevalence of our ancestral belief systems and practice of each tribe, by both Muslims and Christians. Even the concept of monotheism, the bedrock of Christianity and Islam, is undercut and disparaged by the practice of ancient Gambian society practices. What seems so apparent in this proposed Islam state declaration is Yahya Jammeh's perceived ability to circumvent the National Assembly and the Constitution, which says more about the redundancy of the state institutions relegated to a mere tool of Yahya Jammeh.

But for now, even if Yahya Jammeh had meant to turn the Gambia into an Islamic state, he only projected an unforgivable cluelessness about the complexity this effort would require. The cost of turning the Gambia into an Islamic state is enormous and complicated. Even recognizing the absolute power Yahya Jammeh wields, it takes more than just a declaration at an obscure town square to make the Gambia complaint with the dogma and values of an Islamic state. And now that the media misinformation has gone viral, Yahya Jammeh is stuck between a rock and a hard place, in a dilemma, unable to walk back or deny the state Islamization story. Be that as it may, nothing materially is going to change in the Gambia. Turning Gambia into an Islamic state requires significant structural changes; the governing instruments, the legal system, education, and other institutions, as well as making far-reaching cultural changes. Crucially, the task of turning a secular state into an Islamic state will make the Gambia a theocracy, an oxymoron when juxtaposed on Gambia's republican Constitution and jurisprudence. Importantly, an Islamic state requires governing by Islamic Sharia Law without which there is no Islamic state, but even that is only a part of the burdens of declaring the country an Islamic state. Gambians' way of life, regardless of tribe, is incompatible with Islamic state, and there is no indication Gambians want to be like North Sudan or Somalia, where the predominance of Islam means the loss of the African identity, assimilation, and the adoption of Islam's governing legal system. But prioritizing religion as opposed to economic development speaks to Yahya Jammeh's miscalculation or, better still, deliberate attempt to evoke religion as a way to divert attention to the most essential needs and deter public expressions of disenchantment with his regime. It insults Gambians' intelligence and questions Yahya Jammeh's capacity to govern effectively.

To further belabor the issue of Gambia Islamization, it is hoped that, at the minimum, Yahya Jammeh understands that the Gambia's governing instrument, the Constitution, must change before the country can have a legally binding Islamic state, and changing the Constitution requires a referendum vote by two thirds of the Gambian people. But even changing the Constitution with a referendum is also only a part of the hurdle Yahya Jammeh must overcome to make his reality true to Gambians. Changing Gambia to an Islamic state cannot be done by proclamation. The existing Constitution undermines that effort, unless Gambians are to pretend it no longer matters, and Yahya Jammeh is, in fact, the state to quote King Louis XIV of France; "L'État, c'est moi." This also requires a national referendum, approved by the majority of Gambians and ratified by the National Assembly, before it becomes legally binding. In as much as Yahya Jammeh wields more power than Gambian law allows, the Constitution cripples his ability to make life-changing proclamations that alter the nature of the state as instrument of social and political organization. It is an enormous undertaking to change the Gambia into an Islamic state, and the blowback, from secular Gambian Muslims, was fierce, relentless, and unwavering in its support of the nature of Gambia's secular state. The secular state is a default security protocol and altering this balance will relegate non-Muslims to second-class citizenships, in contravention of the Constitution. Whether Yahya Jammeh meant to proclaim Gambia an Islamic state or not, it is clear the damage is already done. And this only proves how reckless Yahya Jammeh was, both in his words and actions. The Islamic state of Gambia, 'not in our name,' is the trending Gambia refrain heard around the globe. "Not in our name."

INVITING RADICAL STRAIN OF ISLAM,
THE RISE OF THE ANTI-THEOCRACY

Pushing citizens against the wall has historical precedence that has often tested the limits of their tolerance and sparked mass resistance and rebellions. The backlashes frequently incite fearless expressions of discontent that spiral out of control into political skirmishes that lead to oppressed peoples' liberation from state tyranny. These spontaneous outbursts of grassroots activism have spawned unrest and metastasized into political movements for freedom that grow beyond the ability of the state to control or manipulate. If this scenario seems familiar, it is because the Gambia is living this reality at this material time. Many things are happening simultaneously in Gambia, all revolving around a political system that for two decades showed disdain and rejection of its citizens, both on political and moral grounds. The Gambia has evolved a political system that mirrors Yahya Jammeh's contempt for political and governance conventions; willfully circumventing the instruments of effective governance, as enshrined in the Gambian Constitution. This intractable mockery of the systems of tantamounts to ridiculing the sacred document of the Constitution, cast Gambia as a nation of lawlessness, and shock citizens by the illegal regularity with which Yahya Jammeh single-handedly passed laws that seek to further entrench his odious military regime in power. The practice of frequently amending the Gambian Constitution by fiat, in complete disregard for the authority of the Gambia's National Assembly, also seeks to suppress citizen's countervailing attitudes toward the laws and expose the state's imperativeness to required mandate for a nationwide referendum for the purpose of amending any part of the Constitution. A case in point is Yahya Jammeh's recent declaration of Islamic state in Gambia, a move that is already manifesting simmering resentment from the powerful Christian community. The rejection of attempts to divide the Gambian people based on Yahya Jammeh's fake religiosity illustrates his deceptive mind-set and has nothing, whatsoever, to do with the divine context of faith and religious beliefs.

To be clear, consequences of illegally declaring Gambia an Islamic state are far-reaching and threaten the existence of Christian belief systems in multi-religion secular Gambian society. Christianity has for several centuries been the vanguard of intellectual and economic development in Gambia, and any attempt to legislate it out of existence is roundly rejected across tribe and faith differentiations. Yahya Jammeh's palpable fear of the spread of Islamic terrorists operating in the region far outweighs his moral obligation to Gambians, as manifested in the fatal religious intolerance foisted on Gambian society. Yahya Jammeh's comical Islamic state will not likely survive and will instead, by popular demand, be rapidly abrogated so Gambians can return to the peace and unity of their secular roots. Injecting religion in the Gambia's body politics also has other sinister motives that, though political, do not at first glance seem nearly as apparent. Nothing has irked Gambians more than Yahya Jammeh's recent promise to substitute the Gambian Constitution and English jurisprudence with Sharia as the basis of Gambian law. This may seem extreme, and even far-fetched, but fits perfectly in his political doctrine of reducing Gambians into the type of filial subservience found only in religion. As Gambia's economy disintegrates and the level of poverty is skyrockets, the exploitation of religion to insulate himself from the wrath of a disillusioned population may seem like a good idea, but reality may catch up with Yahya Jammeh as demands that he step down reverberate across the land and beyond. At no time has hatred of Yahya Jammeh and his cabal been as virulent and dramatically demonstrated as in this year's struggle for electoral equity and open defiance showcased on the opposition campaign trail. As the public urges the recalcitrant opposition into uniting, boycott the impending December elections and create a transitional unity government, the momentum is growing to cancel the elections as echoed in communities where Gambians reside across the globe.

This year, the clamor for change through opposition unity,

previously self-consuming for many, is echoing in every corner of the country, as it alone can guarantee the likelihood of political change. For many Gambians, the realization that Yahya Jammeh is a greedy murderer who is plundering the Gambia's meagre resources is only now beginning to dawn on their consciousness. Ostensibly, the death of fear in the Gambia has propelled the growing nationwide rebellion that promises change, regardless of the apprehension and timidity of a largely moribund opposition political establishment. As Gambians take back freedom denied them for twenty-one years, freedom that truly belongs to them, both constitutionally and by nature of their citizenship, the control by the political parties will be diminished, as every Gambian's control over their own lives becomes the center of focus. In the recent past, both UDP and the new GDC helped spring into life a side of Gambian society that no one knew existed, and helped channel their supporters' anger into solidarity for political change. This year, it is stating the obvious that if elections are free and fair, and the opposition collectively coalesces around one unifying political objective, Gambians would most likely do something very radical, which may also seem miraculous—electorally unseat Yahya Jammeh from power. Overwhelming evidence suggests that this year, Solo Sandeng's martyrdom and the subsequent detention of the main opposition UDP's senior leadership, including the party leader Ousainou Darboe, have snowballed into open popular rebellions that have forever removed the element of fear, which for two decades consumed and paralyzed Gambian society into numbing indifference to the catalogue of political assassinations, murders, tortures, and terror. This year, the political orthodoxy has forever changed, and it is imperative that the paradigm of ritually voting for Yahya Jammeh's regime also comes to a screeching end. Gambians will once again have the freedom to make their choices without the coercion of outside interference, in particular from Yahya Jammeh personally and AFPRC military regime's political party.

FATHER EDWARD GOMEZ, SPEAKING
TRUTH TO POWER

From under the ground in Brikama, like a phoenix, it rises. Its aesthetic calmness evoked a sense of messianic reverence. Even in its tranquil demeanor, the echoes of Fr. Gomez's serene voice transcends the tribal and religious divide, to reverberate in the hearts and minds of Gambians everywhere. Unsurprisingly, Fr. Edu Gomez's Sunday sermon touched on raw nerves and gently challenged our better angels to act with sagacity and moral rectitude as we ride out a dangerous religious firestorm in a country once renowned for its tolerance. The issue that grips the Gambia, this time again, is serious enough that hardly anyone is treating it with levity, and in soaking up Fr. Gomez's dose of wisdom, the pandemonium surrounding the unilateral declaration of the Gambia's Islamic state, a week earlier, resurfaced to nudge Gambians into rejecting the injection of religion in Gambia's body politic. Suddenly, the gravity of Gambia's predicament was not theoretical anymore. It was real. And even as the temper of Edu Gomez's sermon betrayed an Orwellian somberness, which spoke to the solemnity of the moment, only a few Gambians had come to grips with the precarious situation the country was plunged into. Only days earlier, a motley crew of self-serving Islamic clerics and elders had demonstrated their dangerous lack of objective rationality by lauding the Gambia's surreptitious transformation into an exclusive Islamic hegemony; leaving other faiths in the lurch. Yahya Jammeh's customary misuse of Islam and abuse of Islamic clerics to advance a political agenda is unparalleled, but the easiness with which Muslim clerics and elders succumb to the temptations of financial incentives and allow lust for material wealth to override their doctrinal liability tantamount to dereliction of religious responsibilities.

In contrast, in this instance, the Rev. Fr. Gomez symbolized a check back into reality; something evidenced by an underpinning of professional insight and foresight in how a draconian measure could easily degenerate in acts of violence. Fr. Edu Gomez's reference to the tragedy in the Central African Republic, in his sermon, exemplifies the contemporary historical attitude that Gambians can wrap their minds around, in order to understand the full breadth of the unintended consequences of superficial divisions of citizens, based solely on shallow, selfish political considerations. Rev. Fr. Gomez's lecture transported me back in time to another era, so long ago, sitting in church pews, listening to the booming voices of so many priests bellow out compelling canons of wisdom, but with the magic of imagination, that past was soon crowded out by the reality of the grimness of now, and the perils and cataclysm that potentially looms over Gambia. Unlike any other time in history, the sanctioning of inequality, based on religious beliefs will drive a wedge between citizens of different faiths, and incite resentment in a significant subsection of Gambia's population. This convergence of religion and politics has emerged as a centerpiece of the political conversation, a potential flashpoint of bigotry, intolerance, and civil strife Gambia cannot afford. Already, threats to the national security loom large in a political system built to appeal to the worst human instincts and the tribe-based politics that have haunted the majority of citizens, for twenty-one long years. The implications of erecting barriers to opportunity, based on religious beliefs, are frightening to even ponder, considering how, so far, tribal preferences have relegated a section of the Gambian population to second-class citizen status, with a pent-up anger ready to explode into a political conflagration.

A cursory look at anecdotal evidence shows how the seemingly innocuous hyperbole and bluster have historically established footing and turned the insipid into the awakening of the monsters in each of us. What makes Fr. Edu Gomez's story all the more fascinating is his emergence as a national icon, from a faraway parish, invisible behind thick shrubs, and dwarfed by tall, majestic mahogany trees. The town of Brikama, in Kombo North, is an unlikely place for a Catholic cleric to preach a message of wisdom to a local audience, a message that resonates at the national level, and has global reach. The adulation of Fr. Edu Gomez is not limited to Catholics, as the verdict of history has set him apart from other clergies easily influenced by political access and corruption, and material considerations. Fr. Edu Gomez's simple act of reverence has become a national call to reconcile with our better angels, and his moral rectitude has inadvertently turned into a national indictment of the systemic corruption of the Gambia's Muslim clerics. The recent convergence of Muslim quacks at the State House in demonstration of support for social stratification of Gambian society, based entirely on religious affiliation, for now, resides in the depths of Gambians' consciousness. An unpretentious sermon of piety in a backyard chapel, tucked innocently away behind thick shrubs and tall trees, has given rise to a new voice of reason. The towering character of Rev. Father Edward Gomez may not save the Gambia from sliding into the toxic mix of religion and politics, but in this spat between religious excess and simple common sense, this man of God has illustrated how Gambia's cantankerous Islamic clerics have fallen into disrepute as objects of political propaganda and the destruction of Gambian society. This may not be the march of the crusaders, but it is certainly a reminder of the constant struggle to keep the Gambia united by tribe, geography, and religion.

DESECRATING THE CHRISTIAN CEMETERY AND THE CORRUPTION OF ISLAM

Even the dead will have no rest. The living, distraught and in disbelief, are stunned by threats of the improbable becoming the likely. It is easy to script a parody of Yahya Jammeh, based on his tragic history, and digging up the graveyard bones of the long-ago dead, as spooky as that sounds, it would be an ideal starting point. Notwithstanding his legendary perfidiousness, Yahya Jammeh imagines himself as an icon of African liberation, but what he is, is more like the definition of the confusion of historical characters, some good and most not; General Idi Amin, François-Dominique Toussaint Louverture, Jean Bedel Bukassa, and Sekou Toure. Lacking sense of limit to his authority,

Yahya Jammeh, last week, brazenly triggered a proverbial standoff with the Gambia's Christian community over the three-hundred-year-old designated cemetery. This stalemate mirrors the ugly vindictiveness of a tyrant who sadly subscribed to the idea of total subjugation of Gambian society. Already, the Gambia's Muslim leaders have, over the years, cynically allowed Yahya Jammeh to chip away at their rights to worship, to a point of decreeing how they practice their Islamic faith, but the Christian community, unlike their Muslim counterparts, are unlikely to roll over and tolerate intrusion into the practice of their religion, and the hijacking of their faith. Yahya Jammeh's recent efforts to test the resolve of the Christian community is a familiar pattern that, over two decades, permitted him the pleasure of gradually seizing on citizens' perceived weaknesses and exploiting their fears in his perennial quest to leave his stamp on every aspect of Gambian society life. This has resulted in the alarming coersion of the military regime and Islam as institutions no government, altered the constitutional secularity of the state, and evolved a relationship with Islam that was purely political in nature. Islam in the Gambia has effectively been turned into an arm of the state with Muslim leaders assuming, preeminent roles in the harmful subjugation of citizens, and psychological wrecking of the collective Gambian psyche. Evidently, Yahya Jammeh has taken his control of the institution of Islam in Gambia to the extreme, often obliging Muslim clerics to participate in his ritual idol worship, to the chagrin of young Muslims.

The heads of Islam in the Gambia—Imam Ratib, Cherno Kah, of the Banjul Mosque, and Chairman of the Gambia Supreme Islamic Council, Imam Momodou Lamin Touray, Gunjur—had morphed into cheerleaders for Yahya Jammeh and appendages of the regime, having long ago succumbed to coercion into silence and detachment from the state-sanctioned crimes against the Gambian people. Until recently, Christianity as an institution has been the Holy Grail of Gambia's rabid politics of divisions, but the recent burial of eminent dissident radio journalist, George Christiansen, at the Banjul cemetery, has again awoken the evil in Yahya Jammeh, and triggered his challenge of the oldest and most powerful institutions in Gambia—the Church. George Christiansen's burial, which Yahya Jammeh is deceptively using to exert influence, and hold onto power over the Christian community, was preceded by similar denial of the burial on Gambian soil, of three distinguished dissidents, Buba Baldeh, Phoday Makalo, and Kukoi Samba Sanyang. Yahya Jammeh's mutation from ignorance to insanity will not exculpate him from his heinous crimes, and his newly hatched devious plan to flex a degree of control over Christians' practice of their own faith, exemplifies the gruesome Machiavellian ruthlessness with which he has sunk Gambia into the depths of social, political, and economic devastation. To most Africans in the diaspora, the story of Yahya Jammeh seems like fiction, and harder yet for other Africans to understand, is why Gambians have permitted Yahya Jammeh to stay in power so long under conditions of extreme suffering of Gambians, and his cannibalization of Gambian politics. In the developing rumpus between Yahya Jammeh and Gambia Christian community, powerful Muslim voices have offered their unwavering support for the idea of secularizing Gambia's political system, and noninterference in religious affairs. Not unlike exiled Imams Baba Leigh and Ba Kawsu Fofana, who returned to the Gambia, Christianity is not without its champions for secular Gambia: Revs. Fathers Edu Gomez and Peter S Lopez. Their sermons are clear and unambiguous: "diminishing the rights of any citizen diminishes the rights of all citizens." This reality is firmly etched in universal truth.

RAMADAN CHALLENGE FOR IMAM TOURAY, BISHOP ELLISON, IMAM KAH

The seriousness and the enormity of the horrors of Mile 2 Central Prison will not be fully known until after the demise of Yahya Jammeh, but the cruelty behind the tall, forbidden walls of that unholy citadel of misery, agony, and death, is all too real. If anything, the Gambia's Mile 2 Prison personifies the aggregation of the mean-spiritedness of a regime that has barbarized the Gambian spirit into a state of total confusion, and in the process unleashed a crisis reminiscent of the ghosts of Rwanda and Bosnia. The two competing visions of Gambia, one pushing toward a country devoid of the concept of humanity and remade into the image of Yahya Jammeh, and the other, a pull back toward a Gambia founded on the enduring spirit of empathy and dignity bequeathed Sir Dawda Jawara, could not be more starkly different. Today, the terrible conditions under which Mile 2 prisoners live and die plays out much like a Sophocles tragedy whose characters, as in *Oedipus Rex* and *Antigone*, are as bizarre as the tragic images of Mile 2 Central Prison are ruthless.

But unlike the Greek tragedies, products of the geniuses of imagination, the horrors of Mile 2 Prison are real, foreboding, and as cruel in all its manifestations. Mile 2 Prison is also an uncharacteristic departure from the heroism so emblematic of ancient Greek characters; instead, it is a drama that reads like the mesmerizing fantasies of a J. R. R. Tolkien novel, fantasies that capture the cruel antediluvian persona of Yahya Jammeh in its demonic splendor. Today, with the rest of African moving with religious fervor and matrimonial commitment toward democracy and the rule of law, the Gambian regime careens regressively down toward the path of political chaos and civil disorder. The prison system, which has totally stained the Gambia's international image, had their time long ago, and their brutal stories were eloquently documented and memorialized in *The Gulag Archipelago*, a novel by the intrepid Alexander Solzhenitsyn, a victim of the now defunct Stalinist prisons in the defunct Soviet Union.

But just as the Soviet Union broke up into its component nationalities, Yahya Jammeh's desensitized regime will collapse under the weight of its brutality, but unlike the Soviet Union, Gambia will remain a country united, intact and determined to bring back the nostalgia of the glorious era with Africa's inarguably greatest leader, the venerable Alhagie, Sir Dawda K Jawara. Mile 2 Prison could never exist under the venerable President, Sir Dawda Jawara, who, despite the massive economic shortcomings of his reign, made Gambians enamored with the concept of freedom at a time when much of Africa was like what the Gambia had become; ruled by tyrannies. I vividly remember the utter fear of our tour guide when I pointed to the soldiers guarding Benin's presidential palace, the terror and confusion at Lagos airport terminal that day in 1989 when President Sanni Abacha took power, and, of course, my unpublicized experience of the electoral bloodshed in Douala, Cameroon. Africa then was a continent steeped in political violence, and the bruising toll this left in its wake was both mind-blowing and life shattering.

Back at Yundum Airport after a harrowing ordeal around West Africa, I was overwhelmed with emotions of pride, joy, and appreciation for home. But this was Gambia then. Today Gambia has become what much of Sub-Saharan Africa was like back in the bloody seventies and eighties; a terrible place to live and die. But this article is also a challenge for Gambia's religious leaders: president of Gambia Supreme Islamic Council, Imam Momodou L Touray, Rev. Robert Patrick Ellison CSSp, Bishop of Banjul, Imam Ratib of Banjul, Imam Cherno Mass Kah, and State House Imam, Abdoulie Fatty. It is a challenge for the heads of Gambia's religious organizations to remember the incarcerated in their prayers, but above all, form a prison-visiting committee and go to the various prisons and detention centers all around the country to observe the extraordinary deplorable conditions under which prisoners live and die. Gambians have followed the activities of religious leaders over the years, and are stunned at how politics has hindered the proper practice of their faiths.

The cozy relationship religious leaders have developed with Yahya Jammeh over the years and their inexcusable silence in the face of the gruesome murders, extrajudicial executions, forced disappearance, tortures, intimidations, ceaseless arrests, detentions, and incarcerations of citizens, is an indictment of their faith. For the many years since Yahya Jammeh became head of that ungodly cabal that took over power in 1994, there has been an exodus of citizens to find shelter and safety away from the perpetual threats to their lives. They are in Senegal, but also in Mali, Guinea, Guinea-Bissau, Europe, and America. And for the many Gambian families whose loved ones are murdered, executed, incarcerated, or disappeared from the face of the earth, there is never peace; there is never closure. Then there are children whose fathers will never come home after they were taken away by Gambia's security agents many years ago, because they have been murdered.

There are mothers who now shoulder the heavy burden of bringing up kids and putting food on the table with little at their disposal, with kids who will never grow up knowing their fathers. Over five years ago, Sheriff Mustapha Dibba was released from Mile 2 Prison and died barely a week after. And shortly thereafter, a former permanent secretary, Lamin Sanneh, was released from Mile 2 Prison, but he too died a week later. And last year, Tombong Camara died a few days after he too was released from Mile 2 Central Prison. But these deaths are different from the deaths that have occurred there since Yahya Jammeh came to power. In Mile 2 Prison, more than a hundred inmates have been reported dead, and the deaths there never seem to end. In addition, a Nigerian citizen, Michael Ucheh Thomas, falsely accused of being a member of the banned Coalition for Change-Gambia (CCG), died Sunday, July 29, 2012, bringing the total of Mile 2 Prison deaths to well over a hundred, in the past decade and a half. The religious leaders' visits to Mile 2 Central Prison will be greatly appreciated by a suffering country. This is just what religious leaders ought to do, not merely luxuriating in the presence of power at the expense of the weak, the poor, and vulnerable. Visiting Mile 2 Prison visit will bring hope to prisoners, shower them with blessings, and uplift their spirits.

IMAM BABA LEIGH, FAITH, AND THE RAPE OF RELIGION IN GAMBIA

There was a period in Dippa Kunda, Serre-Kunda, when I often woke up early morning to listen to the song of Billali, the early-morning Muslim call to prayer. At first, I planned it, but it grew into a habit, waking me up effortlessly early morning to listen as the gusts of morning breeze carry the calls to prayer westward toward the western reaches of Dippa-Kunda, London Corner, Bakoteh, and even faraway Kololi along the serene Atlantic coastline. I first heard the song of Billali a decade earlier in Dakar, Senegal, and was mesmerized by its mournful melody. Emanating from Sere-Kunda's mosque minaret, the song had a tinge of melancholy that added mystery to the solitude of the early-morning dawn, making the muffled voices of Kombo market women echo sorrowfully in the morning darkness. And barely two miles east of the legendary Sere-Kunda mosque, St. Theresa's Catholic Church bells often peeled away simultaneously, as if providing chorus to the "Song of Billali," further adding mystery to the stillness of the early morning. Quite often, the minaret calls and distant church bells were eerily faint, sounding ghoulishly terrifying, a reminder of the frightening graveyard anthem of Michael Jackson's magnum opus, "Thriller." But that was Gambia when religion was neither tainted by the corruption of politics nor devalued by the idolization of materialism. The Gambia of that bygone era is a far cry to the new Gambia; Gambia permanently locked into a state of perpetual political crisis.

Today, the politicization of the largest religious denominations, Islam and Christianity, have greatly diminished the esteem not of the religions, but of their mindless leaders, to a point of asolute irrelevance. Either totally out of fear, or lack of understanding of the roles of their faiths, Gambia's Supreme Islamic Council, under Imam Momodou Touray and the Catholic Diocese of the Gambia under Rev. Bishop Robert P Ellison, through coercion or by their free wills, have succumbed to Yahya Jammeh's dangerous power, at the detriment of their congregations. The trade-off for financial rewards awarded to Imam Touray and Bishop Ellison and the prostitution of Islam and Catholicism in Gambia has been devastating to Gambians of all faiths. After years of state usurpation of religious authority, the mixture of religion and politics in the Gambia is a stunning reminder of its inherent dangers, particularly in a society with such a tragic history of ignominious subservience to political authority. The years since 1994 have witnessed the lethal intermingling of state and religion, resulting in a kind of political servitude, the like of which Gambia has never seen. The collusion of religion and politics in Gambia has had a mortifying effect on society, judging from the relationship between Yahya Jammeh and the heads of Gambia's religious organizations. Imam Momodou Touray and Rev. Bishop Robert P Ellison's frequent fraternizing with Yahya Jammeh, apart from emboldening his insane rampages, has in so many ways given the regime a license to pillage and plunder scarce natural resources to the detriment of citizens.

Clearly, the past several years have seen a fracturing among the Gambia's Muslim community between those who adhere to the teachings of their faiths and those who have hopelessly been transformed into Yahya Jammeh's bootlickers and political propagandists. In the recent past, Imam Ba Kawsu Fofana of Sanchaba Sulay Jobe mosque was arrested, released, arrested again, thrown in prison, and forcibly expelled from his own country. But even before the storm of his illegal arrest and state overreach had completely subsided, Yahya Jammeh ordered the arrest of Imam Baba Leigh of the Kanifing mosque. Imam Baba Leigh's shocking arrest was precipitated by Yahya Jammeh's bitterness over Imam Baba Leigh's condemnation of the horrific execution on August 23, 2012, of nine innocent Mile 2 Central Prison inmates. For a man with such an infinitesimal religious ingraining, Yahya Jammeh lacks the restraining power of respect ordinarily deferred to persons of faith of every denomination. Now it is painfully obvious that Yahya Jammeh has little or no respect for even Islam itself, and this in spite of his colorful, superficial, and ubiquitous display of religious zealotry and insanely extravagant religious showmanship. But what most stands out most in the eyes of Gambians is Yahya Jammeh's apostasy, betrayed by his ubiquitous and fanatical attachment to ancient idol worship. Yahya Jammeh's superficial adherence to religion is repudiated by the degree of cruel acts of violent murders that his regime has become revoltingly notorious for. His litany of infractions against Islam in recent years are endless, but even Gambia Supreme Islamic Council has been totally powerless in restraining his reptilian cruelty. Moreover, weeks after Imam Baba Leigh Kanifing of mosque was arrested, no one knew his whereabouts, and not even his family was granted access to him.

The unfolding saga surrounding the arrest and detention of Imam Baba Leigh adds to the justifiable condemnation of Yahya Jammeh and further lends credence to the scandalous exploitation of religion, especially Islam, for political reason. Last year, Yahya Jammeh unilaterally banned religious rituals at Gunjur's famous Shrine, a religious practice that pilgrims around West Africa and overseas consistently observed, beginning long before anyone alive in the Gambia was even born. Motivated by a deeply held belief in voodoo Satanism and animist worship, Yahya Jammeh's fear of the use of the Gunjur Shrine to offer sacrifices for his oust from power resulted in the senseless and downright insensitive banning of worship at the renowned shrine. Last year, Yahya Jammeh held up Friday prayers at Gunjur Mosque beyond the time stipulated in the Holy Quran, and in the end, failed to show up there for prayers, after ordering the congregation to wait for his arrival. Additionally, the sight of the Gambia Supreme Islamic Council elders toiling on Yahya Jammeh's farm was shocking. It shows that Yahya Jammeh's disrespect for Gambians has no limit, and the arrest and continued illegal detention of Imam Baba Leigh is just another example that speaks for itself. Gambians and friends of Gambia around the globe demand Imam Baba Leigh's immediate, unconditional release. The rape of religion in the Gambia has gone too far for too long. It must end.

CHAPTER 8

DYSFUNCTION OF INSTITUTIONS

LIVING IN A PARALLEL UNIVERSE

The experience of the last two decades, under the weight of Yahya Jammeh's brutal reign, ought to make every Gambian pause and think. Yet, despite the suffering of fellow citizens, stemming from Yahya Jammeh's brutal and incompetent regime, the emerging tsunami does not seem to register in the minds of many Gambians. As a result, the Gambia is on the precipice of social and political instability, and nothing Yahya Jammeh can do at this moment will mitigate the impending disaster. Whenever the balance of power suffers from artificial dislocation as a result of political activity, the natural tendency to realign power equitably by the force of popular will become an overarching national objective. But at this stage of Yahya Jammeh's nefarious regime, there is no impetus for him to change, because his regime's existence is predicated on the use of fear, intimidation, and brutality, pursuant to his infatuation with entrenching his hold on power. Yahya Jammeh's signature threats, as evidenced by his recent remarks about butchers at the Yundum Airport, though seeming benign, ought to be taken seriously. Historical experience under his regime suggests that the carnage he has committed over the years has provided the impulse to support the juxtaposing of his words against past behavior, to help forestall the malleable complacency that has paralyzed fellow citizens for far too long. Under the threats of losing jobs, going to jail, torture, and even death, Gambians have been forced to defer to Yahya Jammeh's regime, even in cases involving clear evidence of his murder and torture of fellow citizens. We cannot continue this unbridled deference to Yahya Jammeh and the eclectic mob of greedy and power-hungry slime surrounding him. Lack of moral fortitude and pervasive intellectual dishonesty by many in Yahya Jammeh's military regime is destroying Gambia's democratic experiment and turning institutions into appendages enabling the perpetuation of Yahya Jammeh's spineless dictatorship. Anecdotal evidence supports the contention that many citizens are in denial, and that the self-serving rationalization offered by some senior public servants regarding their service under the murderer Yahya Jammeh, will do much to trample down on citizen dissent. This is what is precipitating and perpetuating the slave mentality that is corroding the values, pride, and dignity at every level of social, and economic strata in the Gambia.

There is no doubt that for too many fellow citizens working in the regime, greed and the enigma of power and its influence on the perception of self-worth are motivating otherwise decent Gambians to turn their backs on the value systems that have informed how the tapestry of the nation was shaped. The cruel story of Yahya Jammeh's regime and the irredeemable rancor it epitomizes is causing the fearful submission to his regime's predacious power grab. And recently, when the state Minister, Mrs. Badjie-Janneh, admonished a delegation of WAJA journalists against disseminating news that has the potential to sow seeds of discontent, she could not be more right. By the same token, she ought to have addressed the Gambian culture of political patronage from which she benefited by virtue of being of Jola extraction. More than anything else, the tribal biases that have excluded other citizens from the benefit of accessing equal opportunities in their countries of birth is primarily responsible for the backwardness, destruction, and retrogression in Rwanda, Darfur, Liberia, and Sierra Leone, all countries that Mrs. Badjie-Janneh so eloquently referenced in her speech. Similarly, Yahya Jammeh's Jolanization of the country's civil service, the perpetual hiring and firing, the arrests and detention without cause, the disappearances and murders plaguing Gambia, and Mrs. Fatim Badjie-Janneh's own lack of qualification for the position she is handling are the kinds of examples that cause people to rise up and rebel against their own governments. The Gambia is already on the path to backwardness, but when the country reaches the stage of social upheaval, Mrs. Badjie-Janneh will have only one person to blame, and that is Yahya Jammeh. Obviously Yahya Jammeh has all rights to be as tribalist all he wants, but it does not give him the right to steer the collective national resources toward his fellow Jola tribesmen, at the exclusion of other tribes. This is what will give members of the other tribes a compelling reason to want to rise up and overthrow Jammeh's supercilious and divisive military regime. The vast majority of Gambians are stridently opposed to a dictatorship that has created a wedge between the Jolas and the rest of Gambia's citizens. But, the entire Jola population cannot be blamed for Yahya Jammeh's narrow-mindedness. The emerging distrust of Yahya Jammeh's Jola tribe does not originate from hatred, but from a natural reaction of people who are deprived and treated as second class citizens. The mischaracterization of the values of our Jolas compatriots—a people we all know so well, a people we love, lived with, and shared the good and the bad, the best and the worst moments of our lives—is inadvertently being engineered by Yahya Jammeh through his guiltless commitment to the wanton promotion of tribal bigotry in the country.

After the last general elections, Yahya Jammeh promised to pay the people of Western Division for their overwhelming support of his candidacy. Now, by steering two major development projects to that region of the country, he appears to live up to that promise.

Last week, an agricultural project worth $12.7 million and road construction project worth $7.5 million were approved for the Western Division. Yahya Jammeh has a history of diverting development funds to his native Western Division, and it is deliberate discrimination of other parts of our country. This is unacceptable for many obvious reasons, not the least of which is that deserving citizens and farmers in other parts of the country are deprived of what they are so rightfully entitled to. The development loans made to the regime are paid for, not only by any particular region or tribe, but by all taxpaying farmers throughout our country, irrespective of whether they benefited from it or not. And as far as the failure of Yahya Jammeh's regime is concerned, it was disconcerting to read about the National Assembly's debate relating to this year's trade season. By this time every year throughout President Jawara's thirty-year reign, his government would have announced a date for the beginning of the trade season. It is inconceivable that up to this moment, the military regime has not announced the beginning of this year's groundnut-buying season, but in addition, judging from the National Assembly debate, it appears that the regime has not even provided marketing outlets for farmers' harvest this year. Yahya Jammeh demonstrates that his regime is not equipped to deal with the range of development issues and challenges facing the country, and he is focusing on the perpetual prosecution of innocent Gambians for ridiculous, frivolous, trumped-up charges. The ongoing prosecution of three individuals for the attempted purchases of African idol charms for personal protection is ridiculous at best and downright stupid at worst. It is unimaginable that the issue of charms will be written into the laws despite the fact that 80 percent of citizens believe in voodoo, to the extent that they seek out animist and Islamic charm gurus for personal and family protections from evil spirits and imagined enemies. Clearly, our country is crying loudly for sober and informed leadership, and we have a responsibility to provide that for the benefit of all our people. In short, Yahya Jammeh's overthrow is long overdue. Far too many of our fellow citizens have died. Far too many are hungry and suffering needlessly in our prisons and jails. It is time for this madness to end. It is time to get rid of the tribalist murderer, Yahya Jammeh.

MUSICAL CHAIRS, INTELLECTUAL MIDGETS, AND PERNICIOUS MEDIOCRITY

The concurrent meetings were bound to happen—and to happen at this time, at this moment. With the festering economic hardship in the Gambia and international pressure mounting on Yahya Jammeh, Gambia's feckless regime needed a saving grace, and they got it—not once, but twice. Certainly, the agreements the European Union and the Senegalese government reached with Gambia's sanguinary regime are still unclear, but Gambians remain tepid, securely tethered to the hope that they will not again be victimized by the EU and Senegal's lowering of human rights standards. The crushing weight of mounting political pressure and unflattering irreverence of Gambia's corrupt regime, resonates with regime's that have crossed every known boundary of acceptable behavior. The Gambian regime, in denial of the smoldering bitterness over the total lack of freedom, has ostracized itself into a pariah nation, by the force of its political tyranny and undeniable misanthropist regime. Additionally, Yahya Jammeh's indifference to Gambians craving political change exemplifies his disregard for the social, cultural, and economic realities that have reduced daily life in Gambia to empty aspirations.

By themselves, the EU and Senegal's meetings with the Gambian regime are striking manifestations of Yahya Jammeh's insidious disregard for the competency Gambia requires in the art of governance. In the multilateral meeting last week, the EU delegates demonstrated a high level of professionalism, and their group sharply contrasted the hodgepodge cabal of Gambian delegates, most of who looked more like oddities in a Californian Disney theme park. Under Yahya Jammeh, Gambia has come to symbolize the assault on competence and excellence, thus reducing the Gambian bureaucracy to an unnerving intellectual mediocrity. Yahya Jammeh's unilateral decision-making and Gambia's brilliant manifestation of incompetence, which runs deep at every level of the bureaucracy, is hamstringing the Gambia's development, further plunging the country in a terrifying, apocalyptic economic distress. Further, the prosecution and maligning of innocent Gambians with higher education and intellectual depth is a Yahya Jammeh–instigated subterfuge that speaks to the dangerous tribal xenophobia in Gambia. Yahya Jammeh's regime has demonstrated deep commitment to institutionalized bigotry toward the Gambia's embattled majority tribes, the intellectual class, and dissident Jolas who understand the pernicious ramifications of vilifying innocent Gambian tribes, and in particular, Fulas and Mandinkas.

The absurdity of Yahya Jammeh's intransigence and the hopelessness of his one-dimensional thinking, insult Gambians' primordial instincts to regain freedom, as a right in the human existence. Beyond that, Yahya Jammeh's Gaddafi-like political tyranny is a manifestation of intellectual deficiency and embellishment of his political standing, rather than a reflection of the reality of his political isolation, and susceptibility for removal from office. Since coming to power, Yahya Jammeh populated the bureaucracy with often barely literate individuals, and sometimes with persons who lack the education and experience to handle the positions that are assigned to them. In Gambia, the culture of mediocrity has seeped into every level of the civil service, making failure a function of the lack of intellectual capacity. Today, the Gambia's severe economic challenges are textbook signs of failure to address the jarring poverty and the impoverished population's fearsome hunger to vent their frustration. Last week, after the EU delegates met with their Gambian counterparts, to hash out important national issues, Yahya Jammeh showed his underhandedness and contempt for the European union body by passing draconian media bills that sought to muzzle speech and censure use of the internet. This divergence from international free press norms only adds injury to the culture of intellectual midgetry, and pernicious mediocrity in Yahya Jammeh's Gambia.

THE NATIONAL ASSEMBLY BLINKS SHAMEFULLY

The ostentatious show of what, in hindsight, seems like political bravado was an ambitious departure from the norm. In a way, the move was an innocuous display of political independence, but that elicited Yahya Jammeh's mortifying fury. But the die was cast, and the status quo was stood up to in ways that threatened, or at the very minimum challenged, Yahya Jammeh's hold on absolute power. By every account, it was only a small but extemporaneous challenge of the chronic political powerlessness of the National Assembly, a move arguably made to compensate for years of political complacency and indifference. But, if the National Assembly hoped to burnish its filial servitude in order to secure its place on the good side of Gambia's history, their act of independence turned out to be but an ephemeral taste of political liberty. After many years, the National Assembly had failed to contend with the eccentricity and craziness of their all-powerful demigod, Yahya Jammeh, and they paid dearly for it, with their pride and egos bruised by Yahya Jammeh's retributive justice.

This was exemplified by the National Assembly's recent handling of the GNOC case in relation to the sports minister, Sheriff Gomez, a move that touched on Yahya Jammeh's raw nerves, and quickly degenerated into a bruising exhibition of Machievillian cruelty. What no one saw coming was the ignominious apology letter that the so-called House Speaker wrote to appease Yahya Jammeh's furious blowback. In the National Assembly's disgraceful letter pockmarked with spelling and grammatical errors, the members, in their apology to Yahya Jammeh, shamed both the institution they represent, and the Gambian people, once again recoiling into the apathy and indifference that has brought Gambia to this level of political tyranny. In a few days, the National Assembly oscillated from its exceptionally diligent handling of the GNOC case to extending an undeserved apology to Yahya Jammeh for merely performing their mandate as the elected legislative body. By their apology, the assembly once again retreated into its comfort zone, a place of darkness and ignorance characterized by fear and political ambivalence, and in so doing, left the art of misgovernance to Yahya Jammeh's tyranny and unpredictable savagery. In every way one looks at it, their apology was unprecedented, both in character and tone, and now serves only to consolidate Yahya Jammeh's unchecked power.

At a time when the Middle East and North Africa are literally on fire, demanding change and human rights and civil liberties, one would think Gambians would be motivated to capitalize on the political momentum in North Africa and replicate the acts of bravery and sacrifice exhibited by ordinary people across the Maghreb and elsewhere. Once again, Yahya Jammeh's idiosyncrasies won out, a matter that serves not only as a warning to our docile legislators, but will also force the National Assembly members to self-censure their actions and activities moving forward. Despite its awkward nature, the National Assembly's apology was hardly surprising, considering the intellectual caliber of most of the members who sit as representatives in that sacred national institution. Throughout the military reign, members of this august body have individually and collectively, consciously and inadvertently, helped underwrite the policies that have made Yahya Jammeh's power grab easy and possible, by consistently conceding to his injurious demands and turning a blind eye to his considerable failures of leadership and criminal power abuse, two hallmarks of this criminal regime. To many, this new saga is only a small reminder that Yahya Jammeh's best dictatorship days are incomparable to the worst of Sir Dawda Jawara's long reign, an indisputable reality that brings to mind the late House Speakers, Sir Alieu Jack and Momodou B Njie (BP), whose intellectual maturity, charisma, and nobility contrasted with the boorishness and ignorance of the new Speaker at the helm of the National Assembly. No one can imagine a scenario under which the gentlemen, these models of citizenship, these embodiments of grace and integrity, in their time, under Sir Dawda Jawara, in their capacities as House Speakers, would be coerced into writing humiliating letters of apology to Sir Dawda.

Their pride dictated that they would rather resign than submit to fear, shame, and ridicule; they would choose integrity over material rewards, conviction over lack of moral rectitude. After all these years, Yahya Jammeh is accustomed to having his way with the National Assembly, and now the body elected to represent the voices and interests of the people, has metastasized into a useless institution maligned into irrelevance and redundancy. Everything the National Assembly has done to date militates against the enforcement of our laws and Constitution, having methodically undermined the hopes and aspirations of our people. The National Assembly's morbid display of cowardice in the face of everything that happened in the country is to a degree responsible for the obsequious political quandary into which the Gambia has descended. Beyond that, Yahya Jammeh appears to have demanded the National Assembly apology letter he ordered written be published in the open press, to further maximize humiliation of the Assembly members, and to prove who is in charge, and in so doing, effectively forced members to acquiesce to his orders, in order to mitigate the harsh retribution he would otherwise impose on them. In general, this saga further underscores the moral weaknesses and political immaturity of the National Assembly, underpinnings of an effective representation to that discredited legislative body.

And judging from the reactions of the media and Gambians in general, it looks like everyone was miffed and disillusioned by the National Assembly apology letter as patently wrong, which, apart from consolidating Yahya Jammeh's power, created the conditions for the further erosion of the Assembly's authority. Despite his unspoken threats, Yahya Jammeh had no power under the Constitution to remove an elected National Assembly member; on the contrary, members are elected and empowered by the Constitution to remove him, if he can be linked any of the murders, tortures, and disappearances, either by ordering them, authorizing them, or participating in their execution. But for now, it is a misnomer to call the letter to Yahya Jammeh an apology; rather, it represents a remarkable surrender of the National Assembly's authority and further weakens the Constitutional system of government. The apology letter was surreal, a new first, a descent into political morbidity, and an act of small-mindedness and defeatism that will further engender the political schism in the country. And as Gambians go through the grit, gristle, and grime of everyday life, a life intermittently punctuated by murders of innocent citizens, there still are no demonstrable indications that Yahya Jammeh's regime will change its ways. For the people of the country, the fundamental crucible is how much longer must Gambians continue to endure the deaths and dying, the misery and hopelessness, agony and helplessness, and this abominable nightmare that is Yahya Jammeh.

Truth be told, Yahya Jammeh has efficiently emasculated the entire National Assembly, reduced the judiciary system into a circus, and sapped the life out of the Gambia's superfluous political establishment. As worrisome as all this may seem now, Gambia, as a country, will be burdened by the emotional heft this will leave for a long time. As of now, only a popular revolution or a military revolt will save Gambia from the despicable journey down the path of destruction and anarchy. To save the country from impending chaos, Yahya Jammeh must go while we can still control and manage the emotional outrage that has been building up in the hearts and minds of the brutalized fellow countrymen. The time for Yahya Jammeh to go has come and gone many times.

INDEPENDENCE DAY ANNIVERSARY: THE CELEBRATION OF DYSFUNCTION AND MISERY

In the short space of two and a half decades, the clamor for political independence has become a continent-wide movement that significantly altered global political dynamics between the colonized and colonizers. For postcolonial Africa, it was a revolutionary era that ushered in hopeful signs, but which quickly degenerated into the tyrannical recolonization of the mind of a continent—this time, by Africans. On February 18, 1965, young students witnessed the lowering of Great Britain's Union Jack flag for the last time and the ascension, in its place, of a newly independent Gambian flag. There was enthusiastic applause when Hon. David Kairaba Jawara took to the podium as Gambia's first prime minister. In those early days, the political pundits gave this dusty, little backwater of a country little or no chance to succeed economically as a standalone political entity. The groundwork was set for rampant speculations about the possibility of political confederation with neighbor French-speaking neighboring Senegal. But the Gambia's Sir David K Jawara had a different vision, and his solutions to the country's lack of natural resources persevered to move the country from a political experiment to a country that provided academics to the US and Europe, and bureaucrats to United Nations and its ancillary bodies. By 1994, the public face of the Gambia was not whether the country could survive the challenging viability test as an independent entity, but on how remarkably well President Sir Dawda Jawara's government proved the Gambia's resilience under difficult circumstances, far beyond the pessimism of the pundits and prophets of doom.

The breadth of Gambia's political liberties and expansion of opportunities, under President Sir Dawda K Jawara unleashed the creative ingenuity of citizens, which mitigated the lack of natural resources. There was a time, not so long ago when February 18 each year aroused the passions and recommitted citizens to one another and to the state's well-being. Independence Day was worth celebrating. The reasons to laugh were plentiful. And a nation with vibrant citizens projected itself as a champion of human and civil rights. That was then. This is now. The tail end of the uneventful colonial era and the first three decades of independence are starkly different from the last twenty years of political repression. The independent anniversaries, since the military coup 1994, failed miserably to release the passions of a nation and galvanize its citizens' resolve to advance Gambia towards political and economic modernity. The vehemence with which the military regime skirted the protocols of good governance has baffled both Gambians and the international community, which caused concentration among citizens' collective efforts to bring about necessary political change. In the two decades since Yahya Jammeh came to power, Gambia has developed a subculture that, apart from being alien to Gambian values, has impeded the country's acceptance into the community of civilized nations. And unlike the preceding nineteen years, this is Gambia's golden jubilee anniversary, an anniversary, which is albeit a meaningless milestone, characterized by complete subordination to brutal state power. Every independence anniversary since 1994 has been an absurd celebration of contradictions that made a mockery of the concept of independence from colonial domination.

Today, as the Gambian prisons fill beyond capacity, the death toll increases exponentially, so has the forced disappearances, as even more Gambians flee to the safety of faraway friendly nations, this year's celebration of the independence, like previous years, is a denial of the existence and prevalence of state terror. But it also negates the political circumstances that brought Gambia down to its knees into a state of dysfunction, on the brink of bankruptcy and political disintegration. The Gambia's disastrous human rights records aside, Yahya Jammeh, as a Casamance, Senegal citizen, totally lacks fidelity to Gambians and the Gambian people, which justifies his removal by any necessary means. Gambia's democratic experiment and characterization as the Smiling Coast of Africa, which is proudly sold to the international community for three decades, has, with the advent of military rule, plunged this once universally renowned peaceful country into the dark depths as an African pariah nation. Even by Africa's standards of state-sanctioned brutality, the Gambian regime stands out as particularly ruthless. Gambia's slow drift to political tyranny and tribal bigotry was long ago condemned and, by extension, invited the regime to an inevitable confrontation with an unforgiving population. After twenty years of greed and criminal incompetence, Yahya Jammeh's regime ought to now simply pack up and leave or be forced out. The heinous crimes and incompetence of this regime cannot be undone. And independence celebration or not, it is not going to get better. It will, in fact, get worse.

After twenty years, Yahya Jammeh rules by subverting the Constitution. It is time for peace to return to a traumatized people.

THE JUDICIARY IN OVERDRIVE AND YAHYA JAMMEH'S CORONATION

The Gambia's justice system is in overdrive. And the judiciary is burdened with frivolous lawsuits brought up by the military regime, and with endemic corruption, the rights to freedom is bought and sold like commodities. Mass incarceration has become a mere sport, as magistrates and judges play Russian roulette with people's lives. It seems the judiciary and in the legal system practitioners have no clue that sending anyone to Mile 2 Prison is a potential death sentence. The administration of justice is a sham, a total failure, from the office of the Attorney General and Minister of Justice, to the chambers of the so-called Chief Justice. And last week, according to *Freedom* newspaper, an Arab who was condemned for drug running was let out of prison to freedom, allegedly after a bribery exchange of $1 million, leaving behind Gamian six co-defendants. In any properly constituted legal system, the verdict against the remaining co-defendants would automatically be reversed, overturned, and thrown out, and their release secured by court order. The law ought to not treat defendants differently for fear of losing the legitimacy of impartiality, which is the foundation of every legal system. But this case is not atypical either; rather, it is the norm. This case, or similar cases, made the dispensation of justice by the judiciary a mockery of the laws of the land. This is only a tip of the iceberg.

The legal shenanigans have become inextricably intertwined with the fabric of the legal and judiciary systems, where they continue to fester. Consequently, to take a long view of the law, every case that was adjudicated or tried in civilian or military court and resulted in conviction over the past decade and half ought to be overturned, and victims released in a post–Yahya Jammeh era. And for a long time, even the regime had a sense of uneasiness about the dysfunction of the judiciary, which last week prompted the Gambia's Vice President, Dr Isatou Njie-Saidy to reiterate the regime's commitment to a judiciary unblemished by external political interference. Her statement is a tacit yet veiled acknowledgement of the existence of a chaotic and dysfunctional system; a system that is not in pursuit of truth, but of financial rewards, and the corrupting influences that tag along its corrosive power. But there is only one problem; VP Isatou Njie-Saidy forgot that we have heard this song played many times before—in fact, for the fifth time in as many years, and frankly, the tune is old, the sound is bad music to the ears, and the lyrics pregnant with hypocritical disingenuousness.

And to add insult to injury, Yahya Jammeh made similar assertions the past five consecutive years, yet nothing has changed—nothing. But perhaps this time there is change in the air, and this whiff of optimism is not pegged on anything either Yahya Jammeh or VP Isatou Njie-saidy have said. Instead, in a rare moment of frankness and display of unambiguity, the president of Gambia Bar Association, Sheriff Tambedou, came close to demanding job security for his association's practitioners—in particular, judges and magistrates who Yahya Jammeh often hires and fires at the drop of pin. The independence of the Gambia's judiciary from unwanted interference and manipulation is at the heart of the matter. Judicial and civil service appointments under Yahya Jammeh's regime are like playing a game of musical chairs. There are instances when appointees to positions in government are fired within the week of hiring, and in many other instances, people were fired a month or two after their appointment. The Attorney General and Minister of Justice portfolio alone had over two dozen appointees under Yahya Jammeh. That is one appointment each year, a record for any country.

But, for Mr. Sheriff Tambedou's demand for job security to have any chance of becoming reality, two things must happen: Yahya Jammeh voluntarily concedes to the Gambia Bar Association demands, which is unlikely, or the Bar Association, if it's serious about protecting its civil rights, takes a long overdue united front of civil disobedience against state meddling in judicial matters. After all, it is with the judiciary that the last hope of citizens rests; it is to them that the country must look up to for guidance as last resort, but so far, with everything that has happened in the country, the judiciary record has been abysmal, a downright dereliction of duty. But, it is quite unlikely that the Gambia Bar Association will have legal authority left to accomplish its desire for job security and judicial independence, considering that Yahya Jammeh's coronation as king has the approval of Banjul. This is due to the fact that last week, in what can be described as a stunning and jaw-dropping display of craziness, two National Assembly representatives from Banjul, Seedy Njie and Abdoulie Saine, declared that, "as far as Banjul is concerned, we endorse the idea." The idea, in case you wonder, is the coronation of military leader Yahya Jammeh as king in Gambia.

And if these are the caliber of representatives Gambia has as its lawmakers, the country is doomed to the mediocrity that has ruined every prospect Gambia had for social and economic transformation. And Abdou Jarjue, National Assembly member for Kombo Central, by supporting the campaign to coronate Yahya Jammeh, has demonstrated the same level of craziness. It can be recalled that prior to the last National Assembly election years ago, Yahya Jammeh, in one sweep of madness, fired all the APRC's assembly representatives, including majority leader Churchill Baldeh, and replaced them with his handpicked National Assembly class of lackeys. One the other hand, however, Assembly Member Hon. Momodou LK Sanneh from Kiang showed intellectual maturity in his opposition to the infinitely ridiculous idea of a Gambian monarchy. But not everyone in the country is a court jester, and Momodou L K Sanneh of Kiang has shown, in more ways than one, that there are serious Gambians invested in the country's success and economic prosperity. And that, at the minimum, should give us hope that change can happen. The whole country demands it.

"HOPE LIVES ON, AND THE DREAM SHALL NEVER DIE"

A journey of a thousand miles begins with a simple step, says Lao Tzu, Chinese philosopher. This week's convergence of female voices on Maafanta.com online newspaper, around an issue that has paralyzed the Gambian male psyche, typifies the frustration engendered by the anemic response to Yahya Jammeh's murderous military regime. The eye-catching title of this editorial, borrowed from Senator Edward M Kennedy's 1980 DNC speech, is illustrative of the frustration and hopelessness Gambians feel about the cannibalization of the political system. But more importantly, the pathetic inability to do something, anything, about it, lends credence to what Baboucarr Sankanu would rightly theorize as religion's role in the perversion of the natural instincts to fight for the security of the inalienable rights and liberties of each individual. The flight from the miserable circumstances represents a real failure to rationalize the country's predicament at every layer of the discourse; the failure to wrap minds around the underbelly of deadly political problems that continue to consume the country; the failure to articulate and address the insidiousness of this man-made life-altering political menace; and the failure to imbue the conscience with sufficient doses of willpower and courage to take back the country. Most Gambians, rather than take courage and determination from the atrocities committed under Yahya Jammeh's regime, are frozen in fear, apathy and indifference by the string of forced disappearances, tortures, incarceration, murders by executions, and the traumatizing carnage that took the lives of two dozen young Gambian students back in April 2000.

The brutality of that fateful day continues to paralyze Gambians into a state of dispassionate and, so often, fatal abstraction of reality, and in the process, Yahya Jammeh has the space he carved to further consolidate his stranglehold on power. Those who fight back in every way possible, through every medium available, often go to bed agonizing over the fact that the echoes of their voices perpetually drifting into the melancholic solitude of the vast emptiness of Gambia's political wilderness. These challenges notwithstanding, the distillation of the circumstances surrounding the failure to live up to the collective moral obligation has birthed a new front in the struggle to salvage the country from the tragic overreach of the misguided policies of the Yahya Jammeh regime. This potent addition to the chorus of voices engaged in the political discourse symbolizes the opening of a new front in the perennial struggle for the liberation of Gambia. A critical mass of competing female voices could fortify the standing of the vocal few and be a catalyst in the creation of a riot of defiant voices needed to succeed in the fight for the heart and soul of the country. Gambian women have a long history of defying stereotypical casting imposed on them by religion and society, in order to break with tradition and make themselves heard and visible in what is exclusively a male-dominated political environment. The brainchild of Fatou Jaw-Manneh, "Operation Girls Catch Yahya" or (OGCY) is, for our time, a bold and radical novel idea of defiant inclusiveness, but as the nifty Ndey Tapha-Sosseh, the ladies of Maafanta.com are following a tradition that goes back decades, a reminder of the many still unknown and unresearched institutions venerable Gambian women founded—Florence Mahoney, Cecilia Cole, and ageless Bijou Peters, among others.

Today, with the exception of Ms. Amie Joof-Cole, many of the successors of these pioneers have fallen silent and invisible at a time the pull of their charismas, the draw of their presence, the weight of their rich experiences, and the credibility of their voices could make significant differences in advancing causes for liberty and development of Gambian society. As a new generation of women leaders, like the phoenix, slowly and boldly rise from the ashes of the July 22, 1994, military coup, the inspirations they draw from their predecessors have the potential to offset the pathological fear that has stunted their male counterparts for a very long time. The idea of Gambian women coalescing around similar social, economic, political issues that have persistently haunted their male counterparts could breathe new life in the challenging, if not vexing, political discourse. As the country inches slowly toward a showdown with Yahya Jammeh and his regime, it is not a moment too soon for the new crop of liberated Gambian women to move from the periphery roles assigned them by the limitations of culture and religious biases to assume significant, dynamic, frontline roles at every level of society. The move toward true equality in gender roles in the political arena will potentially sophisticate Gambian society and domesticate our menfolk into recognizing the important station women must hold in society. There is a lot of definitive empirical and anecdotal evidence that correlates women's participation in the social and political discourses with economic success in African societies. The need to break from the convention that limits women's roles is, therefore, in itself, compelling and makes confederating with female activists all the more necessary; perhaps even inevitable.

After all, this is not a new concept that would pose a threat to the egos of the menfolk; if anything, it will help detract from the redundant inclinations toward hegemony of male masculinity, and other narrowly defined preferences that have nothing constructive to offer the broader Gambian society. The focalization of the broad menu of objectives around a well-defined platform and the galvanizing potentials of the advantage of gender are strong incentives to cheer groundbreaking Gambian women organizations, which is more than just symbolism and rhetoric, but the rebirth of a new dawn in the checkered life of the Gambian story. The diversity of the new female voices—Amie Joof-Cole, Adelaide Sosseh, Fatoumata Tambajang, Fatou Jaw-Manneh, Jabou Joh, Sigga Jagne, Ndey Tapha-Sosseh, Sarata Jabbi-Dibba, Fatou Sagnia, Ndey Jobarteh, my sister and best friend, Jainaba Bah, and not the least, Aisha Saidy, among a few others—is a welcome addition to the debate about the future of the country. Hopefully, the fence-sitters at home and abroad will be motivated by the broad coalition of female voices to join the battle of a lifetime, not to dogmatize the political challenges facing the country, but to offer practical solutions so as to move the Gambia forward, and out of the murderous wilderness of Yahya Jammeh and his thugs, murderers, drug dealers, criminals, and semi-educated and barely literate system psychopaths. And to quote that venerable, iconic liberal lion, the late Senator Edward Kennedy, with the role women can play in the Gambia's political life, "hope lives on, and the dream shall never die.

AND SO THE UNCAGED BIRDS SING

Senegal and the United States are epicenters of horror stories told with uncommon eloquence and earthshaking disbelief. They are stories of a nation told in different narratives, by many escapees from political tyranny. It is a bizarre story that portrays the obscene picture of a country devastated by political inertia and glaring ruthlessness. It is also the story of Gambia maligned by Yahya Jammeh's tragic contempt for democracy and ignorance of the rule of law. It is a country on the precipice of unnerving political and economic debacle. Gambia's unfolding story highlights the tragic consequence of tyranny and the extent to which Gambia has become frozen in fear, inadvertently facilitating the mass human rights violations that have made free people around the world stand up and take notice. The bizarre stories told in Dakar, Senegal, and Raleigh, North Carolina, reveal the existential threat the Gambian military regime under Yahya Jammeh and his blood-drenched acolytes have foisted on a country once renowned as one of Africa's undisputed bastions of democracy and rule of law. After prolonged detachment from reality, Gambia's chilling and heart-wrenching stories are finally being told with deliberate poise and easy persuasion, and in much detail and even greater clarity. In a country still speculating about the irksome depth and breadth of the gruesome human rights abuses under Yahya Jammeh—assassinations, murders, killings, tortures, arrests, and forced disappearances—the revelation of brutalities in the Gambia is welcome news.

It is a tragic story that poignantly articulates Yahya Jammeh's attachment to power, but more importantly, the shocking brutality that underpins the tactlessness of his demonic regime. Gambia, a country that once offered shelter to Africa's victims of political repression is now transformed into the emblem of repression and vexing lawlessness. But the country's crushing oppression goes far beyond Yahya Jammeh's lust for power, to illustrate his lunacy, devastating incompetence, and ignorance of the values of moral and ethical rectitude. The Gambia's unfolding story catalogues the sanguinary character of Yahya Jammeh's puzzling insensitivity and total disregard for human life. Gambia's anachronistic descent into political and economic tragedy, and the consequences of the social, political, and economic disruption, is bound to have profound repercussions on Gambian society for years to come, judging from the viciousness of its recent state-sanctioned crimes. The dangerous ramifications of Yahya Jammeh's self-serving political manipulation and social engineering of Gambian society will preface the gruesome chapter of a history written in blood by Yahya Jammeh's persistent undermining of the human rights of citizens and unyielding abuses of civil liberties. For years now, Yahya Jammeh's ad nauseam destruction of Gambia's character on the international stage, and the country's social, political, and economic foundering, has lent itself to an avalanche of speculations about the extent of the crimes, but new developments have left Gambians dumbfounded and the international community aghast.

At issue is the anticipated confession of Yahya Jammeh's former close aides, former members of the secretive military assassin group known as Jugglers. The Jugglers, a dangerous group modeled after Haiti's infamous Ton Ton Macoute assassins, are complemented in lethality by an equally ruthless civilian killer group known as the Green Boys. The two secretive groups are primarily responsible for Gambia's state-sanctioned killings over the eighteen years. But the first to confess their involvement in the crimes against Gambians to the online media, more than three years ago was a former member of the Green Boys, who, for security reasons, gave only his last name as Mendy. Mr. Mendy narrated in chilling detail how Yahya Jammeh composed the group of assassins consisting primarily of young, innocent Jolas and a few Manjagos, and released them around the country to wreak terror on the Gambian civil service. Their work, according to Mendy, was partly to falsely accuse Wollofs, Mandinkas, Akus, and Fulas in the civil service of criminal conduct, so as to replace them with Jolas. The accused would be fired immediately, dragged into the kangaroo court system before criminal-minded Nigerian judges, and often imprisoned. As incredible as this seems, it is the confession of an exiled former Green Boys member who is tormented by guilt for his role in causing the Gambia's darkest hour. But perhaps the most damning confession came from Gambia's exiled star witnesses and former officers in the Gambian military, Bai Ebou Lowe and Sheriff Gissey.

The depth and breadth of Officer Bai Lowe's intimate knowledge of the litany of murders ordered by Yahya Jammeh is downright breathtaking. From the assassination of journalist and Gambia Press Union cofounder Deida Hydara, the forced disappearance of Chief Ebrima Manneh, execution of Daba Marenah and company, to the butchering of forty-four innocent Ghanaian immigrants bound for the Canary Islands, Bai Lowe's scary accounts of Yahya Jammeh's gross human rights violations provide a background and reasons for his removal from office and trial for crimes against humanity, not in the Hague, but in Gambia's court system, the same court system Yahya Jammeh falsely relied on to execute nine prisoners from the notorious Mile 2 Central Prison. Bai Ebou Lowe's shocking testimony, which was recently buttressed by Sheriff Gissey, another confessed ex-member of Yahya Jammeh's assassin group, has cast the Gambian regime as the worst Africa has seen since Idi Amin Dada. Bai Ebou Lowe and Sheriff Gissey, in separate marathon interviews with *Freedom* newspaper's Pa Nderry, divulged damning information about Yahya Jammeh's orders to execute Gambians opposed to his reign of terror. And today, as Gambians remember the nine prisoners whom the regime confessed to executing at Mile 2 Central Prison, the *Freedom* newspaper's interviews with Bai Lowe and Sheriff Gissey will refresh Gambian memories of the horror surrounding the deaths of so many Gambians and non-Gambians on Yahya Jammeh's orders. As the unchained birds sing to a dumbfounded audience, hopefully more Gambians involved in the murders will be incentivized to come forward and confess their roles in Gambia's killing sprees, but more importantly, to tell the world about Yahya Jammeh and his regime's criminality.

STATE OF DENIAL AND A NATION IN SLOW ECONOMIC COLLAPSE

Nothing about Gambians' herd mentality is organic. That happens in the movies and the animal kingdom. But again, Gambia's recent history is an unending movie, a perpetually rewritten script that changes with the emotional disposition of one person: Yahya Jammeh. Yet it takes a tremendous amount of moral courage to drift away from the truth, particularly in cases of undeniable evidence, but then the Gambia's contemporaneous story is like an act that inhibits the resolve to defy the ubiquitous and paralyzing fear, marked by powerless indifference to reality. The naiveté, or better still, willful denial of reality among Gambians averse to the idea of conceding to the stressful social, political, and economic conditions in Gambia has degenerated into an acrimonious relations with former dissidents. The benign demonstration of fidelity to the truth about the wretchedness of conditions Gambia is suffering from has devolved into the pitiless stigmatization of victims who are unable, any longer, to tolerate the scourges of military rule. In the Gambia, a significant number of citizens have been forced into a state of detachment from the reality, a pathology that borders on insanity. Unfortunately, that same predicament has made inroads into the diaspora, where Gambian refugees, who until recently demonstrated strident opposition to the savagery in the Gambia, now manifest a less than flattering filial piety toward Yahya Jammeh, consistent with collaborators with bygone ruthless regimes. And of great interest to the Gambian people are the motives for the sudden philosophical conversion by former dissident refugees whose vehement degradation of the Gambia's regime is casting Yahya Jammeh as a moral abomination.

The puzzling change in support of Yahya Jammeh's regime by Gambians at home and abroad is a testament to the personal character flaws of dissidents and nondissidents whose indecisiveness and vacillation on such crucial matters has stunned Gambians struggling to be free from the vicissitudes of dictatorship. As the dark vein of political tyranny casts its long shadow over a once peaceful nation, Gambians are faced with the timeless challenge of the basic rule of survival—to surrender, fight, or flee. The window to take concrete action to end twenty years of one-man rule is now. If anyone is less concerned about the appalling desperation in Gambia, it must be Yahya Jammeh. The growing poverty, killings, disappearances, and exodus of Gambians illustrates a slow decline into political dysfunction, but Yahya Jammeh's mortifying fear of the ramifications of his brutality has hampered his ability to change political orientation. Yahya Jammeh is helplessly wedged between a rock and a hard place, no longer able to experience normal life, and despite his ostentatious display of bravado, realization of the likelihood of his sad end has steered him toward a familiar fatal error dictators make with incredible regularity. Both politically and economically, Gambia is in a precarious state, but despite the gravity of the situation, it seems the tipping point has not been reached yet. Historically, economic deprivation and its associated indignities have had the ability to inspire the moral courage to force political change. And in recent months, several indicators have collectively confirmed what Gambians lived through for the past twenty years; political tyranny, economic deprivation, social alienation and endemic corruption. But this political fiasco notwithstanding, Yahya Jammeh's oppression of Gambians has continued to manifest itself in many different ways, not the least of which is the enslavement of the population of a once free people.

One of the most depressing occurrences in the Gambia in recent years is the sight of civil servants, cabinet members, the vice president, National Assembly members, the Supreme Islamic Council, the military, the security forces, students, farmers, and citizens from every walk of life frequently coerced into participating in free slave labor in one of Yahya Jammeh's several dozen farms dotted around the country. But perhaps more startling still is the sight of soldiers fishing under the pretext of a Yahya Jammeh philosophy of food self-sufficiency. And beyond the physical labor under the hot African sun, the control and subordination of citizens is the principal reason for organizing these slave labor events, and this strategy is working. What it tells us, more than anything, is the depth to which Yahya Jammeh will descend in order to control the Gambian people, under any circumstance, to achieve complete domination over their lives. During his reign, Yahya Jammeh has broken every known political convention in order to assert his rule. Still, the collective will of the people to fulfil their patriotic obligation, in pursuing justice, is sadly lacking. And when, last week, rumors swirled around, at home and abroad, of Yahya Jammeh's resignation, it was clear that there is a public underestimation of the total inability of tyrants to succumb to reasoning. More broadly, rather than focus on Yahya Jammeh's possible resignation, which goes against common sense, Gambians should be planning his exit through protest marches and demonstrations. Gambia's inconsolable story under Yahya Jammeh's terror, is an embarrassment of epic proposition, a tale of overbearing misuse of power and cruelty. More striking still, the state of denial, in Gambia and abroad, even as Gambia's economy sinks, has never been so apparent. And what speaks most to Gambians is the unravelling of an economy, which is causing dire hardship for Gambians across the country. In Gambia and around the globe, citizens' will to be free was never so compelling and forcefully expressed.

OPPOSITION UNITY PUTS GAMBIA ON PATH TO FREEDOM; ASSEMBLY BLUNDER

No one saw it coming. It hit the airwaves like a thunderbolt. Its effects, apart from being euphoric, are giving back to the Gambian people the long-lost sense of hope. The skepticism surrounding the opposition parties, which for long seemed locked in a state of permanent conflict and grandstanding, has historical precedence, but again, reconciliation among parties has always been a possibility. There is need for the Gambian opposition to overcome the insignificant bottlenecks that stood in the way of their coalescing around the life-and-death issues affecting the Gambia and begin the process of reengaging citizens across tribes and political affiliation, on matters germane to Gambia. Gambia's future is a collective responsibility, and the established political parties need to lead, and their unity last week burst out like spring desert flowers and mark the beginning of reestablishing the citizenship of blue-blood Gambians. For a significant number of diasporans, opposition unity, though desirable, has always seemed elusive. Now, it is the diaspora civil society organizations that are stalled in conflict and petty quibbles, even as Gambians' suffering continues to escalate. The support for opposition unity is reverberating in Gambian communities all around the world, and its promise is galvanizing citizens clamoring for political change. This time, the opposition unity glue seems to hold, even as fears of past self-serving efforts at unity cloud the public judgment with apprehension. Hopefully, political events around the world will, this time around, change Gambians' mindset about the political possibilities, even as the opposition and civil society face stiff resistance from a regime that, by its murderous history, long ago ceased to have a legal reason to exist. The opposition needs to leverage the combined power of civil society and the people, which is no match for the guns and bullets that Yahya Jammeh relies on, to keep him in power. After all, if Guinea-Conakry did it, Senegal did it, Ivory Coast did it, Mali did it, and Burkina Faso did it, it should be a cakewalk for a united political opposition, the Gambian population and civil society at home and abroad, to collapse Gambia's murderous, kleptomaniac regime.

Unlike any other year, since 1994, Gambia is confronting challenges that resonate with citizens of ECOWAS who successfully turned decades of political inertia into extraordinary determination to change their political circumstances. The political worldview in ECOWAS member states increasingly has no tolerance for the demagoguery of pariahs like Yahya Jammeh, a view that is supported by the international community, both governments and institutions set up to guarantee human dignity and safety from the political promiscuity of regimes that deprive citizens of their rights. The crux of the mushrooming universal political paradigm centers on returning political power to the people, to give them the tools to make free and unfettered choices. And political systems in West African countries are increasingly rejecting the ingrained notions of state supremacy, instead, constantly evolving to concede power to the lynchpin of democracy, a free people. In Gambia, where politics have regressed from being the most progressive in Africa to its most savage, the political revisionism of the past two decades is unparalleled, as is the high level of brutality and state control of the lives of a battered people. Yahya Jammeh has crossed every known boundary of acceptable human behavior, from daylight fatal shooting, to neck breaking, from public execution, to breast cutting, from economic plunder, to the Jolanization of the Gambia civil service. It is hard, if not impossible, to try to epitomize Yahya Jammeh's crimes against Gambians, even when he leaves office. Importantly, Gambia cannot be the only country left out on this cusp of the political change sweeping the African continent, and in particular, the West African region. Today, Gambia's necessary political change is predicated on the predominance of the regime's demonic moral depravity, which has spurred opposition to the criminal regime, at a time when rapid regional and global political change is transforming the science of politics into a more humane enterprise. Gambians can no longer afford the isolation of the country from the rest of the world, and it is citizens' prerogative to force political conformity to regional and international social and political norms. For it to happen, change is necessary. The Gambia is consequently at a crossroads; allow the barbarity to continue or forge a common path to total freedom.

To say Gambians face some daunting challenges is an understatement, and this has worsened with the passing of an Assembly Bill requiring political leaders to deposit exorbitant sums of money, which they cannot independently afford, as fee to contest the presidential elections. Barriers to political participation underlies the festering perversion of the political system in the Gambia, but the shackling of citizens' inalienable rights to have voices challenging the Gambians people to get more involved in satisfying their fundamental citizenship rights. Yahya Jammeh's fearsome attachment to asinine politics has only succeeded in perpetuating his own undoing, and that of his ruthless regime. When the so-called National Assembly passed the Bill limiting the political space, the outcry was swift and relentless. The rubber stamp National Assembly once again deferred to Yahya Jammeh's illegal manipulation of the political system, causing the descent into a political crisis. The inability of the National Assembly to act in the nation's interest baffled political pundits for two decades, but it is their conscious defense of Yahya Jammeh's seizure of the political space, and in so doing, emasculate the political opposition into an embarrassing redundancy that has left Gambians angry and fuming. And now, some members of the National Assembly, uneasy with the political chaos they have brought on Gambians by passing the electoral Bill, developed intolerance, resorting to the thuggish use of insults to the media who are simply trying to make sense of the political insanity. Gambia's political story has always been punctuated with the actions of the clueless and classless, and the so-called National Assembly has proven once again that they lack the judgment of impartiality, having already mortgaged their souls for money to Almighty Yahya Jammeh, who recently earned the unflattering title of one of Africa's five most uneducated political leaders. The passing of the controversial electoral Bill by the National Assembly yesterday may be a harbinger of what will happen to a Bill intended to amend the Constitution Death Penalty, making killing citizens as easy endeavor. A Gambian dissident aptly characterized the National Assembly this way: "MPs care for their today far more than everyone's tomorrow." This is the wise rambling of an angry Gambian dissident. I couldn't say it better.

THE CHALLENGE TO NOT DIVERGE FROM THE IMPORTANT, NECESSARY, AND INEVITABLE

It was a vigorous back-to-back manifestation of a new breath of political life. First, the Socialist party PDOIS held its annual Congress in Bansang and produced an ambitious seventeen-point action plan. This was followed by the UDP's nationwide tour, which commenced on a rather rough footing, entangled with the regime over what is clearly the party's most fundamental right. As the 2016 elections draw near, the political atmosphere seems shrouded in newfound giddiness, which on occasions burst out in seemingly uncontrollable euphoria. The undeniable success of the UDP's tour is reverberating across the length and breadth of the country as Gambians rediscover the freedom to participate in the electoral process without fear. Political developments back home have had similar effects on the diaspora, who embrace the determination and the path the opposition political parties are taking toward complete freedom from political underhandedness. It is a new day. Gambia is changing, not by the will of the regime, but in spite of it, by the force of the will of the people. For what is still new to the military regime is now old to the rest of the population—the fear, terror, intimidation. Yahya Jammeh cannot stop progress, and he has no option but to relent to the dynamic of the forces of nature in control of the course of change. At the start of this season's political campaign, the UDP slogan, "No Fear," became a fitting encapsulation of the two decades of opposition self-censorship straitjacketing, which often resulted in the ineffective campaign messaging. This year, the political turnaround is visible and profound, and once again, Gambians across the country are taking their solemn duties with patriotic urgency as crowds welcome the UDP at various campaign stops. It was almost like reliving a past that almost died under the weight of a regime whose core belief system is underpinned by a desire to completely alter the character of Gambian political life through social engineering based on tribal preferences and ethnic bigotry.

This political season has become a perfect storm, either by design or by an accident of nature, as the new rediscovery of opposition rights is complemented by the promise of political change from the regional and international communities. Fear of political tyranny across the African continent is exemplified by ECOWAS's recent efforts to twist the arms of the region's imperial leaders by instituting term limits. In their self-serving opposition to the term-limits proposal, Gambia's Yahya Jammeh and Togo's Faure Gnassingbé, succeeded in defeating the term-limit idea, "but it is far from dead," said Gambia's renowned technocrat and former foreign minister Sidi Moro Sanneh. The term-limits issue in ECOWAS will rise again to help limit the powers of ECOWAS's imperial monarchs, bring Africa to modernize its political systems, and stretch the frontier of democracy to its very limits. With human skeletons down in deep, dry wells, hidden graves disturbed by hungry, wild animals, the skeletons of small children, and hunger, emaciated bodies in Mile 2 Prison, Gambia is a political disaster waiting to happen. There is acknowledgment by both Gambians and the international community of a need for political change, and even with the tyranny of the Jola minority cast aside, Gambians have paid dearly with their lives in Yahya Jammeh's perpetual quest of instilling fear for the sole purpose of preempting the likelihood of his forcible removal by the military. Today, the choice is clear, and so are the objectives: removal of Yahya Jammeh's pernicious and dangerously military regime. But what is not clear, however, is the strategy to untangle citizens from the mythical appeal of Yahya Jammeh's tyranny and ways to liberate a segment of society consumed by the allure and the trappings of power, privilege, and tribal affinity. The rationales for rapid political change are abundant and easily definable; not so the strategies for achieving them. The ideas floated by Gambians occupy both ends of the spectrum, from forcible restoration of democracy and the rule of law, to democratic elections. In between both ends of the spectrum lies a range of many other options. What is clear is that political change through the democratic electoral process is not possible—not now, not as long as Yahya Jammeh is in complete control of the levers of power.

The Gambia's hostile political climate makes barring Yahya Jammeh from contesting elections in 2016 a viable and realistic option. This requires the creation of a transitional government of unity that brings the political opposition and civil society working in tandem to replicate a Burkina Faso–type uprising that seeks to return power to the people. With Senegal, Guinea-Conakry, and Burkina Faso acting as frames of reference, Gambians have the capacity to force change and end the long-running carnage. There is nothing more primeval than the desire to live in peace, and with this as a motivating factor, Gambians are obliged to coalesce around a cause that has the promise of removing the threat to their existence. At this stage, it is imperative that political parties continue to educate the population, with the objective of awakening citizens from political apathy and infusing them with the courage to make choices that speak to their collective needs. Crucially, it is imperative to broaden the scope of this political campaign season by not limiting the narrative to simple elections, but first and foremost inform Gambians about the carnage this regime has committed. Gambia is a country in crisis, at the crossroads of five more years of death and destruction, or forcible end to the tragedy that has consumed Gambia for two long decades. The political establishment must respond to citizens' calls with in urgency commensurate with the disaster that has continued to devastate the country. It behooves party leaders to transform the campaign season from its narrow self-censorship, to a broader national character that reaches citizens at a much deeper level of consciousness. As diaspora organizations seek to forge common ground, there are expectations that the political establishment will commit to unity, and working with civil society, there no force on earth that can stop the march to freedom. The executions, killings, mass incarcerations, fleeing of citizens, expulsion of international diplomats, and the high cost of living in the Gambia—there are sufficient reasons for citizens to engage in mass popular unrest to force political change. The stars are aligned for this to happen, and Gambians can no longer wait. Mass popular protests are within the constitutional rights to force change, and as ECOWAS and the free world wait to see change, Gambians are obliged to do what is necessary to bring peace to the Gambia's pitiful political circumstances.

CHAPTER 9

STRUGGLE FOR DEMOCRACY

GAMBIANS ARE FED UP AND HAVE FEARED WAY TOO LONG—NOT ANYMORE

It is a terrifyingly haunting story pregnant with mind-bending twists and sobering turns, a story of alienation with a sinister plot that manifests itself in the horrors and tragedies of death and dying. And it is not a work of fiction conjured up by someone's creative mind, but a story replete with the strain and strife of fear and the anxiety of uncertainty. Only Nietzsche's study of the deities, which obsessed the human imagination for centuries, comes close to the inquiring, thoughtful rigor that Gambia needs in order to study and put meaning to its political madness. The senselessness in the Gambia, unsupported by logic and morality, is a study in the inability to subsume the comfort of apathy and indifference to the disquieting fury of rebellion against state tyranny. But every action has a reaction, and there is no limit to the suffering endured in daily life of the Gambian people. Yahya Jammeh's insidious obsession with power and fixation with imposing fear in Gambian society is now clashing with reality. The Gambian psyche is conscious of Yahya Jammeh's Machiavellian state terror, and the pushback is inevitable, manifesting itself in the increased agitation for urgent political change in Gambia.

Yahya Jammeh's long-established platform of instilling terror in citizens can no longer assume Gambians will just recede in fear as vanquished objects of pity and helplessness. Across the globe, Gambians are defying the regime and, in the process, dismantling the foundation of terror that has long been the hallmark of the dictatorship. The reality of inevitability is finally permeating into Yahya Jammeh's impervious head, causing a seismic shift in his futile effort to mask the obvious signs of Gambia's desperation and international pressure. A sense of an inevitable departure from power looms large in Yahya Jammeh's mind, totally obscuring his sanity and driving him toward the edge of despair. Gambia's unilateral withdrawal from the Commonwealth and threats to sponsor demonstrations at both the British and American Embassies are Yahya Jammeh's way of lashing out at opponents to his tyranny. The inevitability of departure from power is finally transitioning the collective national struggle against tyranny to a critical phase, as citizens struggle to avoid a power vacuum in the event of his surreptitious departure. As political change begins to manifest out of the pain and agony of the past decades, signs of losing the battle are underpinned by a massive exodus from Gambian jurisdiction of a significant number of the Yahya Jammeh's inner circle.

The patently false notion of invincibility and Yahya Jammeh's cynicism contrast with the political undercurrent that is slowly seeping into the broader political landscape. The relentlessly overt and aggressive international pressure exerted by the European Union, the US State Department, African Union, Amnesty International, Media Foundation for West Africa, ECOWAS, Article 19, and the Gambia's relentless dissident movement, have wreaked havoc on the country's economy and silenced Yahya Jammeh's political hyperbole and empty messianic pretensions. In another evident sign of rupture of Yahya Jammeh's stranglehold on power, recent demonstrations in New York and the daring takeover of Gambia's embassy in Washington, DC, directly encapsulate the depth of frustration and the will to fight for political change. The New York and Washington, DC, events, widely supported by Gambians, were vehement portrayals of rejection of the status quo whose history was to silence those who dared to have different political voices. After a long period of fearful silence, Yahya Jammeh's obvious cravenness and ham-handed political manipulation are manifestations of the existential threat that his regime poses to Gambia's political stability.

There are no shortages of ideas about how political change in Gambia ought to look like, but the general consensus is to leverage Yahya Jammeh's economic failure to further garner international support in restoring the Gambia's democratic experiment and the rule of law. But even as the inevitability of change challenges Yahya Jammeh's sanity, he continues to double down on even more pernicious political tactics, which, in the recent past, included the abduction of dissidents from Dakar, Senegal and the recent arrests and incommunicado detention of US citizens vacationing in the Gambia, Alhagi Ceesay and Ebou Jobe. Additionally, Yahya Jammeh's intolerance of the Mandinka people and mortifying fear of the power of the United Democratic Party betray his spinelessness and fear of political change. The ad hominem attacks on Ousainou Darboe and accusations of tribal bigotry are demonstrations of the searing paranoia that tortures Yahya Jammeh's sanity. Matter of fact, Gambians have long been galvanized against Yahya Jammeh's ubiquitous tribal bigotry, and consequently view his baseless accusation of Ousainou Darboe as a cruel joke. After nearly two decades of tactlessness, Gambians are fed up with being fearful of Yahya Jammeh, and are ready for political change. Given Yahya Jammeh's abstraction of reality and preoccupation with political survival, inability to recognize the contours of the end days, by Yahya Jammeh is no surprise. But the fact is; dictators are never rational, and that is also the tragedy of Yahya Jammeh.

WE HAVE FAILED THEM, OUR OWN
WRETCHED OF THE EARTH

The setting sun casts its reddish glow across the whitewashed perimeter fence where the shadow of the tall crimson eastern wall struggles to stretch out across the highway. The aura of serenity and sombreness that surrounds the place was at once strange and awe striking, mysterious and frightening. Darkness was slowly setting in over the imposing metal gate that faces the surging sea where the serenely majestic Gambia River empties into the mighty Atlantic Ocean. And across the Sere-Kunda highway, beneath a canopy of lush green brush, a female Agamidae lizard scampered hurriedly into the underbrush, pursued closely by a much larger, yellow-headed male lizard in much need of reptilian affection. Barely visible in the growing darkness, an eerie sign festooned the imposing rusting metal gate, which long ago began to rust with age. The menacing sign on the heavy metal gate said it all and then some: Mile 2 Central Prison. The name Mile 2 Central Prison conjures up images of brutality unheard of elsewhere on the African continent— images of death, torture, emaciation, and extrajudicial executions.

Mile 2 Central Prison is a place where death and dying have become routine, and visible hopelessness and despair have reduced a once vibrant people to despair and self-pity. For the scores of Gambians who remain locked up in Mile 2 Prison, it is as if time stopped. Behind the impenetrable Mile 2 Prison walls are the desperate people whose reality is confined to what their tormented minds can dream, dreams as real as the ghosts of the whispering hills of Sare Hella. Theirs is a world of fantasy and of make-believe far removed from the real world. Whatever it is, and however much we try to bring their predicament to life, give meaning to the senseless world that surrounds them, and draw attention to their helplessness, one thing is certain: Mile 2 Central Prison is as much a curse and an aberration to the conscience. Mile 2 Prison is cruel and debasing; an eyesore, which under Yahya Jammeh has found its rightful place in Gambia's unwritten history—there to remain etched into our collective memories for the rest of time.

Mile 2 Central Prison is a colonial-era institution, but the genesis of its new notoriety is a Gambian phenomenon, the creation of Yahya Jammeh's military regime. Only a little over a decade ago, Mile 2 Prison did not strike fear in the hearts of Gambians. Today, by a cruel fate, the prison complex has come alive for all the wrong reasons. Around the clock every day, thousands of commuters and hundreds of vehicles ply the Banjul and Serekunda highway, oblivious of the suffering behind the tall, oppressive walls of the prison: the unbearable tortures prisoners are subjected to, the unthinkable cruelty the prison is synonymous with, and the hundreds of prisoners who have given up on life, because no one can help them, and no one can save them from the stranglehold of a madman whose regime brought disrepute to a once peaceful nation. The Gambia is a changed country, for it has turned into a place where its people, once vibrant and hopeful, can no longer think for themselves or pursue their dreams, free, secure, and unafraid. More than any other institution, Mile 2 Prison represents the inveterate canker of a regime whose era came and went long ago, not unlike regimes with panache for drama lies in the graves of the cruel men who gave us an era we will never forget—Idi Amin, Sekou Toure, Mobutu Sese, and "Emperor" Bokassa. As these murderous dictators of a long-gone era rot in their graves and the living of their kind face a hostile new world, the Gambia, of all countries, is living a life of evil and cruelty of a time so long gone, an era of political martyrdom represented in murals and tombstones carved in the blood of those who sacrificed their lives so others may have freedom: Gdansk; Prague; Birmingham, Alabama; Soweto; and Tiananmen Square.

Among the dead are names with faces, and names with no faces, but their spirits still speak to us in our waking moments and in our dreams. Yet Gambians have failed to live up to the causes for which many gave up their lives, the political awakening they banqueted to us, the exemplary lives by which they lived and died, and the freedom inherited in their dying. In the blue skies over Mile 2 Prison, the troubled ghost of Jallow

Union floats above in agony, the mortified soul of Steve Biko, paralyzed with disbelief, and the eloquent spirit of Stokely Carmichael roam in restless frustration. As the bodies of long-ago political martyrs turn into the salt of the earth, they remind us of the freedoms we own, that are taken away from us, not by accident, but by cruel calculation of a tyrant. Today they demand us to take back that long lost freedom, the freedom they championed until they drew their last dying breaths.

Mid-morning around Mile 2 Prison plays out much like nature's theatre in all its awesomeness. To the east, where the blue Atlantic Ocean is locked with the River Gambia in a million-year embrace, the lazy waves flap incessantly against the serene coastline, slowly eating the sandy beach away to create small, fragile sand cliffs. In the distance, across the grayish sea, Barra Town slave fort, in all its medieval allure, is clearly visible below which seagulls, in hunger-driven resolve, dive ceaselessly into the warm waters to pluck out unsuspecting fish from beneath the rippling waves. To the west of Mile 2 Prison, wide expanses of swampland teeming with marine life stretch westward toward Bakau, Talinding, Mandinari, and southward as far as the eye can see. But neither the demeanor of the nearby Palm Grove Hotel nor the unpretentious solemnity that surrounds Wadner Beach can exorcise Mile 2 Prison of its visible deadliness. In a strange way, there was uniqueness about Mile 2 Prison that mirrored images of Dachau, Auschwitz, Tiananmen Square, and Treblinka. Inside the tall fortified walls of the prison, lurks an uneasy quiet behind the innocent exterior look, the captivating manifestation of its unforgiving cruelty.

Everywhere one looks, the invisible scars of Mile 2 Prison saturate the cool ocean breeze to showcase one more place where dreams go to perish. As darkness engulfs Mile 2 Prison, melancholic solitude slowly shrouds the prison in pity and sadness, but inside the prison proper, a hundreds of eyeballs, as bright as the stars, stare listlessly into the nothingness. In a far corner of the prison yard, an emaciated human body, with skeletal bones visible from the distance, stares listlessly at the concrete wall and mutters barely audible gibber to himself. In this oppressive environment, Mile 2 Prison has turned into a place of utter misery, not into a place where people go to atone for their wrongs to society. Mile 2 Prison is a place where people go to die. In the mind's eye, the prisoners are visible, mere shadows of their former selves—the hungry, sick, hardened skin, the skeletal frames of bodies with big, bright, sunken eyes, and the frightened looks that spelled death a million times as in Treblinka, Auschwitz, and other places of darkness. Many Gambians have died in Mile 2 Prison, more in one decade under Yahya Jammeh's dictatorship than the entire history of the prison, and still they continue to die of hunger, sickness, and torture. There are the executed whose gravesites remain unknown, unmarked, and out of sight. They were our friends too, brothers, sisters, neighbors, family, and fellow Gambians. But we seem not to care. We have turned our backs on them, and they suffer in silence as time and the world pass them by. The Gambia's wretched prisoners are defeated and stalked by death, our forgotten, left to their own devices, in despair and without hope, not knowing whether they will live to see one more day. Yet in their hearts, they keep praying to an unknown deity for one more day of life, just one more day.

MORAL JUSTICE, RESPONSIBILITY TO PROTECT TRUMPS THE NONINTERFERENCE CLAUSE

The brazen extrajudicial execution of ten military officers in 1994, was only a sign of things to come. But not even the deadly, primitive 2009 witch-hunting exercise or the 2012 execution of nine Mile 2 Prison inmates could inspire international action against the violence perpetrated by Gambia's terrorist military regime. Over the years, regional and international indifference to Gambia's dire human rights abuses have galvanized Gambians to coalesce around the theme of regime change, in an effort to restore sanity and rule of law by whatever means necessary. Without pressure from the international community, Gambians see the removal of a deadly regime as the only means to end the cruel bloodletting that has ravaged the country for the past two decades. When change of government through the electoral ballot box process becomes impossible, expression of popular discontent through protests and street demonstrations disallowed, Gambians are left with no option with which to change their government. Great Britain, the United States, the European Union, African Union, Senegal, ECOWAS, and the political opposition in the Gambia, the governments and institutions with the economic, diplomatic, and political muscle to bring to bear on the Gambian regime, have not reacted more forcefully to the plight of the Gambian people. This is where the rubber meets the road. Without legal recourse, and with regional and international recalcitrance, should Gambians be forced to accept the disastrous human right abuses as divinely ordained, thus give the human right abuses a veneer of legality, or should Gambians recognize the moral imperative to end the suffering of fellow citizens by any means necessary?

After years of sensitizing the international community to the rights crisis by the terrorist regime and the urgency of political change in the Gambia, across the world, leaders of Gambia's dissident movement have determined that international neglect of human rights crisis in the Gambia was driven by the archaic doctrine of non-interference in the internal affairs of other nations. The Gambians' dissident movement realized early on that they were alone to tackle the problem of regime change to save lives. The determination by Gambian dissidents across the world to return to the rule of law through regime change, which itself came to power through the use of force, was not taken lightly. Equally important, Dec. 30, 2014, would not have occurred if international recognition of the deadly rights abuses in the Gambia was on par with the gravity of the state terrorism. The desperation to change their regime and end two decades of executions, killings, disappearance, and mass incarceration is a no-brainer, and for the Gambians to defer to a United Nations resolution that bans change of government other than through the electoral process is, in light of the barbarism in Gambia, unsupportable, and tactically leaves the Gambia's dissident movement between a rock and a hard place. Indifference to the plight of Gambians has emboldened Yahya Jammeh to push the boundary of gristly human rights abuses, and in the aftermath of the foiled Dec. 30, 2014, coup, the crackle of machine-gun fire, the rivers of blood as victims cry of agony, and the corpses of the dead fed to zoo animals, and Gambians will once again cry for their dead.

As it is, US and Senegal's intelligence investigation into the December 30, 2014, activities has left Gambians with the challenge of choosing between legal right versus moral responsibility. The international community, led by the United States, appears to support the doctrine of noninterference in other nations' internal affairs, thus creating a conflict with a new United Nations law, which gives weight to the "responsibility to protect" citizens of nations under tyranny. In support of the recently failed effort to restore the rule of law in the Gambia and end the state sanctioned executions, murders, mass incarceration, Gambians will resist laws that kneecap their exercise of moral responsibility in protecting their fellow citizens. Gambia's dissident movement is firmly anchored in the belief in the responsibility to protect fellow citizens from state terrorism, and will use every means necessary to achieve that goal. The responsibility of the international community at this point is to prevent the revenge bloodletting of accused victims, and assist Gambians in changing their political circumstances. The December 30, 2014, effort to protect Gambians from a terrorist regime has failed, but the determination to restore sanity in the Gambia is a powerful commitment that has basis in morality. Against all odds, the Gambia's relentless online media has put a small African country devoid of natural resources on the map of political consciousness. The responsibility now is for the US, Great Britain, EU, AU, ECOWAS, and the Senegalese government to determine whether Gambians deserve protection from the executions, murders, disappearance, and mass incarcerations perpetrated by Gambia's terrorist regime.

The international community has a moral responsibility to uphold the doctrine to protect Gambian citizens, and US Justice Department must recognize the December 30, 2014, event as an effort to end twenty years of state terrorism. In light of this, Gambians call on Attorney General Eric Holder's Justice Department to help set free Gambian Americans in custody. The protection of Gambian lives is always an act of moral righteousness that should never be subjected to legal scrutiny, or the US Justice Department risks alienating Gambians and exposing US stubborn indifference to the plight of Gambian citizens. Gambians stand firmly for the dead and the living dead who attempted to give their country the freedom they yearned for. And Gambians will never deviate from the determination to free their country from the clutches of a murderous tyrant, and in that alone, every Gambian citizen can be counted as complicit in the December 30, 2014, effort to save lives and free its people. If that is grounds to be cast as acting illegally, then Gambians will plead guilty as accused. More important, Gambian Americans should never be tried for being concerned about the genocide in the Gambia. The "Responsibility to Protect" or "R2P" UN doctrine elaborates that I, "the State carries the primary responsibility for protecting populations from genocide, war crimes, crimes against humanity and ethnic cleansing, and their incitement; 2; that the international community has a responsibility to encourage and assist States in fulfilling this responsibility; and 3; the international community has a responsibility to use appropriate diplomatic, humanitarian and other means to protect populations from these crimes." The R2P adds, "if a State is manifestly failing to protect its populations, the international community must be prepared to take collective action to protect populations, in accordance with the Charter of the United Nations. Moral Justice would be judging things according to their subjective rightness or wrongness, as opposed to strictly following the law."

THE BECKONING OF RALEIGH AND THE
HARROWING CALLS TO SWEET CAROLINA

There is growing resistance to the Gambian regime; a coalition forming to coalesce around a central theme that has dominated Gambian life and politics for more than a decade and a half. It is belated, yet it is coming not a moment too soon. Raleigh, North Carolina, represents more than just the condemnation of Yahya Jammeh's cruel perversion; it is a prelude to Gambia's emerging history, and the preface of a new dawn. Raleigh symbolizes a history written and recited in our collective weary voices, voices that echo the hopeless cries and the painful agony of our citizens. North Carolina is where the beautiful poems and the delightful narratives of sages and budding minds will go to slowly die, only to be resurrected by the dreadful reality of the Gambia's impossible story of deaths, executions, and disappearances. The British High Commissioner in Gambia, David Morley, last week echoed the moment's urgency in a damning Human Rights Report (HRP) on Gambia, and this week, the US Secretary of State John Kerry, in his 2012 Gambia Human Rights Report, echoed the British High Commission's painfully agonizing frustration with Yahya Jammeh's politics, and Gambia's nauseating story of executions, a country once dubbed Africa's smiling coast, now turned into Africa's most notorious rogue nation. The story of how Gambia got to this painful moment of anguish will be told by those yet unborn. Our collective responsibility as Gambians is to deflect the story and rewrite the history so that tomorrow they will tell the tale of the hardship endured in the struggle so that we can leave them a country and a free people free, liberated once again.

As it is, Gambians today occupy places high and low around the world, and their signs of distress and determination embody an intense desire for political change and the reestablishment of democracy and the rule of law. Eighteen long years after the ascension of Yahya Jammeh's military AFPRC regime to power, the disaffection with military rule has prompted stubborn resistance from Gambians around the globe.

Yahya Jammeh's Machiavellian motivation is underpinned by more than just a fantasy for longevity in political power, but by a rapaciousness that make Ferdinand Marcos's rape of the Philippines resources look like child's play. Gambia's human rights record remains disastrous, the economy is gradually heading down the gutter, living conditions are slowly moving toward sustainability, businesses are fleeing the climate of intrusion, and Gambians are distressed and demand political change. After all the pain, silent suffering, and lonely weeping, Raleigh offers an avenue for change and a promise to carve out a niche for Gambia's massive diaspora population working around the globe. Crucially, the agitation for change is unequivocal, inspiring a new frame of mind that promises to draw Gambians to coalesce around the seminal issue of unity. Alkali Conteh, head of GDAG, Raleigh, may still be a new name to many, but Banka Manneh, head of STGDP and CSAG, is a household name and a powerful voice in the diaspora community, and together they are unequivocal in their determination for political change. As Raleigh, promises to begin the removal of the horrifying scepter of Yahya Jammeh, the terrible necessity for national unity is the single most important and dominant force.

To date, Gambians have experienced numerous false starts in the unending struggle to remove Yahya Jammeh from power, but Raleigh, this time, is pregnant with the promise of hope. This year, the brilliant concept of Raleigh is more than a flight of fancy; it is a studied architecture of the mind of a people, above all, a true reflection of the collective will of the Gambian people. With the addition of Gambia's world-renowned diplomat, Dr. Momodou Sedat Jobe, to the struggle, the stage for political change has been set. Dr. Sedat Jobe, renowned for his weekly scathing attacks on the Gambian regime, symbolizes the jettisoning of inertia and the rebirth of a new revolutionary mind-set. And Gambian professor. Abdoulaye Saine, more than anyone else, is an unsung hero of this moment, whose inspiring presence in Raleigh, is crucial to the meeting. Moreover, Gambians of significant stature are expected to grace Raleigh next month, including former vice president

BB Dabo, and recently released Dr. Amadou Scattered Janneh. This year, the arch of history is calling, above all, Raleigh portends the demise of our abstraction of reality and cynical detachment from the relentless barbarity that has devastatingly consumed Gambia for so long. But in Raleigh, there is a dream for a new Gambia where citizens will unfold their wings and fly again, where they can talk to the invisible spirit fearful where the haunting night sounds of Dankunku and Sambang *sabarrs* gripped my childhood mind in awe and joy, and where from Koina to Kartong, the winds of political change will once again cry out, "Never again."

RALEIGH AND THE URGENCY OF POLITICAL CHANGE

It is now an integral part of Gambian history. The Raleigh Conference, that is. But it is not history as in things past. Raleigh is still ongoing, still under a slow, painful birth, still emerging out of the dark shadow of the Gambia's tragic story, and still being crafted into Gambia's political reality. One can rightly argue that Gambia is exceedingly messy, both in its politics as well as its economics, even laden with smoldering bitterness beneath the surface of tranquility, and some Gambians are divided by the nonsensicality of their individual illusions of egotism, but there is nothing idealistic about aspiring for a Gambia that is free from the vicissitudes of corruption and political tyranny. The right to freedom is a natural instinct, essential to living like a being human, and its supremacy must never be compromised or subject to the whip of despots and political manipulation. The meticulous planning that went into making Raleigh a reality reflects the pathetic political conundrum that has wreaked havoc on the Gambia's cultural homogeneity and moral rectitude, which for generations had defined the true Gambian spirit. The surprising 1994 coup, which initially generated a groundswell of support, irreversibly devastated Gambia and led to the ongoing social disarray and political confusion, but not even the cruel bloodlust could confound Gambians' sense of nationalism and patriotism.

The true meaning of Raleigh was, therefore, to arouse our jealously guarded nationalistic fervor for a cause greater than our individuals inflated senses of our worth. But Raleigh also questioned the depth to which Gambians would go, the breadth to which they will venture, and the extent to which they will sacrifice in order to restore dignity to a brutalized country. Raleigh, as an event of historical significance, may now belong to the past, yet its aims and visions live on in our collective commitment to a free Gambia. The resolutions that came out of Raleigh are a mature and balanced approach, with potentials for success in lieu of Gambia's notoriously partisan electoral system. To further foil prospects to alter the political landscape, Yahya Jammeh, over the past several years, stripped the Gambian military of its intellectual capacity, moral fortitude and ability to force regime change in Gambia. But Raleigh has come to signify the opening of an avenue that will carry Gambia toward a new political dispensation. Raleigh crafted a resolution that is striking in many ways, but particularly, because it called for the formation of a steering committee. From personal knowledge, different Gambian groups and individuals support different individuals to head a united civil society; nonetheless, we have a unique opportunity to end the unnecessary bickering over this issue.

As it stands, the new and still-forming Gambia Consultative Council (GCC), which has the most comprehensive list of Gambian organizations and individuals involved in the liberation struggle, originally planned to hold the election of an executive committee to lead the struggle, but the recent UK Congress and Raleigh Conference have together preempted much of GCC's original plans and forced the organization's rethinking of a new direction. It is worth noting that prior to the Raleigh Resolution, GCC concluded that the divisiveness that could result from electing its executive committee was unnecessary and preventable. GCC, therefore, proposed the formation of a steering committee, which incidentally the Raleigh Conference proposed as well.

Now that a common ground is created between Raleigh and GCC, we should collectively agree that Gambians need to put our best feet out to lead the effort in regaining our country. Gambians who GCC proposes to lead our collective effort have earned the right, because they have better and more broadly recognizable resumes. In this ongoing struggle, GCC recognizes the selfless efforts of every Gambian, but in order to achieve the success we desire, a leadership organizational structure is required, and the formation of a steering committee is an appropriate beginning.

MY LAST ACT; THE LAST BATTLE

I had a dream. Not a Martin Luther King Jr. dream. A Mathew Kali Jallow dream. I was home and out of my depth. But naivety did not take me back. My dream did. Home had turned into a whole new world of conflict and contradictions. And I was caught in its crossfire. I was a sitting duck in the crosshairs that lent pungency to the fear marked on people's faces. Serekunda was bustling. But not how you think. It was a city in atrophy, the epicenter of a melodrama that was beyond the arch of my imagination. The battlefront had no lines. The war scars were everywhere, enshrined in the timid swagger and muffled voices visible on the hallowed faces of the mosaic and tapestry that is Gambia. The moral limits imposed by social norms left no impression, no imprint on the code of our people's lives. The paradoxically ubiquitous and invisible minefield of state power that demands rigid compliance to unreasonable state order left a blueprint where everyone had to march in lockstep, and retribution against slight, real or imagined, was exercised beyond the forceful use of words. In the quiet back alleys of my old stomping grounds of Dippakunda, Sere-Kunda, mud-drenched roadside ditches, uncongenial moon crater pathways, and Kilimanjaro-high road bumps all seem to predicate the excesses of state power. The fanciful regurgitation of state grit, monotonous and conspicuous on the airwaves, surpassed the limits of propaganda to assume the color indoctrination.

Beyond the nastiness of the ad hominem propaganda attacks on the national airwaves, even the streets seemed to sense the subterfuge that consumes the state's reckless exercise of authority. It seemed the more things changed, the more they remained the same. The art of reasoning was crowded out by the drought of moral and ethical norms and robbed people of their dignities. On my nostalgic walk around the back roads of Sere Kunda, I occasionally was drowned in the unfolding drama of life, often becoming absurdly oblivious of my surroundings. I tripped and stumbled with abhorrent regularity, and in a place where even the subtle nuances in life can be seen to reverberate hostile intent, I seem to have lost the soundtrack of my life. Everywhere I looked, it seemed the blighted dirt roadways were hostile, furious, and unwelcoming. The streets seemed to speak to me laconically in an unintelligible, didactic language alphabetized in the characters of fear and terror. As the epitome of a political gadfly, I lost my edge and, with it, the veneer of moral sanctimony that defined the proud legacy of freedom and liberty to which I am remorselessly wedded. So callously threatening was the invincible state power that ignited the long-running pedantic sermons for civility in the political discourse. But the aberration of the unethical and immoral, exacerbated by brutal ignorance of the state, had a grip on power under the spurious rubric of maintaining public order.

As I walked around the metropolis of SereKunda, in all deliberate haste, my eyes were fixed, for no particular reason, on the oncoming mass of humanity. Minding my business, might I add, my calm demeanor did not betray the intense apprehension that consumed my thoughts. But even in my complacency, whatever could go wrong was far from my mind. I, after all, imagined myself as Gambia's Centurion, with a tint of Wole Soyinka and a tinge of Chinua Achebe, and like T. S. Eliot and Fredric Nietzsche, I belong to the pantheon of thinkers, making no apology for the depth of my curiosity. But now, standing by the dry riverbed on the west side of Dippa Kunda, it soon became clear that in so many ways, Sere Kunda was the poster city for everything that could go so horribly wrong in the Gambia. Gambia was no longer recognizable, and it seemed as if I was walking on enemy territory, a castaway into a pond where reptilian bloodlust threatened to devour me in a pandemonium of carnivorous feasting. It mattered not that I had just returned home, or rather, what I thought was my home, from faraway lands. In the asinine political unorthodoxy shamefully displayed in the hostile language of platitudes and rhetorical flourish, even I was a stranger in the backwoods where I once lived and played. Not even the fiercely apolitical escaped the wholesale victimization of citizens demonstrated by Yahya Jammeh's total lack of objective rationality.

The manifestations of state insecurity, characteristic of the indiscipline of unchecked power, was exacerbated by fear of an intensifying groundswell centered on the singular objective of freeing Gambia from political tyranny. The state's adventure into the depths of ignorance has permeated every aspect of life, and the debilitating consequences of this morass has drawn Gambia toward the inevitable cusp of political change. The constricting and claustrophobic lack of freedom, out of touch with the times, has given rise to the impetus to splurge in a final act of patriotism; to free Gambia. Gambians are increasingly transcending the fear, which for long emasculated the country into a state of apathy, self-pity, and indifference. The corruption of the absolute state power in the Gambia is more than just pithy cliché; it is real and demonstrates the ham-handedness of the state's tyrannical tribal bigotry. But as my nighttime experience demonstrates, it was more than just a dream; it was real, and it exposed a culture brutally rejected by revolutionary Gambians. For a person who lived a life of activism, whose lifetime experiences have more than once pushed him into despair; hunger, and homelessness, accepting tyranny in the Gambia is never an option. The struggle to push Yahya Jammeh out—or die trying—will be the culmination of my life of activism. It will be my last act of patriotism, my last battle.

THE UNFINISHED BUSINESS OF RALEIGH

The idea of the Raleigh Conference was not born out of lofty political ideals or driven by ideology, nor was it impelled by illusions of utopian grandeur. After all, the nineteenth century is long gone, and with it Karl Marx's dialectical materialism and Vladimir Lenin's proletarian revolution, effectively ending the anarchistic revolutionary fervor of political puritanism and egalitarian fantasy of that century. Raleigh was conceived at a time Gambians were wrapped up in fierce political struggle to replicate the story of La Guinea, Ivory Coast, Mali; democratization or risk relapsing into the familiar carnage of 1981 coup attempt. Like the fearsome Libyans, Syrians, Egyptians, and Tunisians who rose to their circumstances and demanded change to the political system, the Gambia is also faced with daunting challenges, which demand unleashing the nationalist fervor and avoid the comfort of partisanship, which is untempered by competence and political sagacity. Raleigh was preceded by the high drama of hope, and even higher optimistic euphoria for the possibilities of coalescing around an issue so seminal in the Gambia's political discourse. Last week, the unveiling of the steering committee was an anticlimactic event, unsettling and incredulous in its daring. Moreover, the process itself was painfully slow, challenged by lack of definition of the broader dissident agenda. The idea is to marry the dissident movement's political and economic agenda with the capacity to galvanize citizens in the political struggle. If the Raleigh select committee was unbound by the contentious difference in political viewpoints or perhaps even dismissive of the need to crowd Gambians into a single unifying mind-set, the unveiling of a steering committee expressed this in the lousiness and amateurism with which the soaring aspirations of the united Raleigh Conference deescalated into crippling manifestation of disunity. Without any equivocation, the formation of the new Raleigh Steering Committee screams out loud for its striking lack of the pretense of pursuing transparency. Even if few representatives of the Gambia's dissident community shroud Raleigh with uninspiring exuberance, the truth remains: its shortcomings outweighs the possibility of the historic conference. For Raleigh promised attitudes that will elevate the political discourse in Gambia and create a cohesive agenda; instead, its display of barriers to its own success is evident in its paternalism and scant analytical decision-making.

The absence of key voices from the Raleigh Steering Committee does raise serious questions, but equally important, the deliberate surrender to mediocrity, so painfully obvious, has stained the hope that Raleigh represents. Effort to create a unified Gambia political force has become more challenging, as obstacles to create cohesion have been created by the Raleigh Conference. But the arch of history has always bent to the need for change, and that could ensure that the promise of Raleigh is not flamed out by the unflattering failure of unifying Gambians. At this point, the reconstitution of the Raleigh Steering Committee is the sticking point, which stands in the way of a unity against Gambia's brutal dictatorship. Raleigh's dismissiveness of dissenters in its steering committee shows intolerance, but above all, highlights the deep differences in understanding of the needs of the Gambia's dissident movement. The withering criticism of the composition of the Raleigh Steering Committee, besides echoing apparent misunderstanding of the dissident movement's direction, is an expression of the difference in strategy. Meanwhile, as the Raleigh Conference enters its second week, the chances of reconstituting the steering committee to create a united front are challenged by the readiness to open a new front in the struggle for political liberation. Until then, the unfinished business of Raleigh, its mediocrity and amateurism will stand out as relics of the incompetence that belies the historic failure that Gambian's past unity efforts are renowned for.

THE GAMBIA'S LOOMING ECONOMIC
AND POLITICAL CRISIS

For those Gambians with even the most basic knowledge of economics, it seems inevitable. And it is. It is only a matter of time before the looming economic implosion—not whether. For something that began on that fateful July day back in 1994, the unraveling of the Gambian economy is a long time in the making. The dire consequences of Yahya Jammeh's Armed Forces Provisional Ruling Council's (AFPRC) voodoo economics are coming back to bite, and no amount of glowing World Bank and IMF economic reports can restrain the hardship precipitated by Yahya Jammeh's economic blunder. For nineteen years, Gambia willfully operated outside the Weberian administrative system and Keynesian economic model, adopting, instead, a paternalistic brand of African economic management and bureaucratic administration that is impulsive, arbitrary, capricious, and erratic. Since Yahya Jammeh's reign of horror began in 1994, the Gambia has witnessed a steady economic decline, from the robust civil service and state bureaucracy and market economy of the Sir Dawda Jawara era, to an austere descent into social and economic entropy. Yahya Jammeh's spiteful disregard of the universal principles of bureaucratic administration and economic management combined to ruin Gambia's governance; plunging its once vibrant civil service and bureaucracy in deleterious dysfunction and state of utter hopelessness.

Gambia's slow slide into administrative and economic paralysis is evidenced by the chaotic and senseless hiring and firing of civil service managers, as well as a runaway price increases of basic commodities. For the first time since political independence, Gambians are literally starving, and a significant number of families can only afford one square meal a day. The price of food, which increases every few months, are out of reach of most Gambian families. Gambia's worsening food security crisis is far removed from the Sir Dawda K Jawara era, when agriculture accounted for 75 percent of the national GDP, and employment was at par with the productivity levels. And additionally, Sir Dawda Jawara's successive governments subscribed to economic and administrative policies that supported robust GDP growth, individual productivity, and higher employment rates. Under Sir Dawda K Jawara, Gambia's civil service and public bureaucracy were accredited authority to set national goals and objectives, design annual agency and departmental plans, and set budgets specifically designed to respond to departmental and agency goals and benchmarks, diffusion of authority in the civil service, total noninterference in the business and commercial activities, and the absence of impulsive and arbitrary manipulation of the financial market. Sir Dawda K Jawara's renowned deference to the tried and tested market economy and bureaucratic management, truly set him apart from most African leaders.

The policies Sir Dawda Jawara adopted heralded, were a dawn in Gambia's social and political awakening, economic development and intellectual evolution, unmatched by any African country. The administrative and economic template Sir Dawda's successive governments embraced supported economic growth, though his efforts were subverted by pervasive corruption and a civil service that was nonetheless saintly in comparison to Yahya Jammeh's notoriously criminal regime. Unlike Sir Dawda Jawara's ruling political party, Yahya Jammeh's ruling military AFPRC party lacks a defined political ideology, and, by extension, a governing philosophy that could dictate a viable course of social and economic development. Yahya Jammeh's governing mentality, rather than empower the bureaucracy, instead emasculated the civil service and rendered the bureaucracy inefficient, dysfunctional, and in total disarray. Yahya Jammeh's dependence on primitive African witchcraft and sorcery as governing ideas plunged Gambia back into its pre-religion animism and devil worship, and his ignorance of tribal history are regenerating dangerous tribal divisions of our ancestors. Few in the civil service, from secretary general to the rank and file, possess the qualifications, other than being praise singers for Yahya Jammeh, or belong to his Jola tribe. But, worse still, the never-ending harassment of businesses and the recent clamp down and seizure of millions of dollars from business entrepreneurs has turned Gambia into Africa's most unfriendly business environment.

Today, Gambian businesses face relentless harassment for kickbacks, and wealthy Guinea Fulas are closing their businesses, forced out by harassment for bribes, for opportunities in Senegal and back to West Africa's wealthiest country, Guinea-Conakry. The proliferation of banks to launder money from the Gambia's drug-infested economy, Yahya Jammeh's monopoly of most businesses, constant currency manipulation, total lack of guiding principles, arbitrariness of economic and administrative decision-making, an investor-hostile environment, political and human rights crimes, which include mass executions, murders, and disappearance, and the arrests and detentions that perpetually hangs over citizens have singly, and in combination, made Gambia's slogan as West Africa's smiling coast a ridiculous joke. And potential investors lured to Gambia with empty promises, outright lies, and propaganda are forewarned that Gambia is awash with illegal drug money, and the country is a major transit point for illegal South American drugs bound for the US, Europe and other destinations in West Africa. Due largely to the deadly human rights abuses and adverse business environment, Gambia's economy will, sooner or later, collapse under the weight of the regime's tyranny and hostile business environment. In a meeting last week at the State House, *Freedom* newspaper reported that Secretary General Lamin Sabally pleaded to religious leaders to ask Gambia's online papers to desist from criticizing the regime, and Alieu Mboge interjected that his son knows online media owners and can prevail on them to stop criticizing the regime. We are still waiting anxiously to hear from religious leaders and Alieu Mboges's son.

THE IMF IS WRONG AGAIN ON
THE GAMBIAN ECONOMY

The report that the Yahya Jammeh regime bribed IMF auditors to write, so that these corrupt officials will prepare a glowing report on Gambia's annual economic performance, is shocking. In a country where data collection is nonexistent, and the economic performance is not recorded, where the economy operates outside the ambit of the market economy, where the GDP, important indicator of a country's economic progress, is not measured, and where the informal economy cannot be recorded with any degree of accuracy but accounts for a significant amount of the in-country, cross-border, and regional trade, any report prepared by the IMF and other institutions, rather than do justice to the Gambia, will instead give the regime an illusion of accomplishment, when, in reality, the economy is going down the drain, due to the lack of productivity, endemic corruption, mismanagement, and waste The financial records of the Central Bank indicate a different reality from what Gambians live every day. It is not a secret that everyone with an ounce of common sense knows that African institutions and their governments are notorious for cooking their financial records in order to fool international institutions that audit them into believing their countries are making economic progress, when the reality on the streets and countryside tell a different story. The Gambia is perhaps the most notorious fudger of records in Africa. But the dubious IMF reports on the Gambian economy are not unlike fake reports prepared for the Commonwealth secretariat, relating to the massacre of forty-four Ghanaian nationals in Gambia. That report, on this heinous act of brutality committed at the behest of Yahya Jammeh, is incomplete, the investigation was a farce, and the conclusion makes a mockery of the justice systems of the Gambia and Ghana, who prepared it. It is clear that Yahya Jammeh will give anything to make this Ghanaian massacre story go away, but until the full accounting of this barbaric incident is provided to the satisfaction of Gambian civil society organizations, at home and abroad, this story will remain open so long as the regime's accountability to Gambians and Ghanaians falls short.

The citizens of our two countries demand that the Gambian regime uses its infinite power to bring this saga to a truthful conclusion, by confessing its role in the massacre and by finally bringing the guilty to account for their crimes. And while we are at it, the broke Jackson brothers, led by their self-loathing sibling Jermaine, need to be told that they are doing Gambians a disservice by associating with the criminal murderer, Yahya Jammeh. More importantly, any dollar taken from Yahya Jammeh is food taken from the mouths of poor Gambian children. Gambia is a poor country, and the millions of dollars Yahya Jammeh will give Jermaine Jackson is money our country owes to the World Bank and the IMF. The Gambia is already an impoverished country, and this should not be made worse than it is. But I cannot reference the lack of dignity of the broke Jermaine Jackson without remembering Mr. Khan, the idiot that Yahya Jammeh recently appointed ambassador to Sierra Leone. For not even Alieu Mboge, Lamin Sabi Sanyang, Famara Jallow, or Yankuba Drammeh letters to Yahya Jammeh can match Mr. Khan's in unadulterated stupidity and disgraceful subservience. But Mr. Khan's reaction, like the rest, is typical of people who are psychologically abused, but above all, who feel they don't deserve what they get. Last time I checked, every Gambian is entitled to work and make a living, and further, no one owes Yahya Jammeh for working for the country. It appears Mr. Khan qualifies as ambassador only in a country where mediocrity reigns and where placing square pegs in round holes is standard practice in the job-hiring process. Mr. Khan must remember that Famara Jallow was dismissed for the second time the month he wrote his letter of gratitude to Yahya Jammeh. It's the same fate that awaits Mr. Khan and everyone serving under Yahya Jammeh. Within the next few months, everyone serving at the top of this crazy regime will be fired or arrested, and some tried and sent to prison. It just never ends. Speaking of end, it is good to see my political party coming alive again. I mean the NRP. Mr. Hamat Bah is making waves once more, and that can only be a good thing for the Gambia's struggle to democratize. Further, comments will be reserved for my new proposals to Mr. Hamat Bah for a relaunching and possibly renaming the NRP, and if funds permit, to be held outside the Gambia but closer to home.

Finally, congratulations to the PDOIS executive member who recently scaled the political wall to join the UDP, and welcome him to the world outside PDOIS's doctrinaire politics and unhealthy political propaganda, where vulnerable young men and women are turned into political zombies. In normal politics, there is no need for saints or cult following, and every normal human being must think for themselves and act according to the dictates of their consciences. The exercise of politics is a human endeavor, and there is no expectation for anyone to behave like divine reincarnation. The freedom and the ability of the mind to wander freely in search of knowledge is what helps humans to grow intellectually. When actions of others can be anticipated, which includes the words they use in communication, we have almost become the same in thinking. When that happens, what makes us special and individual will no longer exist. We must never allow that to happen.

ECONOMIC GAINS BENEFIT INSIGNIFICANT FEW

To understand how Gambia's economic engine functions and the forces that are driving it, one has to examine how the Gambia's economic policy objectives are operationalized. First, the point of departure has to be Yahya Jammeh's perspective on how the state ought to operate in the process of implementing policy objectives in an increasingly globalized and competitive market. To begin, Yahya Jammeh's rejection of the democracy and development dichotomy, equating it to corruption, is perhaps the most intellectually bankrupt argument that can be made against the duality of democracy and development. Democracy is designed to provide social, economic, and political stability, engage people in their development, and encourage by unleashing the creative genius of citizens. There is no institutionalized system of social organization that has proven more effective; in fact, all other competing forms of social organization have failed to deliver a more effective system of human organizing. By agreeing with the theoretical definition that a state consists of an eclectic group of individuals with conflicting and contradictory interests, with each pursuing dissimilar objectives and each utilizing means and platforms that intrude in and potentially limit the success of other competing interests, we can then value the crucial role that democracy can play in harmonizing naturally occurring human conflicts engendered by the existence of individual interests. The totality of state interest, consisting of civil society, the media, the business sector, communities organized by geography and by other interests, political parties, and other group interests, constitute the state, and to the extent that each pursues interests that benefit the country, each in their own different ways, often means that their interests sometimes overlap, and their methods of achieving their singular objectives are often in conflict with one another.

Clearly, tensions arise from this dynamic relationship, and in the Gambia, the perennial state and media-strained relationship over the past decade and a half is an example of this conflict. For, a government like ours, which operates in secrecy and has something to hide from public scrutiny, has developed into the natural enemy of our media, which, acting in the best interest of the state and its people, is equally determined to bring government activities into the open for public examination. The limited definition often attached to the concept of Jeffersonian democracy, particularly in most developing countries, has not done justice to the broad spectrum of its reach. The practice of democracy transcends the issues of human rights and recurring electoral cycles; rather, it is a necessary and imperative conduit to good governance. The rule of law, a pillar in the broader definition of democracy, is crucial in engendering security and stability in a country to ensure the operation of a stable business environment that allows entrepreneurship to flourish and prosper in order to create jobs and increase the revenue base government needs to provide public services to the citizens. In a nutshell, a democratic system of government promotes public accountability, citizens' participation, equal opportunity, equality before the law, and citizen responsibility, so government works in the interest of all the people. The success of business and the expansion of capital investment in the Gambia are directly tied to the institutionalization of democracy. But democracy also espouses a legal and regulatory infrastructure, which allows the harmonious interplay of conflicting and often contradictory group interests, and when seemingly irreconcilable conflicts do occur, mechanisms for resolving them exist in the structure of democratic rule of law. In the Gambia, Yahya Jammeh has replaced existing legal and regulatory structures of the state by directly engaging the business community and making laws, often in a threatening manner, which over time have harmed business and negatively impacted economic security.

Yahya Jammeh's relationship with the business community is not unlike the contentious and certainly deadly one that has developed between him and the Gambian media, and in an increasingly globalized world, this antagonistic relationship can potentially have a lethal effect on foreign investment and Gambia's crucial bilateral and multilateral relationships with foreign governments. The more Yahya Jammeh assumes the role of the legal and regulatory body, the more he usurps the remediation powers of the law. The constitution of the civil and administrative laws should be broad enough to provide effective and efficient regulatory mechanisms that can protect consumers from abuse and government from corrupt business practice. Any implementation of economic development policies in Gambia must be preceded by far-reaching legal reforms, from the Constitution to local and municipal level regulations, to ensure that we lay a strong and vibrant economic growth foundation. So far, anecdotal and empirical evidence suggests that the Gambia has neither the ability nor the capability to implement a structured development program that encompasses the main highlights of good governance: financial accountability, operational efficiency, predictability, probity, and regulatory guidelines that support an efficient and effective utilization of time and resources. By default, every country is endowed with the necessary basic framework to engage, produce, participate, and compete in the global marketplace, the most important of which are the available human resources and the creative ingenuity of its people.

The primary function of the state is, therefore, to facilitate the release of the creative genius of its human capital by establishing an enforceable regulatory framework that expands the scope for innovation and human and capital investment. It is necessary to underscore the word *enforceable*, since officials of the state have the proclivity to break the rules and render existing legal and regulatory frameworks not only redundant but unenforceable. The economic policies constructed by government must be supported by a strong and enforceable legal and regulatory structure that rejects the paternalistic and nepotistic geography of our cultures. Gambia's weak legal system has compounded the challenges of our economic development, particularly relating to investors who suffer economic losses due to unscrupulous state officials, lack of effective legal recourse, and absence of effective and efficient legal enforcement mechanisms. But in addition, the cost of doing business in the Gambia has become prohibitively high, both in terms of capital outlay and the amount of time needed to secure business licenses, and such costs primarily relate to bribery of officials during the process of establishing new businesses. There are other cultural factors that, like our deeply ingrained cultural paternalism, inhibit business development; consequently, the climate for business development in Gambia is not favorable to investors. To make matters worse, Yahya Jammeh's overreach and constant meddling in the activities of the business sector have proven to be problematic and a disincentive to investors both local and foreign.

MAKING LAWS, ISLAMIC STATE, DOCILE NATIONAL ASSEMBLY, AND THE UNRAVELING OF A COUNTRY

Despite Yahya Jammeh's excessive power, criminal regime, and illegal lawmaking authority, the expectations of periodic elections in the Gambia are almost an article of faith. The management of the electoral process, in all its tediousness, fulfills a cardinal democratic benchmark, which, in the Gambia, is all but democratic. As the 2016 elections draw closer, at stake is not necessarily who will occupy Gambia's State House but how the democratic process holds up in the face of Yahya Jammeh's absolute contempt for the integrity of the process. In July this year, Yahya Jammeh made a knee-jerk decision to increase the fees for opposition presidential contestants in the 2016 elections, to GMD one million or $25,000, up from GMD 50,000 or $1,250, in 2011. This illegal form of taxation, apart from assaulting the citizenship rights of every Gambian, also stifles the democratic process in order to pave the way for a one-party state in Gambia. The Gambia National Assembly, renowned less for any meritorious accomplishment and more as the quintessential rubber stamp representation of the people, passed the measure as a bill, without giving regard to Yahya Jammeh's ultimate goal of decimating the democratic process and obliterating the last visages of our democracy. But last week's proclamation of an Islamic state awoke Gambians to a new reality, Yahya Jammeh's efforts to overthrow the Gambia's republican constitution and foist the dreaded Islamic state upon the people. Clearly, historical evidence is replete with cases of Yahya Jammeh's public demonstrations of contempt for the Gambia's colonial heritage and Western way of life. There is no line he will not cross to display his puerile tantrums and gibberish rants against what he perceives as colonial handiwork. Far scarier than that, Gambians have for long grappled with Yahya Jammeh's slow march to absolute power by systematically weakening Gambia's National Assembly and the judiciary. Yahya Jammeh's ultimate goal is to eventually abolish any impediment to his creeping rise to absolute power, and unilateral imposition of the

Islamic state is a means to that end. It is his blueprint for achieving unfettered power.

Unfortunately for Yahya Jammeh, Gambian cultures, regardless of tribe, are apathetic to the idea of government by theocracy and its application of Sharia law. The Wahabist tradition of Sharia law, exercised with such inhuman brutality, is a misplaced concept in Gambian society. But Yahya Jammeh's ostentatious disdain for democratic institutions is routinely and methodically expressed in the ways he has often bypassed the Gambia's lawmaking body, the National Assembly, and promulgated laws that harm the separation of powers clause enshrined in the Constitution. The unilateral Islamic state decree clearly establishes Yahya Jammeh's indifference to the concept of tripartite system of government. Above all, it brings into focus the weaknesses of the National Assembly and the judiciary as bulwarks to the erosion of citizen rights and citizens as the center of political power. The National Assembly has, historically and inexplicably, deferred to Yahya Jammeh, even in cases of clear violation of the Constitution. Yahya Jammeh's reckless determination to thwart the laws of the land by consistently undermining the democratic system of checks and balances in government is designed to extinguish every effort to hold him accountable for his atrocities and ruination of Gambian society. Even more than that, the Gambia is culturally and traditionally antithetic to the concept of Islamic state, and the country's status as a secular state is, in the eyes of its citizens, sacrosanct and immutable. Yahya Jammeh's unilateral declaration of Gambia as an Islamic state is a criminal subversion of the republican constitutions and a serious felony crime of treason, not unlike any armed insurrection. The consensus among Gambians across religion, tribe, and geography unanimously rejects the Islamization of life and politics in Gambia. Yahya Jammeh's Islamic state, like his established tribalism, is detrimental to national security and has absolutely no foundation in ECOWAS and Africa Union principles, set up to guarantee civil rights and economic justice. The open rebellion against the imposition of Islamic state in a country with a long secular tradition impugns Yahya Jammeh's authority to make law and sneers at the Gambia National Assembly for acting like incurable dumbasses in allowing Yahya Jammeh to get away with defecating on our most sacred document, the Constitution. The disastrous Islamic state idea, unlike any other since 1994, has excited passions and spawned the collective rejection of Yahya Jammeh's efforts to create religious divisions in a volatile region of Africa.

Over the years since 1994, Gambians have consistently coalesced around events and incidents that have tested the limits of their tolerances—the December 2014 incident, the Mile 2 Prison executions, the 2009 witch-hunting, the 2006 executions, the 2000 student massacre, the November 1994 executions—but the Islamic state declaration has sparked unanimous rejection rarely witnessed in Gambia. The bold and loud rejection of the silly Islamic state idea is particularly intense, considering the ways in which religion has historically degenerated into civil conflicts across many African countries. Not unlike Yahya Jammeh's disastrous tribal agenda, religion too has an overwhelming ability to engender chaos and lawlessness, and Gambians cannot permit this to pile up in a country already strained by Yahya Jammeh's tribal bigotry. This is not lost on Ousainou Mbenga, head of DUGA, a Gambian human rights organization, who was uninhibited in his criticism of Yahya Jammeh's frivolous Islamic state scheming. "This regime has lost all legitimacy, and this division of Gambians by religion. is dangerous and alien to the lost cultural homogeneity Gambians hope to bring back. Yahya Jammeh's purpose is to create more acrimony and conflict among people who have lived as one family for generations," Mr. Mbenga said. "We already see the effects of Yahya Jammeh's tribalism affecting so many Gambians in ways that have the potential to create problems for us in the future," added Mr. Mbenga. Tijan Massaneh Ceesay, a leader in the Washington, DC, area Gambian Catholic community, was philosophical in his condemnation of the idea of divisions by religion, quoting a revered pioneering African statesman, Sir Dawda Jawara. "We will be able to demonstrate to the world how a group of people from different religious backgrounds and different origins can live together in peace and harmony." "What sets Gambians apart, adds Tijan, is that as a secular state, Gambians don't care who is Muslim and who is Christian or pagan. This Islamization of the Gambia should never come to fruition." The consequences of Islamizing the Gambia are enormous, both psychologically and materially. Among others, it will cast the influential Christian community as less than equal, downgrade them to second-class citizen status, and discriminate them in jobs, economic opportunity, and a slew of other areas. Clearly, Gambia's Islamization idea is a flashpoint for discord and civil strife, which Gambians don't deserve or desire. The unanimous decision by Gambians is very loud and clear in its simplicity: Islamic state, "Not in our name."

OF NEOPHYTES, ACOLYTES, AND POLITICAL CHARLATANS

In a country with a system that harbors little or no regard for the practices of good governance, Gambia's anachronistic descent into amateurism forced the previously imperfect democratic government to slowly slide into the regime's current state of utter dysfunction and absolute chaos. Today, the Gambia is cast as a total failure by every matrix that measures effective bureaucratic functionality and government efficiency. Clearly, the floundering of the regime is not quite without valid reasons, but more significantly, it is explainable by the way a perpetual state of social and political instability is built into the governing protocol to ensure the regime's maintenance of unfettered control of the mechanisms of governance. And in disregard of the citizens' constitutional rights, decisions as to who gets hired and who remains unemployed and destitute are used effectively as instruments of control, resulting in deleterious repercussions to the nation. Thus the withering criticisms of Gambians, who continue to deliberately blind themselves to the severe economic hardship, the traumatic psychological impacts, and crippling indifference to the shameful abuse are not without moral justifications. The reason Gambians continue accepting positions in the regime, despite the certainty of victimization, continues to mystify citizens and challenge the deep denial by regime collaborators and their mendacious efforts to obfuscate the reality of Gambia's ostentatious history of state savagery.

Gambia's renegade collaborators continue to draw bruising criticisms from fellow citizens and invite the not entirely undeserved scorn of countrymen and women who are left to speculate how religion and our collective moral foundation have lost their divine force in our society. Yet it is patently false to conjecture that every Gambian who has accepted employment with the regime did so for selfish ulterior motives. And for a country that lacks an educated workforce and professional expertise, the circle of talent has dwindled dramatically as professionals flee to safe countries. In a climate of professional shortage, the regime is compelled to hire the majority of its civil servants from an available pool of low education and highly unqualified cadre who commit not to a national interest but to the unwritten goal of entrenching the regime. But among the Gambians ensnared in the regime's political and tribal machinations is an educated minority who are the subjects of often abusive but always fiery rhetoric condemning their roles in prolonging the deadly regime. The riveting ad hominem attacks of educated collaborators projects frustrations toward educated Gambians' subservience to dictatorship. The timeless assumption that education empowers a sense of liberty and independence has turned out not to be a defensible truism in Gambia's case, as the highly educated line up for job offers in the regime even before the ink on dismissal letters of their predecessors runs dry.

The vehemence with which regime collaborators are held in absolute contempt is matched only by Gambian citizens' asinine hatred for Yahya Jammeh. The unflattering disenchantment with the regime's enablers is the single most important question swirling in Gambian minds. Do Gambians who accept work in the regime and, therefore, enable the torture, murders, mass incarceration, forced disappearance, and exodus of other Gambians really care about their fellow citizens, or are the financial incentives and ostentatious show of social class too great to resist? From the highly educated to intellectual nonentities, the challenge to accept or reject positions in the regime is a decision each individual has to make for themselves, but the risks are great. For, history has proved that working in Yahya Jammeh's regime is not unlike playing cat and mouse in a crocodile pond; sooner or later, one will get devoured. Those who escape scotch free from Yahya Jammeh's grip and live to tell it are few and far apart, for cavorting in a crocodile hole is like walking into a death trap, a risk only neophytes, acolytes, and the cabal of political charlatans can wish for themselves. Yet despite the undeniable hazards of working in Yahya Jammeh's regime, soulless Gambians dare to line up for their certain disgrace, incarceration, or even death. For no matter what happens, in the end, Yahya Jammeh will always have his last hurrah with the weak of heart and mind. The overwhelming historical evidence against collaborators notwithstanding, Gambians still refuse to learn, and in so doing, contribute to prolong the regime's executions, murders, mass incarcerations, and exodus from that hellhole that is Gambia.

GAMBIA, NOT YET FREEDOM

It was a week of surprises, cheers, laughs, smiles, hugs, kisses, tears of sadness, and tears of joy, all in one hell of a family reunion. Prisoners who had languished in dreary prison cells for years were finally set loose from the dungeon of death, Mile 2 Prison, to a waiting crowd of family and curious onlookers. For those condemned to death or on life sentences, it is like the miracle at Mile 2. But this is still the Gambia, where justice and the rule of law are foreign concepts, and Yahya Jammeh is renowned more for his double dealing and duplicitous nature than for the honor of character. The relentless efforts of foreign governments, national and international institutions and organizations, Gambian online media and civil society organizations, and many others combined to make Yahya Jammeh miserable, isolated, and desperate to the point of relenting on the political prisoner release condition imposed by the European Union. Finally, the incarcerated prisoners whose physical movements were restricted are released from detention, but this is not the end; it is only the beginning of their freedom. It was not surprising that every one of the released prisoners paraded before the Gambian people extended gratitude to Yahya Jammeh, and some signaled readiness to return to work with him. What clearly came out was the visible faces of anguish of a broken people, the emaciated, too weak to savor the moment. How old they looked, and how desperate some were to throw themselves back into the demonic grip of an unforgiving megalomaniac, Yahya Jammeh.

But the dramatic prisoner release happened because of growing pressure condemning Yahya Jammeh's unilateralism and primitive styles, which most of the rest of African nations scorn at as caveman. It was evident from the very beginning that the released prisoners had critical decisions about their future to make: to stay and work for the regime in order to prolong its chokehold on the Gambia and Gambians, to stay in the Gambia and pretend to live a peaceful life, or leave Gambia to avoid further victimization and be a free man once again. In the end, some will be compelled to return to Yahya Jammeh's circle of orbit by economic circumstances, and in so doing, submit themselves to Yahya Jammeh's dangerous political machinations. For those who choose this path, to prove their undying loyalty to Yahya Jammeh, one thing is certain: you have not seen the end of Mile 2 just yet; in fact, part of your destinies are still residing in the hellhole of Mile 2 Prison. And to those who choose to leave, it is not all that easy outside. You will be compelled by your terrible Mile 2 Prison experiences to be an advocate for those you left behind, those who wake up to the terrifying clang of cold steel doors, those who wake up in dark, dingy, concrete, fortified coffin cells, and the listless, whose fixed gaze on the distant blue horizon encapsulate the vicissitude of a regime on the verge of breaking the Gambia apart into a thousand little pieces. Staying silent is not optional, unless you don't care about those you left behind. You experienced the horrors of incarceration, Gambians; therefore, hope that your time behind bars has taught you a lesson in compassion.

Finally, to those who choose to stay, even if you are not hired by the regime, the least Gambians expect is to not, in any way, shape, or form, do anything to prolong the regime's grip on power. But the prisoner release is not complete yet as long as Amadou Sanneh, a member of the leading opposition party, the United Democratic Party, and two United States citizens, Alhaji Mamut Ceesay and Ebou Jobe, who were abducted back in May 2013, remain in prison. In addition, the fates of others abducted—some since back in 2005, Chief Ebrima Manneh, Kanjiba Kanyi, and nearly twenty others—is still being questioned. Are they alive? Are they dead? Where are they? The released prisoners who decide to stay and perhaps work for Yahya Jammeh to drag Gambia in the mud, particularly Lang Tombong Tamba, Ngor Secka, and other former military or NIA agents, with a history of torturing Gambians and directly or indirectly being linked to their deaths, Gambians await to see if you will relapse into your former old selves, instilling fear, terrorizing citizens, causing the tortures of many citizens and noncitizens, and even be tangentially linked to the deaths of others. Gambians invested too much to secure your freedom, and some died trying do just that. Now don't throw away their sacrifices by turning yourselves into lapdogs for Yahya Jammeh. You are obliged by the sad fate of your fellow countrymen and women to help restore Gambia's lost dignity and save your fellow countrymen and women from the brutal Mile 2 Prison life. Everyone has an option to leave the country and join the struggle to help lift Gambians out of its misery. For as long as Yahya Jammeh remains, no one is yet free. Some have tortured for Yahya Jammeh, helped kill for Yahya Jammeh, and worked as slave laborers on Yahya Jammeh's farms. The only thing you have not done is wipe his ass clean. One day soon, you may do just that if you don't make a wise decision about what you want to do with your life, after life in Mile 2 Prison.

FROM THE RIDICULOUS TO THE ABSURD

After years of unprecedented brutality, hundreds of people tortured, executed, disappeared, or dying slowly behind the Gambia's notorious Mile 2 Central Prison walls, the world is finally coming to grips with the Gambian regime's mind-numbing corruption, divisive tribal bigotry, incompetent management, and incorrigible stupidity. Gambians who experienced the freedom and laid-back attitude of the era of former president Sir Dawda Jawara reject Yahya Jammeh's decade-long frenetic rule. The Gambia's rule by fear, the imposition of a de facto martial law, the acquiescing to the regime's pitiful intimidation, and the effort to reduce Gambians to compliant slaves have combined to erode the collective psyche of our national pride. Today, it is an understatement to say that far too many of our fellow countrymen and women have succumbed to Jammeh's cunning exercise of absolute power. In the face of his bewildering cruelty, Gambians have surrendered to his will and denied themselves the dignity of life and liberty. After years of pernicious rule, the fear and terror to which our fellow citizens have for so long been subjected to is paying off for the military regime. Nowadays, a significant number of greedy, selfish, and sycophantic Gambians are riding Jammeh's bandwagon and enabling the weakening of our people's resolve to stand up for the values of human dignity. Gambia's radio and television airwaves and the regime's mouthpiece, the *Daily Observer*, are bombarding our fellow citizens with meaningless propaganda in an attempt to mystify and venerate the insipid monster, Yahya Jammeh. A casual look at the Gambia's spurious home newspaper articles and aggravating television and radio newscasts will reveal the disturbing direction to which the corrupt and compliant media is heading toward. As the media attempts to rewrite the story of Yahya Jammeh's hypocrisy, brutality, and selfishness, Gambians can only watch helplessly with disbelief all the media propaganda. The tragedy is that, in many ways, Gambians are complicit in debasing the timeless cultural values that have carried us through the ages. The relentless media propaganda in the Gambia is designed to satisfy the ego of a maniac whose vision of changing the Gambia into his image has no boundary. Over the past four weeks, the Gambia television and radio airwaves and the hallowed pages of the regime's newspaper, the *Daily Observer*, have revealed the burgeoning of a different type of propaganda, one that is imposed by state directives and motivated by the desire to secure a place in Yahya Jammeh's good books. A case in point, the addition of "professor" to Yahya Jammeh's collection of meaningless titles speaks to his assuming arrogance, but more importantly, it confirms that Yahya Jammeh holds Gambians in regard. By assuming many questionable titles and collecting so many useless certificates from dubious institutions that have no credibility anywhere in the world, Yahya Jammeh has turned himself into a laughingstock. But Yahya Jammeh continually exposes his megalomania to remind Gambians of lessons gleaned from dictatorships around the world. The more entrenched dictators become, the harder it is for them to differentiate between the state and themselves. In extreme cases, dictators assume the role of deity to blur the distinction between God and man, and although this is not the case in Gambia, mystifying Yahya Jammeh is the beginning of this process. Kim Il-sung is still worshipped as god in North Korea, even though he has been dead for more than two decades. In Central Africa, Jean Bedel Bokassa's subjects were beginning to worship him at the time he was removed from power. In the context of the Gambia, which is not in this position yet, the tipping point may soon be reached as Yahya Jammeh becomes increasingly invincible. For now, it is safe to say that religion has done much to emasculate Gambians, rendering the country impotent to do anything to stop the heinous crimes perpetrated by the state on a daily basis. Today, the indistinguishable relationship between the state and religion makes demarcating the boundary between religion and government hard, if not impossible. In Gambia, the apparent synonym of religion and the state is compelling Gambians to condone the subhuman treatment that pervades every level of society. Religious indoctrination has done much to mold Gambians into weak and helpless slaves to authority, and Gambians have surrendered their collective dignity to Yahya Jammeh. In the end, Yahya Jammeh will have neither mercy in his heart nor motivation to stop murdering innocent Gambians, if that is what it takes to keep him in power. In true Machiavellian fashion, Yahya Jammeh exercises no restraint in obtaining and retaining power and has jettisoned even the values that identify the human character. And in the end, Yahya Jammeh has had a lot of inadvertent or deliberative help making Gambia what it is now. But for now, if the directive to call Yahya Jammeh "professor" bears truth, and the murder of Lt. Bubacarr Bah of the Gambia National Army is affirmed, Gambia will have moved one more step toward absolute power. The question that challenges fellow countrymen and women now is, how much longer are Gambians going to say nothing as their countrymen continue to die? As the saying goes, "If you don't stand for something, you'll fall for anything."

LIST OF YAHYA JAMMEH'S VICTIMS

As Gambians remember two decades of unprecedented human and civil rights abuses, we endeavor to put names to the many Gambians who lost their lives, were tortured or imprisoned, fled, or suffered injustices under Yahya Jammeh's military. This is the updated list of the executed, murdered, and disappeared and those being tried, facing charges, exiled, or languishing in Yahya Jammeh's prison system and jailhouses around the country. These tell the story of the brutal legacy of Yahya Jammeh's military regime over twenty-two long years. But this list is by no means complete, since we believe there are more that Gambians don't know about.

The following were arrested, tortured, and killed in prison on April 15, 2016:

Solo Sandeng Youth Leader
Mariama Jawara Youth Activist

The following were arrested and are unaccounted
for since their abduction on April 14, 2016:

1. Ousianou Darboe (leader and SG of UDP)
2. Momodou Sanneh
3. Lamin Dibba
4. Kemeseng Janneh (former minority leader in the National Assembly)
5. Femi Peters (publicity secretary)
6. Fakebba Colley
7. Lamin Jatta
8. Jukuba Suso
9. Lamin Ceesay-Kiang
10. Tapha Makalo
11. Fanta Darboe
12. Doudo Ceesay
13. Ismaila Ceesay
14. Kebba Khan
15. Amadou Saho
16. Alhagie Fatty
17. Omar Drammeh
18. Lalo Jawla
19. Arfang Amadou
20. Saho Jesuwang
21. Lamin Manjang
22. Alhagie Njie
23. Abdou Camara
24. Lamin Komma
25. Solo Sandeng (died in police custody)
26. Falang Sonko
27. Modou Ndom
28. Lang Marong
29. Fatoumatta Jawara (beaten to a coma and feared dead)

30. Nokoi Njai
31. Fatou Camara
32. Baba Ceesay
33. Jula Jah (commonly known as Omar Jah)
34. Baboucarr Touray
35. Baboucarr Giteh
36. Lamin Janneh
37. Kebba K. Bojang
38. Tapha Makalo
39. Fatou Darbo Jawara
40. Bamba Jallow

**The following were prisoners executed in
Mile 2 Prisons, August 23, 2012:**

1. Lamin B. Darboe
2. Alieu Bah
3. Lamin Jarju
4. Dawda Bojang
5. Malang Sonko
6. Lamin F Jammeh
7. Gibril Bah (Senegalese)
8. Tabara Samba, raped multiple times before her execution (Senegalese, female)

**The following were Gambians murdered
on orders of Yahya Jammeh:**

Abdoulie Colley, Abuko Village
Musa Badjie, collapsed and died in Mile 2 Prison, August 25, 2012
Wuyeh Colley, Kanunorr village, murdered August 22, 2012
Enor Colley, Kanunorr village, murdered August 22, 2012
Regime's witching-hunting kangaroo trials
GAMCOTRAP's Dr. Isatou Touray and Co. trials

GNOC's Beatrice Allen and Co. trials
Suruwa Wawa B. Jaiteh and Dr. Loum's trials
Dr. Amadou Jallow and Co. trials
Dr. Alasan Bah and Co's trials

Recent Arrests, Detention, and Charged with Treason

Amadou Scattred Janneh, former minister of information
Ndey Tapha Sosseh, former president of the Gambia Press Union
Mathew K. Jallow
Famara Demba
Modou Keita
Ebrima Jallow
Michael C. Uche Thomas (died in prison)

Torture and Yahya Jammeh's Convoy-Related Deaths

Demba Sibey of Numuyel village
A third grader from Saaba Primary School
A young girl killed by Yahya Jammeh's motorcade / Gunjur prayer fest
Paul Bass NIA operative killed by Jammeh's convoy
Arab businessman dead in collision with Jammeh's convoy
A soldier from Sintet village killed escorting Jammeh's convoy
A little girl killed by convoy during Mauritanian president's visit
A child killed by stampede for Jammeh's biscuits at Sere Kunda market
In total, since 1994, nearly twenty people—children and adults—
    have died as a direct result of Yahya Jammeh's speeding convoys
    and biscuit throwing to crowds.

Recent Arrests of Journalists

Sports editor Nanama Keita, facing witch-hunting/kangaroo trial
Ahmed Alota, arrested, detained, released

Executed and Murdered Civilian and Military

Ousman Koro Ceesay, former minister of finance
Deyda Hydara, founder *Point* newspaper / president of Gambia Press
    Union
Sidia Sanyang
Ebrima Chief Manneh
Omar Barrow
Lamin Sanneh
Ousman Ceesay
Sarjo Kunjang
Ebrima Barry
Ousman Ceesay
Saja Kujabi
Haruna Jammeh
Yaya Jammeh
Daba Marena
Staff Sergeant Manlafi Corr
Sergeant Major Alpha Bah
Lieut. Ebou Lowe
Lt. Alieu Ceesay
Sgt. Fafa Nyang
Lt. Basiru Barrow
Capt. Sadibou Hydara
Lt. Almamo Manneh
Lt. Abdoulie Dot Faal
Lt. Bakary Manneh
Lt. Buba Jammeh
Lt. Momodou Lamin Darboe
Cadet Officer Sillah
Lt. Basiru Camara
Corporal Mendy
Lt. Gibril Saye
Sergeant Dumbuya
Momodou Sowe

The following were Gambians Detained, Released in Jail, or Murdered between 1994 and 2012:

RSM Alpha Bah (executed)

Major Ebrima Bah

Lt. Momodou Alieu Ba

Corporal Samba Bah

Tijan Bahoum, Power Supply director, NAWEC

Kemo Balajo, ex-National Intelligence Agency

Foday Barry, ex-NIA; director of Intelligence

Ourani Barry, ex-senior civil servant

Lamin Bojang, Medical Research Council

Ebrima Camara, ex-police officer

Omar Barru Camara, ex-MP APRC

Captain Wassa Camara

2ⁿᵈ Lt. Alieu Ceesay

Lamin Ceesay, politician

Madi Ceesay, president, Gambia Press Union

Awa Darboe Cham, wife of alleged coup leader Ndure Cham

Lamin Cham, ex-*Daily Observer*, BBC correspondent

Lamin Cham, politician

Momat Cham, former minister

Momodou Cadi Cham, former politician

Superintendent Abdoulie Colley, ex-police officer

Retired Colonel Abdoulie Conteh, former KMC Mayor

Staff Sergeant Manlafi Corr

Captain Bunja Darboe

Lamin R. Darboe, politician

Lamin Saiba Darboe

Captain Yaya Darboe

Adama Deen, former managing director, Gambia Ports Authority

Demba Dem, ex-MP APRC

Momodou Demba, politician

Mariam Denton, human rights lawyer

Raif Diab, businessman
Ramzia Diab, former nominated MP, APRC
Musa Dibba, ex-NIA director of Finance
Sheriff Mustapha Dibba, ex-Assembly Speaker
Baba Drammeh, ex-Independent Electoral
Commission (IEC) officer
Omar Faal, Marabout
Ansumana Fadera, ex-senior civil servant
Jerreh Fatty, politician
Lamin Fatty, journalist, the *Independent* newspaper
Mariama Fatty, politician
Kebba Faye, ex-senior civil servant
Tamba Fofana, headmaster
Abdou Gafar, journalist, *Daily Express* newspaper
Lamin Gassama, security manager, Banjul International Airport
Antouman Gaye, lawyer
Pa Njie Guirigara, general manager, VM
Sarane Hydara, ex-senior civil servant
Captain Abdoukarim Jah
Karamo Jaiteh, former managing director, Gambia Roads Authority
Suruwa Wawa B Jaiteh, former permanent secretary
Staff Sergeant Buba Jammeh
Haruna Jammeh, villager
Kebbaringo Jammeh, councilor
Marcel Jammeh, villager
Lance Corporal Babou Janha
Amie Jarju, villager
Cherno Ndure Jarju, politician
Lamin Jarsey, politician
Tamsir Jassey, ex-deputy inspector general police, director of
    Immigration
Dudu Kassa Jatta, politician
Ousman Rambo Jatta, councilor

Colonel Vincent Jatta, ex-chief of defense staff (deceased)
Momodou Jaw, ex-IEC officer
Abdoulie Kanaji Jawla, MP, APRC
Baboucarr Jobarteh, ex-protocol officer
Maimuna Jobarteh, politician
Abdou Jobe, managing director, NAWEC
Alieu Jobe, ex-accountant general
Duta Kamaso, ex-MP, APRC
Kanyiba Kanyi, politician
Lamin Keita, ex-senior civil servant
Nato Keita, politician
Abdoulie Kujabi, ex-director general, NIA
Jasaji Kujabi
Dr. Badara Loum, ex-permanent secretary
Lt. Ebou Lowe
Mustapha Lowe, college student
Bamba Manneh, ex-NIA operative
Chief Ebrima B. Manneh, journalist, *Daily Observer* newspaper
Fatou Jaw Manneh, journalist
Kebba Yorro Manneh, politician
Daba Marena, ex-director general, NIA
Malick M'boob, ex-*Daily Observer*, RV
Sulayman Sait M'boob, ex-minister, IEC commissioner
Sergeant Buba Mendy
Captain Pierre Mendy
Omar Ndow, former managing director of Gamtel/Gamcel
Ndondi S.Z. Njie, former chairman of IEC
Alhagie Nyabally, ex-president, Gambia Student Union
Alassan Nyassi
Balla Nyassi
Dr. Badara Loum, former permanent secretary, Agriculture
Private Alagie Nying, Gambia National Army
Sam Obi, *Daily Express*, RFI correspondent

Baba Saho, ex-NIA director, External Security
Musa Saidykhan, former editor in chief, the *Independent* newspaper
Betrand Sambou
Dodou Sanneh, former journalist, GRTS
Ebrima Sillah Sanneh, ex-IEC officer
Lamin Sanneh, former permanent secretary
Sergeant Abdoulie Sanyang
2nd Lt. Pharing Sanyang, Gambia National Army
Commander MB Sarr, Gambia National Army
Lt. M. Savage, Gambia National Army
Ebou Secka, ex-senior civil servant
Nourou Secka, ex-NIA operative
Momodou Senghore, ex-senior civil servant
Ousman Sey, Marabout
Musa Sheriff, journalist, *Gambia News & Report* magazine
Amie Sillah, journalist, women activist
Alieu Singhateh, ex-NIA operative
Kebba Singhateh, politician
Modou Sonko, journalist, *Daily Observer* newspaper
Private Ebrima Sonko
Juldeh Sowe, journalist, the *Independent* newspaper
Issac Success, journalist, *Daily Express* newspaper
Azziz Tamba, politician
Ebou Waggeh

Arrests and Detentions of Journalists

October 2005: Abdoulie Sey
2005: Musa Saidykhan
March 2006: Musa Saidykhan
March 2006: Madi Ceesay
April 2006: Lamin Fatty

Journalists on Exile in Senegal, Europe, and the US

Pa Ousman Darboe
Alieu Badara Sowe
Pa Ousman Darboe
Musa Saidykhan
Sulayman Makalo
Omar Bah
Alhagie Mbye
Ebrima Sillah
Augustus Mendy
Bankole Thompson
Papa Colley
Sulayman Darboe
Fatou Jaw Manneh
Pa Omar Jatta
Momodou Thomas
Musa Saidykhan
Ansumana Badjie
Pa Samba Jaw
Sarjo Bayang
Pa Nderry Mbai
Cherno Baba Jallow
Ebrima Ceesay
Baba Galleh Jallow
Ebrima G. Sankareh
Yankuba Jambang
Mathew K. Jallow

Military/Security Mysterious Deaths

Captain Tumbul Tamba
Captain Musa Jammeh
Colonel Vincent Jatta

Lt. Solomon Jammeh
Pa M. Jallow
Manlafi Sanyang
Boye Bah
Momodou Bah
Sgd Illo Jallow, chief bodyguard for Lady Zaineb S Jammeh

Military/Security/Civilians Recently Detained

Lang Tombong Tamba
Bore Badjie
Omar Bun Mbye
Demba Njie
Lamin Fatty
Yankuba Drammeh
Malamin Jarju
Kawsu (Bombardier) Camara
Ngorr Secka, NIA
Ensa Badjie
Bun Sanneh
Sarjo Fofana

Military/Security/Civilians: Detained, Tortured, Released, Fled

Ebrima Chongan, ex-assistant inspector general of the Gambia Police
Lieutenant Binneh Minteh
Captain Bunja Darboe
Capt. Yahya Darboe
Capt. Wassa Camara
2nd Lt. Pharing Sanyang
Alieu Jobe
Tamsir Jasseh
Omar Faal
Demba Dem,
Col. Ndure Cham

Abdoulie Kujabi

Kemo Balajo

Alieu Singhateh

Foday Barry

Landing Sanneh

Executed Military and Security Officers, 2006

Alieu Ceesay

Alpha Bah

Manlafi Corr

Ebou Lowe

Daba Marenah

Students Massacred on April 11, 2000

Reginald Carrol

Karamo Barrow

Lamin A. Bojang

Ousman Sabally

Sainey Nyabally

Ousman Sembene

Bakary Njie

Claesco Pierra

Momodou Lamin Njie

Ebrima Barry

Wuyea Foday Mansareh

Bamba Jobarteh

Momodou Lamin Chune

Abdoulie Sanyang

Omar Barrow

Burama Badjie

Gambians Missing and Disappeared Since 2005

Ebrima (Chief) Manneh, arrested July 2006

Kanyiba Kanyi, arrested September 2006

Haruna Jammeh, arrested in 2005

Marcie Jammeh, arrested in 2005

Alfusainey Jammeh, arrested in 2005

Momodou Lamin Nyassi, arrested in 2005

Ndongo M'boob, arrested in 2006

Buba Sanyang, arrested in 2006

Alieu Lowe, arrested in March 2006

Sgt. Sam Kambai, arrested in 2006

Bakary Gassama, arrested in 2007

Kebba Secka, arrested in 2007

Ebrima Dibba, arrested in May 2008

Ebrima Kunchi Jammeh, arrested in May 2008

Cases of Regime-Ordered Arsons and Arrest Orders against Media Personnel

On August 8, 2001, radio station I FM was set ablaze around two in the morning, after proprietor George Christensen and his watchman were doused with hazardous chemicals in the hope of incinerating them. The two victims survived the ordeal, but the station was a total loss.

On August 10, 2001, the home of Alieu Bah, Radio I FM journalist, who moderated debates and discussions between prominent personalities, was set ablaze around three in the morning while he, his wife, and children were asleep. The family narrowly escaped death, but the house was gutted to the ground.

On October 17, 2003, the *Independent* newspaper premises were set on fire around three in the morning when three unidentified masked men stormed the building, assaulted the night watchman, and then sprayed him with a fire hazard chemical in the hope he would burn to death.

But he luckily survived the assault. The premises were destroyed beyond recognition.

On April 13, 2004, the Kanifing printing facilities of the *Independent* newspaper were set on fire around two in the morning by six individuals dressed in military fatigues. The printing machinery and other hardware equipment were destroyed.

On August 15, 2004, the home of BBC reporter Ebrima Sillah was set on fire as he slept. He narrowly escaped.

Arrests and Detentions of Journalists
On September 19, 2003, around six o'clock at night, Abdoulie Sey, the editor in chief of the *Independent* newspaper, was arrested in his office by intelligence agents and held incommunicado. He was released four days later.

In September 2005, Musa Saidykhan, editor in chief of the *Independent* newspaper, was detained for interrogation for a brief period, shortly after returning from a South African journalist conference.

On March 27, 2006, Musa Saidykhan, editor in chief of the *Independent* newspaper, was arrested again by security agents a few days after publishing an article critical of Yahya Jammeh's reactions in the wake of an alleged coup attempt on March 21, 2007. He was released after three weeks in detention.

In March 2006, Madi Ceesay, the *Independent*'s general manager, was arrested by the regime's agents and then released after three weeks of detention.

On April 10, 2006, *Independent* reporter Lamin Fatty was arrested in his home by NIA agents and released after two months in detention and being charged with false publication.

On April 25, 2006, *Independent* receptionist Juldeh Sowe was arrested and released after several hours.

On July 7, 2006, *Daily Observer* journalist Ebrima Chief Manneh was arrested by NIA officials from the *Observer* premises and was seen in public once after two years of detention, at the Royal Victoria Hospital, sick and emaciated. Six powerful US Senators—Edward Kennedy, Richard (Dick) Durbin, Russell (Russ) Feingold, and Joe Lieberman, among others—wrote to Yahya Jammeh asking him to release journalist Manneh after being held for nearly three years. Manneh has since been confirmed murdered by Jammeh's agents.

On May 24, 2006, following the hacking of the online *Freedom* newspaper, five Gambian journalists whose names appeared on the paper's readers' list were arrested and detained for different lengths of time. After several months, they were released. They are the following:

Musa Sheriff
Pa Modou Faal
Lamin Cham
Sam Obi
Malick M'boob

Arbitrary Arrests and Detention
Dodou Sanneh, a journalist in September 2006 and a Gambia Radio and Television
Services reporter, was arrested and detained, then later fired, rehired, and fired again from his government job.

On March 28, 2007, Fatou Jaw Manneh, a US-based Gambian journalist, was arrested at the airport, her traveling documents seized, and charged with sedition. Her kangaroo trial lasted more than a year.

Her heavy fine was paid with donations from family and friends from all around the world.

On December 16, 2005, police roughed up Ramatoulie Charreh after the participants in a conference she attended attempted to visit the spot where journalist Deyda Hydara was gunned down.

In 2006, Njaimeh Bah, *Point* newspaper reporter, was attacked by unknown assailants and severely beaten.

On December 12, 2006, Baron Eloagou, reporter for the *Daily Express*, was severely beaten by unknown assailants.

In December 2006, Abdougafar Olademinji, reporter for the *Daily Express*, was attacked by unknown assailants and beaten severely.

On June 14, 2009, seven journalists and members of the Gambia Press Union (GPU) were rounded up from various locations by heavily armed paramilitary agents and detained at NIA headquarters before being transferred to the notorious Mile 2 Prison outside Banjul. The group listed below was granted bail and charged with publishing seditious material. Their case is ongoing, despite protestations by regional and international organizations such as Media Foundation for West Africa, Amnesty International, and Community to Protect Journalists. They are the following:

Emil Touray, secretary general, Gambia Press Union
Sarata Jabbi Dibba, vice president, Gambia Press Union
Pa Modou Faal, treasurer, Gambia Press Union
Pap Saine, managing director, the *Point* newspaper
Ebou Sawaneh, editor, the *Point* newspaper
Sam Sarr, managing editor, *Foroyaa* newspaper
Abubakr Saidy-Khan, journalist, *Foroyaa* newspaper

On June 16, 2009, Abdulhamid Adiamoh, publisher of *Today* newspaper, was arrested for false publication and detained at National Intelligence headquarters. Forced to plead guilty or face deportation back to Nigeria, he was fined an extortive amount of money or would face six months of jail time.

On June 22, 2009, Augustine Kanja, a reporter for the *Point* newspaper, was arrested and detained by security agents. He was released June 25, 2009.

In 2012, Baba Mansally was among ten Gambians who fled the country after it was discovered they were supplying information to Gambian media in the US and UK. Two of those arrested by the regime have since died in the notorious Mile 2 Central Prison in the outskirts of the capital.

Lawyers Who Fled Gambia after Attempted Murder

Ousman Sillah
Mai Fatty

Foreign Nationals Executed in Gambia

Forty-four Ghanaians
Two Senegalese
One Togolese
Two Nigerians

Seventy-Two Ministers, Appointed and Fired

Dr. Momodou Lamin Sedat Jobe (resigned)
B B Dabo
Dr. Sedat Jobe
Sidi Sanneh
Mass Axi Gai

Angela Colley
Kanja Sanneh
Neneh Macdoual-Gaye
Therese Ndong-Jatta (resigned)
Maba Jobe (hired and fired before taking office)
Momodou Lamin Sedat Jobe (resigned)
Joseph Henry Joof (resigned)
Satang Jow (retired)
Yankuba Kassama
Margaret Keita
Ousman Badjie
Samba Bah
Lamin Kaba Bajo
Musa Bittaye
Amie Bensouda
Fatou Bom Bensouda
John P. Bojang
Momodou Bojang
Nyimasata Sanneh
Bojang Mamat Cham
Ebrima Ceesay
Momodou Nai Ceesay
Ousman Koro Ceesay (murdered)
Sulayman Massaneh Ceesay
Bakary Bunja Dabo
Fasainey Dumbuya
Samba Faal
Omar Faye
Sadibou Haidara (murdered)
Sheikh Tijan Hydara
Blaise Jagne
Balla Garba Jahumpa
Momodou Sarjo Jallow

Dr. Amadou Scattred Janneh
Manlafi Jarju
Tamsir Mbowe
Dominic Mendy
Alieu Ngum
Bakary Njie
Omar Njie
Susan Waffa-Ogoo
Hawa Sisay Sabally
Sana B. Sabally
Abdoulie Sallah
Hassan Sallah
Momodou Sallah
Sidy Morro Sanneh
Kebba Sanyang
Samsudeen Sarr
Cheyassin Secka
Musa Sillah
Edward Singhatey
Raymond Sock
Amina Faal Sonko
Baboucarr Jatta
Famara Jatta
Kumba Ceesay-Marenah
Mustapha Marong
Fafa Mbai
Musa Mbenga
Sulayman Mboob
Bolong Sonko
Bai Mass Taal
Fatoumatta Tambajang
Bemba Tambedou
Yankuba Touray

Crispin Grey Johnson
Antouman Saho
Lamin Bojang
Marie Saine Firdaus
Edward Gomez
Mamburay Njie

Compiled by Mathew K Jallow

ABOUT THE AUTHOR

A naturalized US citizen exiled from the Gambia, West Africa, Mathew K Jallow is a practicing journalist, writer, political activist, and human rights advocate with a broad knowledge of African affairs. Mr. Jallow has been consulted by UN experts, development executives, and international nonprofit managers. He has extensive experience in organizational administration and nonprofit management and holds undergraduate degrees in business administration and hospitality management, as well as a graduate degree in public administration from the University of Wisconsin-Oshkosh. In 2012, Mr. Jallow was sentenced to death in absentia, which was commuted to life sentence, for his role in efforts to hold public demonstrations against the military dictatorship in his native Gambia. In Wisconsin, where he now lives, he has worked in state government and nonprofit organizations assisting marginalized segments of society. Prior to fleeing to the US, Mr. Jallow worked in senior executive positions in two of the largest international nonprofit organizations, Freedom from Hunger Campaign, Germany, and Action Aid International, London, UK.

Lightning Source UK Ltd.
Milton Keynes UK
UKHW012129270122
397812UK00001B/128